Reading and Reasoning Beyond the Primary Grades

- *Joseph L. Vaughan*
- *Thomas H. Estes*

Allyn and Bacon, Inc.

Boston London Sydney Toronto

Acknowledgments for Quotations in Text:

Page viii: Reprinted by permission of Judy Baca.

Page xi–xii: Reprinted by permission of Belita Gordon.

Page 3–5: Excerpted and adapted with permission of Macmillan Publishing Company from *The Naked Children* by Daniel Fader. Copyright © 1971 by Daniel Fader.

Page 58–60: Permission has been granted to use the excerpt "The Most Common Drug" from *Building Better Health, Red Level,* © 1983 by McDougal-Littel Co. All rights controlled by McDougal, Littell & Co. World rights secured. All rights reserved. Used with permission.

Page 138–140: Reprinted by permission of *The Wall Street Journal,* © Dow Jones & Company, Inc., 1980. All Rights Reserved.

Page 240–241: Reprinted by permission of Susan Drigant Robinson.

Series Editor: Susanne F. Canavan
Developmental Coordinator: Lauren Whittaker
Senior Production Administrator: Jane Schulman
Editorial Production Services: Kailyard Associates
Copyeditor: Susan Mesner
Text Designer: Judith Ashkenaz
Cover Coordinator: Linda K. Dickinson
Cover Designer: Christy Rosso

Library of Congress Cataloging in Publication Data

Reading and reasoning beyond the primary grades.

Includes bibliographies and index.
1. Reading. 2. Reading comprehension.
3. Reasoning. 4. Learning. I. Vaughan, Joseph L., 1942–
LB1050.2.R43 1986   428.4'07   85-15628
ISBN 0-205-08599-7
Printed in the United States of America.

10 9 8 7 6 5   92 93 94 95 96

Contents

Preface

Reading comprehension is among the most vital skills one can learn today and many teachers are seeking to learn strategies that will improve their students' ability to understand and remember what they read. It is for those teachers and for other concerned educators that we have written this book. While primary level educators have vast resources available to them for the teaching of reading comprehension, we believe that middle-school and secondary-school teachers need this knowledge and these skills as much as their primary-level counterparts. This book is addressed, therefore, to the reading teacher and all teachers in grades three through twelve who use reading in their classroom.

It is our belief and the underlying theme of this book that, given at least a minimum verbal competence, the essential prerequisite for successful reading is that students have the ability to monitor and control their own reading. Too many elementary- and secondary-level students read everything in one way, with no regard for variations in texts, their reasons for reading, or for the difficulty they have comprehending. While more strategies for the teaching of reading are available to teachers today, little seems to have surfaced that helps the reader become more independent and accomplished. Our focus here is on developing independent reading and learning in students beyond the primary grades.

While we offer suggestions for students, we also devote considerable attention to ways teachers can facilitate readers' comprehension. We believe that reading needs to be perceived as a reasoning activity and as such the teaching of reading should be founded on a process that emphasizes reasoning. Therefore, we include many activities and strategies teachers can use to develop the reasoning power of readers.

We have organized this book progressively according to basic elements of instruction. In chapter 1 we set the stage for our concerns, focusing particularly on students who need help with their reading.

In chapter 2 we address one of the oft-forgotten partners in reading—namely books, specifically textbooks found in classrooms. We consider the issue of readability of textbooks and then consider the more important topic of the appropriateness of textbooks found in classrooms. We offer ways to evaluate textbooks on the basis of criteria essential to appropriate texts—ways that extend beyond the superficial assessments offered by readability formulas.

In chapter 3 we propose a system of understanding reader comprehension, for we have found that the teaching of reading can best be served by an awareness of what readers do and do not comprehend. This approach helps teachers perceive comprehension from several points of view.

Beginning with chapter 4 and extending through chapter 7, we explore the reasoning process and how it is taught best in a framework that consists of anticipations, realizations, and contemplations; or, in terms of what readers might do before, during, and after reading to facilitate their comprehension. In chapter 4 we offer examples of the content reading lesson, a strategy that helps teachers build readers' comprehension systematically. In chapter 5 we elaborate on numerous strategies for the development of readers' anticipation of what they will read. Such anticipation helps readers relate their knowledge of the topic to their new learning. In chapter 6 the focus is on reader strategies appropriate to the realization, or apprehension, of meaning in text, such as imaging, look-backs, paired reading, a novel notetaking approach called INSERT, and a self-monitoring activity we call SMART. In chapter 7 we complete the cycle of reasoning with suggestions of various strategies for synthesis designed to facilitate remembering. We include various interactive activities as well as several basic spatial learning strategies.

In chapter 8 various strategies are proposed to develop critical reasoning skills in the context of reading instruction. Closely related is the topic of vocabulary instruction in chapter 9. These two chapters function together to stress the need for concept development in conjunction with critical thinking skills.

In chapter 10 we address the relationship between comprehension skills and attitudes and interest. Here we operate on the assumption, grounded in our experience and our research, that a positive predisposition toward the act of reading and the topic of a reading bears significantly on the success of reading.

In chapter 11 we discuss the issues involved in the art of study and suggest ways that readers can become better learners by adjusting their study habits to fit their reasoning strategies. Throughout this book our goal is to encourage independent learning, and in this last chapter we bring our theme to the specifics of successful study.

We hope that your study proves successful and rewarding and that the skills and knowledge you acquire within these pages serves you well in your efforts to teach the vital skills of reading and reasoning.

To the Reader

. . . and what is it about reading and reasoning that inspired this book? We were guided by the conviction that real reading matters to those who understand—those like you and your students whose bright eyes and expectant hearts long for reading to be really meaningful. And those like Belita Gordon, friend and colleague, who understands all about real reading. We are grateful for the inspiration her poem gave us and for permission to share it with you here:

**If Wishes Were Horses,
Emperors Would Wear Clothes**

If wishes were horses,
Beggars would ride.
If real reading mattered,
We'd measure the pride.
We'd assess the excitement,
We'd quantify tries,
If real reading mattered,
We'd norm "Heh teacher, why?"

If real reading mattered,
We'd count satisfaction that
Comes when you've struggled
And puzzled and tried til
The meaning breaks through and
Share it you do
Cause you've just got to show
That you *know* that you know
That you *like* that you know.

If real reading mattered
We'd subtest reader pride.

If real reading mattered
We'd validate ease
Item specs would require
Our readers we please
With words that delight

Questions that tickle
Phrases that soothe,
Thoughts that yet linger.
If real reading mattered,
Involvement we'd provoke;
If real reading mattered,
Immersion we'd invoke.

If real reading mattered
We'd count up the giggles
The laughter the play
We'd count the worn pages
Torn pages these pages would please....

If real reading mattered,
We'd subtest reader ease.

If real reading mattered
We'd reference
Heh-teacher-look-
I-can-read-
I-can-do-it-
I-can-read-the-whole-book!
Heh, aren't I smart,
Wow, ain't I grand And

Oh teacher, please-
Can I read this to
Mommy and Johnny and Jill?

If real reading mattered,
Success we'd instill.

If real reading mattered
We could and we would ...

if wishes were horses.

If real reading mattered ...! We believe students and teachers alike want to make reading matter. In this book we elaborate on all those ideas, strategies, concepts, and understandings that we have been led to by colleagues like Belita, by our students, and by each other. We share these things with you in the hope that you will instill success in your students.

What is this book about? Judy Baca, one of our students, says it for us in a cinquain. We hope that this book is about

Children
Opening doors
Learning, Thinking, Growing!
Teachers cultivating tomorrow's hope.
Reading.

Enjoy.

1

A Learning Strategies Curriculum

THE STARTING POINT: THE STUDENT

Educational scholars throughout history, from Socrates to notable contemporary authorities, have maintained that schools exist to provide a structured opportunity for children to develop intellectually and personally. This development is attained only when learners are given the opportunity to *make connections* between what they know and what they are trying to learn. John Dewey (1902) was speaking of this when he wrote, "The child is the starting point, the center, and the end. His development, his growth, is the ideal. It alone furnishes the standard. . . . Abandon the notion of subject-matter as something fixed and ready-made in itself, outside the child's experience; cease thinking of the child's experience as something hard and fast; see it as something fluid, embryonic, vital." (pp. 95–97)

Dewey suggests that we consider the student more important than curricular content and that we adapt the content of study to the student's needs and potentials. This does not mean a watering down of subject matter; on the contrary, the change in emphasis may imply adjusting the subject matter in the direction of increased rigor for many learners.

Much has been reported recently about what is going on in classrooms. Goodlad (1983) recorded a somewhat passive clientele; he observed that

students listened; they responded when called on to do so; they read short sections of textbooks; they wrote short responses to questions or chose from among alternative responses in quizzes. But they rarely planned or initiated anything, read or wrote anything of some length, or created their own products. And they scarcely ever speculated on meanings, discussed alternative interpretations, or engaged in projects that called for collaborative effort. Most of the time they listened or worked alone. The topics of the curriculum are something to be acquired, not something to be explored, reckoned with, and converted into personal meaning and understanding. (p. 468)

We concur with Goodlad's concerns, especially since we have observed similar behaviors in classrooms.

Recently we were involved with the evaluation of a junior high school reading program in a major metropolitan area. Students were asked to identify those activities which they most disliked in the program. They overwhelmingly listed two activities: those that isolated them from one another (for example, isolated drills and practice) and the omnipresent questions and answers after reading. The students suggested that those distasteful activities be replaced with more time for reading, more time to *discuss* what they read, and some time when they could get help with homework assignments for other classes. In this last alternative, we surmise they were saying "help us learn how to learn."

We have also interviewed students about how they read and study their school assignments. During one session, the students were working individually. They were to read a chapter in a health textbook and then answer the questions at the end of the chapter. Stanley seemed to be having some difficulty; instead of interrupting him, we sat down nearby to observe. Eventually he looked up and asked, "Can you help me?"

"Sure, what's the problem?"

"I'm having trouble with this book, you know. I can't figure out what's going on. I can't find the story."

Stanley couldn't find the story in a health textbook. Why was he looking for a story? Health books don't usually have stories; they contain information, explanations. Here was a student who was given an assignment to complete on his own and who wanted desperately to succeed, and yet, he couldn't because he didn't know how.

Why, we wondered later, was no one else aware that Stanley looked for stories in health books? Why hadn't anyone ever told Stanley that you don't read health books to look for stories? Is it that no one ever asked? Is it that Stanley felt safe telling a stranger? Daniel Fader (1971) recounts a similar occurrence in his book *The Naked Children*.

It began on Thursday morning when I sat in his English classroom during the first period of the day. Charles Dickens would have recognized the teacher. Invented and educated in another age, she was uncomfortable and unhappy in the seventh decade of the twentieth century. If silence is golden, her classroom was the Fort Knox of the neighborhood. Thirty-eight children in her room that morning, breathing not apparent in thirty-five. They had long since gotten the message: Keep quiet. Keep your mouth shut and nothing can happen to you.

Wentworth sat second seat from the front, second row from the wall. I sat in the last seat of the row next to the wall; the teacher's desk was diagonally across the room from me and at right angles to Wentworth. She had a view of his left side and front while I could see his right side and back. What she saw from the left-front was one more of the silent creatures who inhabited the room. What I saw from the right-rear was a boy slowly turning the pages of a hot-rod magazine.

Wentworth turned pages in his magazine while the teacher dragged the class through its hour burlesque of "English." Most of the students sat in a disembodied trance, staring blindly into the utter emptiness of incoherence. Some drew pictures, others put their heads down on their arms, a few unbroken ones whispered.

Then it happened. The teacher meant her question for the girl just east of Wentworth; her glance wasn't off by more than two degrees. Wentworth meant to look west through the windows; at worst, he looked west-southwest. The teacher looked at Wentworth, he looked at her. Neither meant it; both wanted to withdraw, but honor demanded engagement. Helplessly eye-locked, they stared at each other until Wentworth broke the strangled silence by speaking.

What he said doesn't matter. Perhaps he even tried to answer the question—if he heard it, remembered it, understood it. Whatever he said was dreadfully wrong. Without a visitor in class, she might have left him to his invisible magazine. As it was, she blushed, he stammered, she upbraided his inattention, and the neighboring machine supplied the answer. Everyone was upset, the visitor included.

When the bell rang, I tried to be first out the door.

"Doctor Fader," she said, "you know what's wrong with that boy? He's so upset and mean and acts so dumb because he's frustrated. He's frustrated because he can't read. I mean he can't read at all. That makes him feel evil. And then he acts like that. All because he can't read."

She continued to talk but I didn't hear. Can't read? I had just spent forty-five minutes watching him turn the pages of a magazine. Can't read? Can he really have spent all that time looking at pictures? Because I had to believe my eyes, I couldn't believe my ears. Who can give that kind of attention to printed page after printed page—no matter what the quality of the illustrations—and not be able to read? Certainly not an upset, dumb, evil kid.

For all that remained of Thursday and again on Friday I followed him from class to class. By Friday nooon I had seen enough; we spoke in the cafeteria:

"She says you can't read. I don't believe it."

"Maybe she jus' puttin' you on."

"Maybe you're just putting her on."

"I ain't doin' nothin' to nobody." And suddenly he turned away from me—we had been standing together in the cafeteria line—and took a place farther back.

When the last teacher left the cafeteria, five expressionless children got up together and walked toward me across the room.

"Why you messin' on Wentworth?" The only girl in the group was speaking to me. No preliminaries. Just the question.

"I'm not messing on anybody," I said.

What were you looking at during your English class yesterday and today?" I asked Wentworth.

"He don't wanna talk to you," she said.

"But I want to talk to him. He could help me a lot if he wanted to."

"He don't want to."

"He should."

"Lookin' at a hogbook," he said slowly, a smile lighting his face.

"Which one?"

"Don't know the name."

"*Hot Rod*?"

" 'At the one."

"You like it?"

"Some."

"Where'd you get it from?"

"Teacher had a pile of 'em onna table."

"You know where *she* got it from?" An eloquent movement of his shoulders and eyes. "I gave it to her," I said.

"You the one brung all them newspapers and magazines?" The girl was interested. So were the others.

The bell rang and the girl spoke: "We gotta go now. After school we meets on the corner 'cross from the front door." She turned and led them out of the cafeteria. None of them even glanced back at me as they left.

I was waiting on the corner across from school. It was Cleo who brought them to see me. She was in front, with Wentworth, Snapper, and Rubbergut walking together in the rear. Because I was sitting, she sat too. Snapper squatted behind me, Wentworth and Rubbergut leaned against the telephone pole, while Uncle Wiggly continued to shadowbox in the street.

"You still wanna know?" she asked.

I told her that I did.

"All right," she said. "Go on, Wentworth. Tell him."

Wentworth told me. "Sure I can read," he said. "I been able to read ever since I can remember. But I ain't never gonna let *them* know, on accoun' of iff'n I do I'm gonna have to read all that crap they got."

I knew what he said was true. I knew it was true because I had seen him reading; I knew it was true because I'd seen the brightness in his eyes and heard the deft quickness of his responses. (pp. 11–18, 22)

Time and time again the Stanleys and Wentworths encounter learning situations that seem to contradict the object of education. Kids seem to get pushed aside to make room for content. But it need not be that way, and, thankfully, it isn't always.

We've all seen kids excited about learning but rarely about worksheets, vocabulary drills, questions at the ends of chapters, or, to quote Wentworth, "all that crap they got." Our visits to classrooms, some like your classroom and others not, have convinced us that students may not be involved, *but they want to be*. Students in all grades, in all kinds of classrooms, want to learn; they want their learning to be meaningful; they want their learning to be successful. Students of all ages, colors, creeds want to be encouraged, not frustrated; they want to be stimulated to learn, not bored by enforced passivity; they need to be supported instead of pushed aside to be replaced by curricular matters. In short, learning must be student-centered, not curriculum-centered. Eliot Wigginton (1973) recounts a wonderful scene that clearly articulates these principles of learning.

> Suzy was in the outside room and I heard her laughing—as usual—except she was really cracked up this time, and so naturally I had to go out and see what was happening, and she said just be quiet and listen. And Carlton, one of the tenth grade kids, had been in the darkroom alone for an hour and I had forgotten—and God he was missing his English class—and this string of muffled swear words suddenly drifted through the darkroom door. Yep. Carlton was still in there . . . trying to make a double exposure print for Karen's and Betsey's burials article. And he was trying to figure out how to do it and burning up all this printing paper and coming closer and closer to getting it just right and talking to himself explaining what was wrong like there were seventy-eight people watching. And Suzy had been listening to the struggle, laughing, when—Bam—out he came with a dripping wet print and a *There how does that grab you*—and it was beautiful, and we used it on the cover of the magazine that had that article in it. . . . And Suzy and I were both laughing and then Carlton cracked up too. And we slapped him on the back and he punched us and we laughed some more. And then he went to English.
>
> And when he got to English, he had to write five hundred times, "I will not be late to class any more."

> And the teacher read some poems aloud that nobody listened to, so she spent the whole hour reading to herself while the kids hacked off—or slept. . . . You know. (p. 9)

Yep, we know. And we also know that although reports such as *A Nation at Risk* and *A Place Called School* consistently report the difficulties, even the demise, of our schools, we might take heart from Mark Twain who, upon learning that the Associated Press had included his name in the obituary column, retorted, "The reports of my death are greatly exaggerated."

While everyone agrees that conditions in schools today could be improved, we believe the emphasis should be on the positive rather than the negative. Our goal in this book is to mention the negative only when necessary and to bring positive resolutions to the plights of Stanley, Wentworth, Cleo, Carlton, and others like them.

READING AS LEARNING

Among the most important characteristics of successful students is the awareness of how to learn. In our research we have sought to determine what students do well and not so well; our object has been to clarify what can be done instructionally to help students succeed more frequently. Thus, throughout this book we will discuss those strategies and activities we have found most helpful to students and teachers alike. Our discussion of instruction is within the framework of reading and reasoning, with little distinction made between reading and reasoning when a student is seeking to learn from expository textbooks. We will focus on expository textbooks, for our major concern is to help readers of all levels understand and remember more of what they read in such informational textbooks.

Accomplished Readers

Our goal is to help your students become accomplished readers, and we define accomplished readers as those who

> —seek to understand,
> —control the reading activity through an awareness of learning strategies,
> —can identify why they have difficulty understanding when comprehension falters,

—associate strategies and purposes for a specific reading task, and

—monitor comprehension and adjust their strategy if comprehension falters.

These abilities develop over time as the result of multiple experiences with reading. More technically, we are discussing what cognitive psychologists and reading researchers call *metacognition*. Metacognition is the knowledge one has about how to learn *and* one's ability to act upon and control that knowledge. An accomplished reader is metacognitively sophisticated when he or she understands what is involved in reading and reasoning and can apply that knowledge to his or her own reading and learning.

Before launching into the details of becoming an accomplished reader, however, let's explore what we mean by reading. To do this we will engage you in a bit of inquiry. Examine the following question and as you consider each part, reflect on your response either by yourself or, if possible, in discussion with someone else. What does reading have in common with taking a walk, riding a horse, seeing the sun rise, enjoying a concert? What do these activities have in common? In our view, each of these is an event, and as with any event, when one reads, things happen. Open any book and you can become anyone or go anywhere or do anything; all you have to do is follow your imagination. So, follow along while we take you on a little adventure through an event called reading.

◼ Reading as an Event

Begin your journey by reading the following untitled poem from Dooling & Lachman (1971). Note the exact moment at which you understand what this poem is about. Feel free to reread the poem as many times as necessary. When you've finished, we'll have another task for you.

With hocked gems financing him,
Our hero bravely defied all scornful laughter
That tried to prevent his scheme.

Your eyes deceive, he had said;
An egg, not a table
Correctly typifies this unexplored planet.

Now three sturdy sisters sought proof,
Forging along sometimes through calm vastness
Yet more often over turbulent peaks and valleys.

Days become weeks,
As many doubters spread
Fearful rumors about the edge.

At last from nowhere,
Welcome winged creatures appeared
Signifying momentous success. (pp. 216–222)

Now, before you forget anything, on a sheet of paper (1) briefly explain your meaning of the poem, perhaps by providing a title, and (2) identify the word or phrase in the text that triggered or sparked your understanding.

We often call this experience "an occurrence of meaning" because as you read, you reach a point where a meaning pops out at you. In this poem, the thought "Columbus" abruptly appears and all the pieces become connected. Suddenly everything makes sense and you know that your meaning is the correct meaning. This is what Roger Brown (1958) calls the "click of comprehension."

How, though, did this click occur? If you asked that question, then you are raising the critical issue we want to address. Before we share our ideas, we want you to reflect on your experience with the poem and see if you can answer the question, "What happened that enabled you to understand this poem?"

The event of reading involves three major factors: a reader, a text, and a context. Each of these contributes to the click of comprehension or can be examined to determine why the click did not occur. Every time these factors interact, things happen and each occurrence is a unique event. It can happen only once; it can never happen the same way at any other time. Louise Rosenblatt (1978) compares this transaction among a reader, a text, and a context to an electrical circuit: "As with the elements of an electrical circuit, each component of the reading process functions by virtue of the presence of others. A specific reader and a specific text at a specific time and place: change any of these, and there occurs a different circuit, a different event. . . ." (p. 14)

Let's explore each of these factors, one by one. Keep in mind, however, that this separation is artificial; in a reading event, the factors are inextricably interrelated.

☐ *Text*

How does a text contribute to reading? Until very recently, printed text was viewed primarily, if not exclusively, as a repository of information. But that view is changing, in part due to the research of linguists, psychologists, psycholinguists, and educators (for example,

Anderson, Armbruster, & Kantor, 1980; Halliday & Hasan, 1976; Schallert & Kleiman, 1979; and Tierney & Mosenthal, 1980). Unquestionably texts do contain information in one sense of the word "contain," but texts are not simply information containers. In fact, there is nothing simple about what texts are and how they contribute to reading. Let's examine the untitled poem as an example.

The poem originated with two authors, Dooling and Lachman, who had some ideas, feelings, and inclinations that they wanted to share. They chose precise words and phrases with which to construct their poem, words like "hero," "three sturdy sisters," and "turbulent peaks and valleys" to convey their view of Columbus, his daring, his courage, his foresight. Everything the authors wanted to impart is conveyed through the words, phrases, and figures of speech they chose to reflect their thoughts, attitudes, and inclinations; the authors' language became the text for the poem.

A text, then, consists of language and comprises a series of symbols that represent an author's understanding, experience, and point of view. Rosenblatt (1978), in her transactive discussion of reading, has this to say abut text: "Text designates a set or series of signs interpretable as linguistic symbols. The visual signs become verbal symbols, become words, by virtue of their being potentially recognizable [to a reader]. . . . Thus, in a reading situation, 'the text' may be thought of as the printed signs in their capacity to serve as symbols." (p. 12)

Notice again, ". . . the visual signs become . . . words by virtue of their being potentially recognizable [to a reader]. . . ." Not all readers will associate something with the symbols; some will, others will not. Hence, the symbols themselves do not *contain* ideas; they have the potential to *convey* ideas. The symbols have *potential* to be meaningful for a reader. In the untitled poem, each phrase has a potential meaning; for example, "with hocked gems" refers to the source of funding for the voyage. Had you not known that Isabella sold some jewels to finance the trip, the symbols "with hocked gems" would have been meaningless. Still, the phrase would have potential meaning for anyone who knew that fact. What we want you to realize is that language is the vehicle for communicating the ideas, feelings, and inclinations that people have. Hence, language is a conveyor of understandings and experiences, while a text is a conveyor of linguistic symbols representative of the thoughts, feelings, and point of view of an author.

How, though, does a text convey an author's message? Again, let us call on Rosenblatt,

> The text is a stimulus (not in the sense of a stimulus-response) activating elements of the reader's past experience—his experience both

with literature and with life. . . . [It also] serves as a blueprint, a guide for the selecting, rejecting, and ordering of what is being called forth; the text regulates what shall be held in the forefront of the reader's attention. (p. 11)

Thus the text is a guide, a blueprint to an author's ideas. A text is able to convey ideas because it consists of linguistic symbols that have the potential to cue a reader to understandings, experiences, and a point of view similar to that of the author. This is the contribution a text makes to any reading event. The text cues the reader to think, to feel, to imagine, to act. Assuming certain things are right with the text rhetorically and structurally, then the text is a conduit linking author and reader, *assuming certain things are right with the reader*.

Text is the only constant in the event called reading. A text never changes, except of course through editing and revising. A reader's experience with a text does change. How else would *Alice in Wonderland* mean one thing to a six year old and something different to the same person as an adult? Such changes are explained by the reader and the context, the other partners in this *menage á trois*.

☐ *Reader*

A reader's contribution to any reading event is based upon all the experiences that have accrued for the reader up to and during the time of the reading. These experiences serve as the foundation and direction for learning, and they can be classified into three areas: knowledge, feelings, and inclinations. **Knowledge,** more technically known as *cognition,* encompasses thoughts, beliefs, ideas, imaginings, and rememberings. **Feelings,** or *affect,* include sensations, emotions, and moods. **Inclinations** encompass desires, motives, and intentions. Inclinations are, perhaps, the most ignored of the factors and may be the most important. A more technical term for inclination is *volition,* the motive factor underlying what each of us does. You remember the adage, "You can lead a horse to water, but you can't make him drink." Volition is the desire or intent that determines how inclined the reader is toward imbibing the text.

Perhaps you realize that everything we have just described relative to a reader applies equally to any person in any conscious activity and is hardly unique to reading. During reading, the reader draws primarily on those prior experiences that apply to reading: experiences with language, with types of text and their organizations, with the topic of the text, and with reading itself. Thus, when a reader attends to a text and tries to make sense of it, his or her existing knowledge, feelings, and inclinations contribute to that attention and sense-making.

Though a reader draws on knowledge, feelings, and inclinations in an effort to make sense of text, the most apparent contributor is knowledge. Without intending to slight either feelings or inclinations, we will focus our attention here on how a reader's prior knowledge contributes to a reading activity. For example, a question that may already have occurred to you is, What determines the elements of one's prior knowledge that are activated at any particular moment? When you were reading the untitled poem, why did certain ideas come to mind and others not? This is a vital question and one that can be used to explore the interaction between a reader and a text.

Recall that a text provides cues to regulate what is held in the forefront of the reader's attention. As the reader is guided by the text to pay attention to certain visual symbols (and what those symbols represent), those symbols cue the reader to recall certain prior knowledge that is related to those symbols. Try now to recollect what came to your mind as you encountered each of the major cues in the poem. What did you think of as you read "With hocked gems," "financing him," "our hero," "tried to prevent his scheme," "an egg, not a table," "this unexplored planet," "three sturdy sisters," "fearful rumors about the edge," and "welcome winged creatures"?

What word or phrase enabled you to put it all together? Why did that word or phrase cause a click for you? In fact, the text directed our attention to specific symbols chosen to reflect the ideas, attitudes, and point of view of the authors. Those symbols cued you to think about certain specific concepts with which you had some prior experience. As you examined the symbols, they evoked certain familiar associations for you. You, in turn, activated the associations and began linking the concepts that were racing through your mind. Eventually, an acceptable link, one that made sense, was made among all the ideas cued by the text and an understanding emerged out of what had seemed nonsense only moments before.

What then is reading? Reading is *thinking* cued by text. A text guides and cues a reader to think. As connections are made between the symbols provided in the text and the prior knowledge of the reader, meaning emerges. It is these connections that are the "grits and gravy" of reading.

But what about the reader who does not make the connections? A symbol cannot cause an association to occur if related prior knowledge does not exist. Successful reading requires cues within the text that the reader can recognize (note: recognize = re + cognize, that is, to cognize *again*). Regardless of the reading, however, the activity is the same. The text cues; the reader associates and thinks. The key to successful reading is the reader's ability to explore the cues and the prior knowledge necessary to make those associations, those links, those connections.

☐ *Context*

The third factor that contributes to any reading event is context, and here we refer to the setting of the event. While context is an elaborate facet of reading, it is situational context to which we will limit our discussion and we will use the definition put forth by Smith, Carey, & Harste (1982):

> Situational context, a concept akin to Malinowski's (1923) 'context of situations', is the setting in which a reading event occurs; it includes the linguistic text, the individuals involved (e.g., a student and a teacher), the location (e.g., in a classroom or at home), the expectations (e.g., that a recall test will be given over the material), and all such other factors impinging immediately on the event. (p. 22)

Furthermore, the reader-text interaction has its own context, such as reading to take a test, to make notes for a report, to enjoy, to find a specific piece of information (for example, a date or telephone number), or to appreciate a poetic effect. These are all different situations, each with a purpose that seems to demand some variation in reading strategy. You probably read the untitled poem differently in this book than you would have in a magazine or in its original setting (a research report in cognitive science). The situation of a particular experience strongly influences the purpose for reading and the way the reading will be conducted, and all of these influence what will be gained from a given reading activity.

Context is a major fixture in the electrical circuit to which Rosenblatt refers. You will read differently if someone else sets the time, place, purpose, and expectation than if you set those things for yourself. As those contexts change for your students, you will find that your students read differently too. Throughout this book we will suggest ways that you can increase your students' learning by manipulating instructional contexts.

FRUSTRATION POTENTIALS

■ ■ As we know all too well, reading is not always a successful endeavor. For elementary, junior high, and senior high students, reading is often filled with pitfalls and frustrations. One characteristic of an accomplished reader is an ability to deal with the frustrations that arise and to locate the source of the difficulty. As we have talked with students in numerous learning situations, we have tried to specify the kinds of problems that occur most frequently so that we could offer reasonable resolutions. We have identified five major factors that tend to contribute to readers' difficulties:

1. Textbooks that are unclear, incomplete, and difficult to understand;
2. A lack of essential background information or necessary experiences on the part of the reader;
3. A lack of familiarity with effective and efficient strategies for reading and reasoning on the part of the reader;
4. An attempt by the reader to remember before being sure of understanding; and
5. Inflexibility on the part of the teacher in determining what a text *should* mean, playing the role of surrogate author and insisting on the correctness of one interpretation.

These issues will be examined in the following chapters, with the exception of number five. An understanding of various solutions to the other problems can effectively neutralize the fifth problem. But it can't simply be ignored, as one particularly astute elementary student pointed out. Prior to giving a presentation to a group of teachers a few years ago, we asked some students what they might like to say to some teachers about the teaching of reading. Jeff, a fifth grader, considered the question and eventually responded, "Tell them to ask me what I think the story is about before asking what the author meant."

Jeff's suggestion made us aware of how often we interpret texts for students instead of exploring the ideas with them. We realized that teachers are often tempted to explain to students what an author meant. For example, what did William Faulkner mean by his "Bear"? And Frost, what was he trying to say in "Stopping by Woods on a Snowy Evening"? And what right do teachers have to tell students that the rose outside the prison in *The Scarlet Letter* was Hawthorne's way of foreshadowing hope? Jeff was right. Students do have the right, or even more, the *responsibility* to share their ideas with others and reason out their meanings just as authors always insist they want them to do.

Although the temptation to assume the role of surrogate author, to tell readers what a text means, is most formidable with narrative or poetic texts, the subtle temptation is omnipresent even with expository texts. With all the expert information and background knowledge teachers bring to the reading event, they are that much more confident than students of what a text might mean even if it doesn't say it in so many words. To avoid this autocratic snare we suggest you inform the readers about your interpretations in a manner that asks students to reason out what the text means. Helping you learn to do this is among our primary goals.

■ Foxfire: An Experiment in Learning

While considering the issue of teachers as surrogate authors, we recall the exploits of Eliot Wigginton who, in his first six weeks of teaching, had his lectern burned, his yellow chalk stolen, and his chart of the Globe Theatre mutilated. In the next ten years, he and his students published seven best-selling collections of articles from many issues of *Foxfire,* a magazine distributed by subscription in every state and many foreign countries. Recently Jacque Weurtenberg, a noted lecturer and workshop leader in language arts, told a conference audience that when her family decided to build a log cabin in Michigan backcountry, the best source they could find on building log cabins was *The Foxfire Book*.

    Foxfire is a testament to the resolution of one frustrated English teacher and an inspiration to others like him. Today, almost two decades later, Foxfire has become a concept; Wigginton calls it "a tremendous new experiment in education." It served as a prototype for other similar innovations in education around the country, and Wigginton has provided a guide, called *Moments: The Foxfire Experience,* for educators who seek to implement their own Foxfire experiment.

    It is easy for most educators to empathize with Mr. Wigginton in his nearly disastrous first-year experience. Unfortunately, most teachers, like him, began their careers teaching as they were taught, with greater regard for the subject matter than for the students. Undoubtedly, this is because most of us have spent many more hours studying whatever we were to teach than in coming to understand the nature of the students whom we were to teach.

    Wigginton realized that salvaging his teaching career demanded a new approach. To foster growth in his students (his readers), he would have to manipulate the *text* and *context* of their instruction. He decided that English could be defined as "communication—reaching out and touching people with words, sounds, and visual images." (1972, p. 13) His goal was to facilitate his students' mastery of the communicative art, and to accomplish this goal he had to begin with them as they were—a unique composite of knowledge and experiences, feelings, and inclinations. He realized that to reach his students he would have to use subject matter they could relate to and activities that would involve them. In a stroke of genius, he decided that the lore and legend of Rabun Gap, Georgia, would be interesting, and if communicated through the format of a magazine, it would be enticing. Right he was! The success of the Foxfire experiment is now established. Its success is due largely to Wigginton's recognition of the needs, interests, and abilities of his students, and to his own ability to allow them to use material of relevance and to perform activities aimed at achieving a common purpose. Interestingly enough, however, all this change in text, context, and students' involvement began when Eliot Wigginton changed, when he realized that all he had learned about teaching was getting him further from his goal to help students learn. In his own words, "Wig" says,

> And it was with a deep sigh that, as I launched one of several paper airplanes within easy reach, I began to ponder greener pastures. Either that or start all over.
>
> The answer was obvious. If I were to finish out the year honorably, it would be necessary to reassert my authority. No teenagers were going to push me around. Besides, my course was too important. First offense would be an "X" in the grade book. Second, a paddling. Third, to the principal. Fourth, out of class for two weeks.
>
> It frightens me to think how close I came to making another stupid mistake. First, I had bored them unmercifully. Now I was about to impose a welcome punishment. Two weeks out of that class would have been more pleasure than pain. . . .
>
> The kid who scorched my lectern had been trying to tell me something. He and his classmates, through their boredom and restlessness, were sending out distress signals—signals that I came perilously close to ignoring.
>
> It's the same old story. The answer to student boredom and restlessness (manifested in everything from paper airplanes to dope) maybe—just maybe—is not stricter penalties, innumerable suspensions, and bathroom monitors. How many schools (mine included) have dealt with those students that still have fire and spirit, *not* by channeling that fire in constructive, creative directions, but by pouring water on the very flames that could make them great? And it's not *necessarily* that the rules are wrong. It's the arrogant way we tend to enforce them. Until we can *inspire* rather than babysit, we're in big trouble. (1972, pp. 10, 14)

And inspire he has. Involving all of the students in the Foxfire project is a persistent problem. "It hasn't always worked, but we try" is Wigginton's understatement. To involve everyone requires attention to the range of individual abilities and learning styles in a classroom, a goal to which we'd like to dedicate this book. It won't always work, but, like Wigginton, we're willing to try.

If all students are to be involved in learning in the same classroom, where reading abilities may span eight years or more and where interests vary as surely as height and weight, students must be given opportunities to learn as individuals. Students may need to do different things in order to learn, but those differences can lead to and indeed encourage, similar educational goals. Some of Wigginton's students found it possible to write feature articles; for others copying and placing paragraphs in a layout was at first a challenge. But all were involved and all were learning, because each was allowed to function first as an individual and second as a member of the class.

Principles of Learning

Eliot Wigginton found no need to be tempted by the role of surrogate author, once he and his class were transformed to focus on students instead of curriculum. To conclude our discussion of the surrogate author as a potential contributor to learners' frustration, let us note several key principles of learning espoused by Carl Rogers (1969; 1982) that were implemented by Wigginton.

First, Wigginton believes, along with Rogers, that *human beings have a natural potential for learning*. He acknowledges their natural curiosity and creativity and recognizes that his success in teaching them depends on his ability to shape and direct that curiosity and creativity. He made no attempt to teach things about which his students were not curious and would likely never be made curious. Instead, he found ways to manipulate the curriculum and the context of its study to fit students' curiosity, in turn developing an inclination toward learning.

Two other principles of Rogers to which Wigginton ascribes are (1) *significant learning takes place when students perceive the subject matter to have relevance for their own purposes (and contexts),* and (2) *learning is facilitated when the student participates responsibly in the learning process.* Producing the magazine *Foxfire* was a task in which Wigginton's students became involved. Getting the magazine out became their responsibility, and learning the communication skills needed to accomplish the task became relevant, even vital to their purpose. Teachers will find their efforts much more successful when they are able to correlate their own purposes with their students' purposes.

A third principle is that *much significant learning is acquired through doing*. Actually, learning is an evolutionary process that begins with awareness, then moves through understanding and remembering to application. The verbal symbols through which most subject matter is communicated are by their nature abstract, understandable best in relation to concrete experiences. Wigginton linked the two together, the abstract and the concrete, by getting his students out of the classroom, onto the farms and into the shops where they could see firsthand the activities in which the people of Rabun Gap were involved. Through the student's firsthand experience, a context for meaningful reading and writing and study was created.

Finally, *the most socially useful learning in the modern world is the learning of the process of learning*. One who has learned how to learn can be continuously open to experiences and can incorporate into oneself the omnipresent process of change. In discussing the subject matter of education, John Dewey (1897) proposed "that education must be conceived as a continuing reconstruction of experience; that the process and the goal of education are one and the same thing." (p. 27) No teacher, no society, can afford to be satisfied with anything less than students who have learned how to learn.

Much has been written and presented to encourage content area teachers to incorporate literacy into their subject matter instruction. Reading and writing are cornerstones of learning, and students who become more literate are those who become more learned as content specialists. While it would be a nearly impossible task to estimate how much experience and understanding in a literate society depends on reading, you can gain some insight into a world you take for granted by asking someone who does not read or who can only barely read.

The same message needs to be given to the literacy teacher, at all grade levels. When learning to read and when learning to write, students should read about and write about things worth learning about. Literacy does not exist in a vacuum; reading and writing have no meaning apart from the learning and sharing of ideas and information.

A LEARNING STRATEGIES CURRICULUM

■ ■   It was Mark Twain who said, "Education is what you remember when all your schoolin' is through." Certainly the rationale for our society's effort to educate all citizens has to do with the assumption that much of what is taught will linger beyond school days. In that spirit, our aim in this book is to propose ways a teacher can structure students' schooling so it contributes to their education.

One way of structuring students' schooling is to listen to what students say. Recently, we had the opportunity to collect some information from second graders in a very rural school. We asked them if they would enter into their daily journals, in the coming week, their thoughts in answer to the question, "Why is reading books important?" These were some of the answers, in just the form we received them:

> Karen: "I read books becaue I like to no abot things."
>
> Frank: "I learn fatcks. I get a lot from it."
>
> Mike: "I read becols it is nis to read. And it is fun to read. You can read to your family."
>
> Susan: "I lik to read to get baeter."
>
> Grover: "Books helps you get ager cayshinal. Help you learn."

Grover, you said it all, books can help you get educational.

Considering these students' views on the importance of reading, how might we approach our aim with particular attention towards helping children become able to use their books to get "ager cayshinal"? Recall the five frustration potentials mentioned earlier. Throughout subsequent chapters we will explore solutions to those potential difficulties. Specifically, in chapter 2 we examine ways to evaluate textbooks to determine how clearly they convey their message. In chapters 4 and 5 we discuss specific methods of dealing with students' prior experiences and awareness about a topic they are about to study. In chapter 6 we explore learning strategies that facilitate understanding, and in chapter 7 we focus on the remembering phase of the learning process.

Throughout the book there is a message both tacit and explicit: students need to learn how to learn. Literacy teachers and subject area teachers, parents and librarians, counselors and administrators, all of us need to prepare students for the emerging, and as yet undefined, age of the twenty-first century. Regardless of our specialized training, irrespective of our grade-level experiences, we as educators must put our goals in priority and place students and their survival skills first on our list.

We propose that students today need metacognitive awareness so they can monitor their own learning process, and we hope to provide a framework and specific approaches to allow your students control of their own learning. It is our position that effective, efficient reading and reasoning can best be learned in the context of a learning strategies curriculum, a curriculum in which literacy and subject matter are learned concurrently with particular focus on helping students master the process of learning.

For your students, our goal is for them to become accomplished as readers, as reasoners, and as learners. We want them to be able to monitor and self-regulate their own thinking. We want them to be capable of identifying why any learning is not successful by pointing to the source of the difficulty as the initial step in resolving any frustration. We want your students to seek first to understand and then to identify what they do not understand. We hope your students will be able to distinguish between the important and the trivial amidst the deluge of information they encounter daily. We hope they will be able to relate details and examples to higher and broader level concepts so that the broader concepts are made clearer by the details and examples while the details and examples become easier to remember owing to their association with the more important concepts. Finally, and most importantly, we want your students to possess and to use a variety of learning strategies instead of choosing between tromping and tip-toeing through their assignments.

In the remainder of this book, we will consider such topics as attitudes, vocabulary, reading comprehension assessment, and the art of study. In the words of a Japanese proverb, "Give them a fish and they will eat tonight; teach them to fish and they will eat for a lifetime." Extend the analogy. Teach students the information you want them to learn this week and they will pass the test on Friday; teach students how to learn and they will pass the test for the rest of their lives. We hope to show you how to do both as it applies to reading and reasoning beyond the primary grades. A tall order for a short book, but with a little help from you, we'll fill it!

2

Textbooks in Classrooms

SETTING THE STAGE

Many of the reading problems that interfere with learning can be traced to the books students are asked to read rather than to the students who are asked to read them. Before throwing up their hands in despair or charging headlong into a crash remediation program, teachers should carefully examine the textbooks chosen for their classrooms and determine whether the students can realistically be expected to learn effectively from them.

There are a number of procedures and devices for estimating the readability of written text. Anything with a beginning, middle, and end that is understandable outside the context of other text—books, chapters, sections of chapters, articles, pamphlets—can be evaluated. Different procedures will yield somewhat different perspectives on the same text. Readability formulas attempt to pinpoint difficulty in precise numerical terms, in numbers that convert often to the nearest one-tenth of a grade level. Other procedures, for example the cloze procedure, take the reader's perceptions of the text into account, and in return for better diagnostic information give up a degree of arithmetic precision. No one procedure fits all purposes but a combination of techniques offers the best possibility of obtaining an appropriate estimate of whether students will or will not find comprehensible what they are asked to read. The decision of what to require students to read must be made with as much information as one can obtain so the reading task will facilitate rather than hinder learning.

THE RIGHT STICK

■ ■ When Little League managers begin batting instruction, they haul out a large canvas bag and empty the contents in the vicinity of home plate. Out spill brown bats, white bats, long bats, short bats, skinny bats, and fat bats. The players eagerly scramble among the bats as the manager helps them find the "stick" that best fits each of them. When classroom teachers begin their instruction, they haul out a briefcase, open it, and take out the book for that course. It may be brown, red, green, yellow, or chartreuse—fat, skinny, short, long, easy, or hard. But there is usually only one book. One thing is certain: the Little Leaguers and the readers will not all succeed equally well with their respective tasks, but the baseball players are at an advantage by having the right stick.

Failure to learn in school is often attributed to reading deficiencies in the learner. Efforts are made to correct such deficiencies on the assumption that the students could succeed if only they could read better. Whenever such a tack is taken, the implicit assumption is that the reading material given to the students is appropriate, but that they are inappropriate for the material. That is, the students have the right stick; the problem is they cannot use it. But this assumption is often invalid, and in fact many of the difficulties which exist for readers could be eliminated if texts were chosen on the basis of their appropriateness for the students rather than their appropriateness for the topic or course of study.

READABILITY AND COMPREHENSION

■ ■ Over the years any number of formulas for the measure of readability have come into existence. If you were in a word-association task right now and we said "cat," you might say "dog;" if we said "mother," you'd probably say "father;" if we said "readability," you'd say "formula." Well, maybe not. But the idea of readability and the formulas by which it is measured have become almost synonymous. There is, in fact, no proper view to take of readability except to use every tool available in an attempt to get the right materials into the hands of the right learner at the right time. Formulas for measuring readability are only one type of tool.

The problem we face here is that even if readability is a property of text, comprehensibility is not. Any reasonable view of comprehensibility must take the reader into account. As it is put by Walter

Kintsch (1979), who has been doing very important research on the matter for several years now, "most texts are easy to read for some people but hard for others, or easy to read for some purposes but not for others." (p. 2) Another researcher, E. D. Hirsch, Jr. (1977), recognizes this with his concept of "relative readability." Readability has to be judged in relation to author's and reader's intentions, "not in relation to degree of difficulty on an absolute scale." (p. 85) Hirsch goes on to conclude: "It is in the nature of [readability] formulas that *meaning*— the one thing needful—cannot be taken into account in assessing the readability of prose. . . . By introducing meaning into the concept of readability, we give up the possibility of precise arithmetical formulations." (p. 84–85) This would seem true, at least in part, because readers and text *interact* to create meaning, so that what the reader *realizes* in the text plays as heavily in determining comprehension as does what the author *says* in the text. Some of the text assessment procedures we suggest will be taking this interactionist view for granted, as you will recognize.

One of the assumptions made by readability formulas is that the ability of a reader is a relatively fixed quantity, scaled similarly to the difficulty of a text. Surely no one would want to accept the suggestion that a reader's ability is fixed. And yet even as a reader's abilities vary from situation to situation, we need a way to speak of those abilities in qualitative, if not precisely quantitative, terms. In the language of the reading specialist, three levels of understanding have been delineated and identified as (1) the independent reading level, (2) the instructional reading level, and (3) the frustration level. Each of these levels predicts the degree of success which a person will have with a specific reading task.

The *independent reading level* is the level at which a reader can completely understand material without outside help. That is, the reader can learn virtually everything the author has to offer and can do so with ease. In such situations, the reader is familiar with the vocabulary, has the necessary skills to extract the ideas, and can understand the concepts being conveyed. Thus,

What the Author Assumed		What the Reader Has
vocabulary load	=	vocabulary
skills load	=	skills
concept load	=	conceptual awareness

Unfortunately, such a harmonious match between the author's assumptions and the reader's abilities rarely occurs, especially in classroom situations. Perfect congruence, however, is not necessary for students to learn from a reading selection. When students' skills, vocabulary, or conceptual awareness fall slightly below an author's expectations, they will be able to learn, but not with complete thoroughness or ease. In fact, this is what usually happens in academic situations; students struggle with assignments and learn what they can. If students can learn from material in a limited way, often a teacher can provide instruction geared to helping them read with greater ease and understanding. Thus, when

What the Student Has   *What the Author Assumed*

vocabulary   +   = vocabulary load

skills   +   = skills load

conceptual awareness   +   = concept load

the material is said to be on the student's *instructional reading level*. In essence, instruction can bridge the gap between the student's abilities and those necessary to read with satisfactory understanding.

Sometimes classroom material is so difficult for students that a reasonable amount of instructional assistance is insufficient to bridge the gap between the students' abilities and an author's assumptions. In such cases the learning potential is notably limited by the frustration and anxiety often accompanying the students' efforts. This reaction frequently produces negative results because the student associates failure and frustration with reading. The *frustration level* therefore reflects material where

What the Student Has   *What the Author Assumed*

vocabulary   +   ≠ vocabulary load

skills   +   ≠ skills load

conceptual awareness   +   ≠ concept load

TWO QUICK AND EASY PREDICTORS OF READABILITY

■ ■   With the foregoing material under your belt, now consider some of the available ways for judging whether your students will be likely to understand what you ask them to read. Underlying the application of readability formulas is the premise that material consisting of short, simple sentences and familiar vocabulary is more easily understood by readers than material written with complex sentences that include difficult or unfamiliar words. Consider the following sentence: *Sally ran down the street.* The familiar vocabulary and the simple sentence structure present no obstacles to understanding for most readers. However, many young readers, and even older ones, would not learn much from the following sentence: *The only aim now is to hurt the enemy, in any way possible and, with every available weapon, to destroy not only his will to resist but also to eliminate every ability to implement that will effectively.* Analyses of materials using readability formulas can help to quantify a difference in complexity of structure such as these two sentences exhibit, and they can serve as the basis for a more complete picture of a selection's overall difficulty.

Historically, classroom teachers have not used readability formulas because most of the reputable ones have been very time consuming and complex to administer. These formulas, such as the Dale-Chall (1948) and Spache (1960), have been widely used in reading research and textbook preparation, however, and their complexity lies primarily in the process of determining vocabulary difficulty. Both formulas require that each word in a passage be compared to a graded list of familiar words. Thus, an adequate administration of these formulas may require as much as an hour per book or passage. Few teachers are able to devote the time necessary to analyze all their reading materials unless they are fortunate enough to have a computer program for the formula and a computer to run the calculation.

Fortunately, several short-cut formulas are available which give just about the same accuracy as the longer, more complicated procedures from which they are derived. Two of these formulas, the Fry Readability Estimate (Fry, 1977) and McLaughlin's SMOG formula (McLaughlin, 1969), will be discussed here. References to other formulas are provided in an excellent review by Klare (1982).

■ The Fry Readability Estimate

Fry's formula is actually a graph (see Figure 2.1). Several simple calculations must be applied to a selection and the results then interpolated by plotting them on an accompanying graph. This analysis begins by determining the average sentence length in three 100-word samples and continues with an estimate of vocabulary familiarity by a count of the syllables in each sample. The specific steps suggested by Fry are:

1. Randomly select three (3) sample passages and count out exactly 100 words each, beginning with the beginning of a sentence. Do count proper nouns, initializations, and numerals.
2. Count the number of sentences in the hundred words, using

a fraction to estimate the length of the last sentence to the nearest one-tenth.

3. Count the total number of syllables in the 100-word passage. If a hand counter is not available, an easy way is to simply put a mark above every syllable beyond the first one; then when you get to the end of the passage, count the number of marks and add 100. Small calculators can also be used as counters by pushing numeral 1, then pushing the + sign for each word or syllable when counting.

4. Enter graph with average sentence length and average number of syllables; plot dot where the two lines intersect. Area where dot is plotted will give you the approximate grade level.

5. If a great deal of variability is found in syllable count or sentence count, computing more samples into the average is desirable.

FIGURE 2.1   Fry Graph for Estimating Readability—Extended

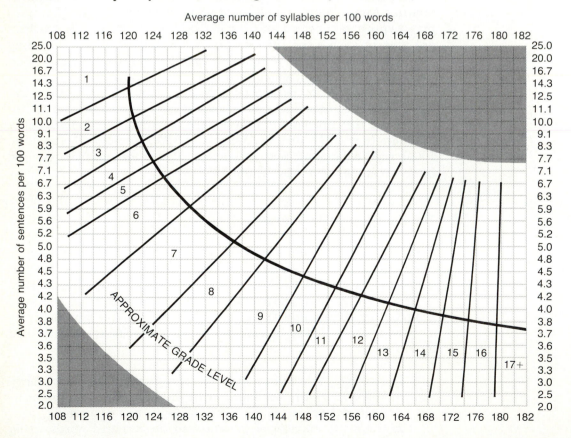

6. A word is defined as a group of symbols with a space on either side; thus, *Joe, IRA, 1945,* and *&* are each one word.
7. A syllable is defined as a phonetic syllable. Generally, there are as many syllables as vowel sounds. For example, *stopped* is one syllable and *wanted* is two syllables. When counting syllables for numerals and initializations, count one syllable for each symbol. For example, *1945* is four syllables, *IRA* is three syllables, and *&* is one syllable.

■ McLaughlin's SMOG Formula

This formula is probably the least complicated of all those available and its efficiency is an attractive feature for many teachers. It is based on the interrelationship of sentence length and vocabulary difficulty, though the inclusion of these two variables is not clearly evident at first glance. McLaughlin has approached these two variables from a slightly different direction than other designers of readability formulas. The SMOG formula requires determination of the number of polysyllabic words in three ten-sentence samples. The premise is, if the sentences are short, then there is a diminished possibility for any polysyllabic words to be included, and thus, the difficulty of the passage can be determined by the number of polysyllabic words in it.

The specific steps included in McLaughlin's formula are:

1. Count ten consecutive sentences near the beginning, ten in the middle, and ten near the end of the selection.
2. In the thirty sentences (total), count every word of three or more syllables when they are read aloud. Recount polysyllabic words (of three or more syllables) if they are repeated.
3. Estimate the square root of the total number of polysyllabic words by taking the square root of the nearest perfect square.
4. If the total number of polysyllabic words falls exactly between two perfect squares, take the lower of the two.
5. Add three (3) to the estimated square root to determine the reading level.

Consider the following example:

	Number of Polysyllabic Words*
10 sentence sample #1	6
10 sentence sample #2	9
10 sentence sample #3	7
TOTAL	22

*words of three or more syllables

The nearest perfect square to 22 is 25 (5 × 5). Add 5 + 3 and the reading level by the SMOG formula is 8. The simplicity of this formula and its slight deviation from the procedures of other formulas, more highly regarded through time and research, has caused this formula to be somewhat suspect among some reading professionals. However, it can serve a purpose for teachers whose time is limited. The major values of all formulas lie not in their grade-level estimate but in their interpretation. (For the curious, SMOG is McLaughlin's acronym for Some Measure of Gobbledegook.)

INTERPRETING READABILITY FORMULAS

Perhaps you think it strange we included two readability formulas. Isn't one good enough? If you try both Fry and SMOG on the same text passages, you'll discover that they tend to produce different results. Mind you, however, both are as accurate as formulas can be! The difference in the formulas lies in the specific procedures and the degree of comprehension each predicts. Vaughan (1976) compared the levels derived by Fry and SMOG and found that they tend to differ by one or two levels, SMOG estimates being higher. The reason for this difference is that SMOG tends to indicate the reading ability required for 90 to 100 percent comprehension while Fry indicates the reading ability required for 50 to 75 percent comprehension.

We should remind you that the estimate of comprehension derived by these formulas should be interpreted in the context of the independent, instructional, and frustration levels that we discussed earlier in this chapter. Thus, we suggest if you intend students to read material without instructional guidance and you expect students to comprehend almost all of it, you should use the SMOG formula to estimate the independent reading level necessary for the material. On the other hand, if you want students to comprehend the selection *with instructional assistance,* they need not be quite as good readers. A quick conservative estimate of how good they should be can be calculated by subtracting 2 years from the SMOG value. More accurately, you could determine the Fry score and consider it somewhere between the frustration and independent reading levels. Try them both and you'll see what we mean.

CAUTIONS WITH READABILITY FORMULAS

Before we move on to other ways of examining text difficulty, we want to offer a caution about inferring too much from a limited sample. If you were to assess the readability level of this book, you would probably find that the chapters, and even sections within chapters, would vary, perhaps even considerably. The same is true for the typical textbook you might ask your students to read. Although efforts are made to stabilize readability levels within a text, it is extremely difficult to do so. Even when those efforts are successful, the meaning is often distorted because of syntactic adjustments that are made to fit the text to a particular readability level. Our suggestion, then, is that you assess the readability level of each chapter as you prepare to assign it so you remain sensitive to the demands of the task required of your students.

Finally, while readability formulas can provide a basis for examining the difficulty of reading materials, they must not be considered infallible or definitive. Properly used, they can be helpful aids in instructional planning, but they provide only an estimate of the difficulty of a reading selection. Thus, anyone using readability formulas should consider these cautions:

1. The criteria for comprehension do vary among some of the formulas, and users should be aware of what they are determining when they use a particular formula.
2. Readability formulas directly tap such linguistic variables as syllables and sentence length, but do not assess conceptual difficulty; these formulas provide *only* a basis from which to extend an analysis of the difficulty of reading material to a consideration of its conceptual difficulty.
3. The scores derived by such devices are only estimates.
4. Readability formulas are not very helpful when used with poetry or other forms of material that do not conform to the basic characteristics of standard prose forms.
5. The true value of such devices can be derived only in tandem with knowledge of the reading skills of the students who will use the material.

It may seem that readability formulas are subject to so many constraints that they are of little value. Consider, however, these realistic and valuable uses:

1. As the basis for quick and efficient analysis of the difficulty of a particular reading selection.
2. As a means of evaluating materials for adoption without having to rely blindly on a publisher's analysis.
3. As a comparison of books to be used within a course to determine

which would be more appropriate for certain times or certain students.

4. As a basis for comparison of stories, chapters, or sections within a required text.
5. As empirical data to indicate whether adopted material is appropriate to the reading abilities of students with whom it is to be used.

CLOZE: A MEASURE OF READABILITY THAT ACCOUNTS FOR THE READER

In 1953, Wilson Taylor introduced to reading specialists a technique of measuring how well students can read a particular text or reading selection. He called it the cloze procedure. Herman Ebbinghaus, a German psychologist famous for his research on memory in the late 1800s, devised the basic procedure around the psychological percept of closure (hence, cloze) and the linguistic concept of redundancy in language. It is a "method of systematically deleting words from a prose selection and then evaluating the success a reader has in accurately supplying the words deleted." (Robinson, 1971, p. 2)

Consider the following sentences. As you read, try to replace the words that have been omitted:

Because materials are adopted for three to five years at a time, the evaluation of materials is a vital issue for public schools. Unfortunately, many schools adopt _____ primarily, if not exclusively, _____ the basis of how _____ content is included. Other _____ of prime consideration are _____ diagrams, glossy photographs, and _____ sidenotes.

Effective evaluation of _____ includes much more than _____ inclusion of certain topics _____ an appropriate readability level. _____ schools excerpt passages from _____ under consideration for adoption _____ ask students to read _____ passages. After reading the _____ passages, the students comment _____ the selections in terms _____ clarity, ease of reading, _____ overall comprehension. Regardless of _____ is considered in an _____ of textbooks, it is _____ to realize that textbooks _____ fail to cue readers' _____ are of little value _____ either the students or _____ teacher.

If you are _____ for a textbook selection _____, you should help others _____ what methods of evaluation _____ are available to the _____. Of course, a textbook _____ be judged for the _____ to which it adequately _____ the content desired by _____ committee. Likewise, a textbook _____ be chosen to fit _____ existing curriculum, rather than _____ to become the curriculum. _____, determination of the readability _____ a textbook can, in _____ final analysis, only be _____ on the readers, rather _____ a formula. If you _____ in a position to _____ textbooks, insist on including _____ readings by students to _____ you know if your _____ are compatible with students' _____. Examine structural elements such _____ unity, emphasis, and format _____ with semantic factors such _____ conceptual appropriateness (or difficulty) for the students who will read the text. Don't rely solely on readability formulas to select textbooks if you and your students are likely to use them for some years to come!

The degree to which you were successful in placing the exact words deleted from the sentences can be considered an index of your ability to read the material from which it was taken. (The words deleted were: textbooks, on, much, factors, good, colorful, textbooks, simple, and, Some, textbooks, and, the, excerpted, on, of, and, what, evaluation, important, that, thinking, to, the, chosen, committee, learn, that, committee, should, extent, covers, the, should, an, chosen, However, of, the, based, than, are, choose, sample, help, judgments, judgments, as, along, as.)

It is important to realize that the cloze test simultaneously measures two variables: (1) it is a measure of the reader's ability to use the language (a combination of language development and reading ability), and (2) it is a measure of the reader's familiarity with the subject matter being presented. The greater the ability of the reader, the less the reader must depend on every detail of letter and word in the text in order to understand the message of the text. Likewise, the more familiar the reader is with the content and meaning of a passage, the less the reader needs to be able to "see" in the text. What the brain tells the eyes of the mature and informed reader will be more important than what the eyes tell the brain, as Frank Smith (1978) puts it. In this sense, cloze takes into account the dynamic interaction of text and reader which results in comprehension.

The following steps are recommended in the construction of a cloze passage:

1. Select a reading passage that your students have not yet read. It should be 300 words in length for readers in middle and upper grades, 150 words in length for younger readers.

2. Type the first sentence intact. Starting with the fifth word in the second sentence, delete every fifth word until you have fifty deletions (twenty-five for younger readers). Replace each deletion with an underlined blank fifteen spaces long.
3. Finish the sentence in which the fiftieth (or twenty-fifth) deletion occurs. Type one more sentence intact.

Once a cloze test has been constructed, it is a simple matter to administer it in a classroom. Provide directions to the students by telling them: "You are to fill in the blanks in the following selection with the words that have been left out. Try to supply the exact words the author used. Only one word has been deleted from each blank. You will have as much time as necessary to complete this exercise." If the students are unfamiliar with the task, show them some examples prior to handing out the exercise. The students are not to use any books or materials when completing the exercise, but encourage them to use context clues to determine what word fits each blank.

Though a cloze test can be administered easily in a classroom, there are potential problems to be avoided if the results are to be meaningful. Often the task itself interferes with obtaining valid scores. If the students have never taken a test like this, they may become very frustrated and not apply themselves. Thus, familiarize your students with the task prior to administering a passage. Initially, let them work on short passages and even let them work in pairs or teams. Try to make the task a challenging game and help them become involved in the process.

The scoring procedure can also cause predictable problems. Only exact replacements are counted correct, and it is not unusual for students to get only 30, 40, or 50 percent correct. Few students are accustomed to being so unsuccessful with a task. Thus, an anxiety factor can interfere with performance, and you need to be prepared to lend support and encouragement during the testing. The first purpose of a cloze test is to measure the harmony between an author's assumptions and a reader's abilities in terms of vocabulary, skills, and conceptual awareness. In great part, as we tried to suggest earlier, the burden of making correct assumptions is on the author. It will please students to be told that cloze is a way of testing whether the vocabulary load, skills load, and concept load the author has built into the text are appropriate.

It is not unusual to hear teachers voice a complaint about the practice of counting only exact replacements as correct. Synonyms so often seem at least as good or better than the original words chosen by the author. However, there are at least two arguments for this apparent inflexibility. (Note, however, that misspelled words and dialectically different words should be allowed.) First, counting only exact replacements does not require a subjective evaluation of the subtle connotations of synonyms, and thus retains objectivity. Second, it has allowed researchers to establish levels of acceptability for percentages of exact replacements. Such figures can be interpreted with reference to independent, instructional, and frustration reading levels.

Once the percentage of exact replacement scores for all students has been determined, *compute the average for the class*. The difficulty of the material can then be estimated by comparing the class average to the following set of criteria deriving from research by Rankin & Culhane (1969):

If the average score is:	*The material is probably:*
above 60%	Easy for this group and will be on its independent reading level.
40%–60%	Suitable for this group and is within its instructional reading level.
below 40%	Difficult for this group and will be on its frustration level.

These average scores can be deceiving, however. All they really say is how difficult the "average" reader finds the text. If the individual scores are not spread too much from the average score, this is useful to know. However, the greater the spread of scores, the less representative the average score becomes and the less generally appropriate is the categorization of the material by reading level. Notice that throughout this discussion, we've been talking about mean cloze scores, not about individual scores. There is no evidence to suggest that an individual's raw cloze score is a valid index of that individual's reading ability.

JUDGMENT ANALYSIS OF TEXT APPROPRIATENESS

■ ■ George Klare (1982) points out that the major methods of determining readability fall into three classes: *predictors* of readability, in the form of readability formulas: *measures* of readability, usually involving performance of readers on some sort of test; and *judgments* of readability, based on analysis by experts. We have discussed two predictors, the

Fry and the SMOG formuals, and one measure, the cloze test. (In chapter 3 we will consider measurement analysis in greater depth.) Now we turn to judgment and the criteria by which you might become expert in assessing the suitability of text for the purposes you have for it.

If you were to set out today to buy a new car, you would be faced with judgments ranging from safety, economy, and general suitability, to style, make, and color. To make those judgments, you would rely on a more or less subconscious preconception of what the ideal car might be for you. Likely, it would get very high gas mileage, or perhaps be fueled by something very cheap; it would probably be very safe to drive, virtually incapable of killing you or anyone else. In sum, the ideal car would express and fit your personality and perfectly fit all your needs for a car. But of course the perfect car does not exist as yet, and may never exist, leaving you forever in the very troublesome position of having to decide what compromises you are willing to make, what features you are willing to sacrifice in favor of others.

The process of selecting a new car is in some ways analogous to the process of selecting a book for use in your teaching. Though the ideal text does not, and probably could not, exist, there do exist certain text qualities on which you will have to decide how far you are willing to compromise. Such an important decision as the selection of a text will certainly have to take into account a number of considerations beyond readability values. The difference in the case of selecting a text, by comparison to selecting a car, is you may be even less sure of your conception of the ideal text than you are of the ideal car. Here we'd like to help by suggesting a few qualities you might want to bear in mind in the process of evaluating a text for possible selection and use. To facilitate your use of the criteria we suggest, they are presented as a series of questions. Each question is accompanied by a brief explanation of why we think it a useful question to ask, and examples are included of actual text selections to illustrate the criterion which gave rise to the question.

Several sources and researchers have guided our thinking in the formulation of criteria for selection and use of textbooks. Two fundamental sources are Brooks & Warren (1958) and Christensen & Christensen (1976). We are also indebted to Elizabeth Wetmore for research reported in a paper entitled "Restructuring Text to Improve Comprehensibility" (1984). Wetmore's research provides evidence that text comprehensibility can be improved using a number of rewrite rules to manipulate the *way* a text says what it says without changing the contents of the text. In addition, we were influenced in our thinking by the research of Armbruster & Anderson (1982) and Anderson,

Armbruster, & Kantor (1980) of the Center for the Study of Reading at the University of Illinois. Each of these researchers has pointed the way toward specific criteria for textbook evaluation. Drawing on their and our own research (Estes, 1982; Vaughan & Vaughan, 1983; Estes & Wetmore, 1983) we have formulated a series of questions for judging the appropriateness of text.

CRITERIA FOR SELECTION OF TEXTBOOKS

As you consider these criteria and examples of each, think about what it means to become a judge of textbooks. Our aim here is to help you become aware of the elements of texts influencing readers' comprehension. Before we explain each of the elements we consider important, let us simply identify them so you can see the forest before we get too closely involved with the trees. The eight elements of text that contribute most significantly to comprehension, or create potential frustrations for readers, are the following:

1. Emphasis
2. Unity
3. Coherence
4. Appropriate Repetition
5. Clarity in Exemplification
6. Appropriate Vocabulary
7. Audience Appropriateness
8. Format

Now let's examine each in its turn.

Emphasis

Are the main ideas of the text clearly stated for the reader, and are ideas given appropriate emphasis relative to their importance to the intended meaning of the text?

If you look at the title and headings of a chapter, you may get some idea of what the author wanted to stress in the text. But look carefully at the paragraphs and sentences in the text. Ask yourself: is the information in the paragraphs clearly stated, leaving no doubt in your mind what the chapter or subsection of text is about?

Ideally, important ideas should be stated in positive, not negative, terms and should be highlighted by position and repetition. Important principles are better retained if stated at the beginning or end of sections of text, rather than being buried in the middle, and if they are repeated in the discussion, both by restatement in different words and by an example or two. Furthermore, when several important ideas are being presented, they should be clearly enumerated or set off from the rest of the text.

The following example illustrates just how far off the point an author can stray, in this case with the effect of giving emphasis to quite the opposite idea intended.

Two Methods of Classification

The basic idea of classification is not difficult to understand. We all do some informal classifying, and almost anything may be classified— stamps, rocks, clouds, even the kinds of weather. The words in a dictionary are classified. They are classified according to their spelling—that is, alphabetically.

In classifying objects we could use an alphabetical method, arranging them according to the alphabetical order of their names. Suppose a supermarket manager arranged his merchandise alphabetically. Think of the varied goods to be found under the letter A: abalones, almonds, apples, apricots, artichokes, and many more. These would be followed by bacon, baking powder, beans, beef, beets, bread. . . . Imagine the practical difficulties in such a system! Refrigerators for perishable groceries would have to be scattered throughout the store. Actually, in any supermarket we find that the merchandise has generally been grouped according to the nature of the product. In one section we find various kinds of canned goods; in another, fresh fruits and vegetables; in a third, meats. Moreover, each of these sections may be further divided. Familiarity with this system of classification enables the shopper to locate groceries easily and quickly.

Thus we can classify in either of two ways: according to likenesses in names or according to likenesses in objects themselves. For biological classification names of organisms are certainly of much less importance than characteristics, so the alphabetical method is not satisfactory.

Readers asked to recall what they can from this selection usually talk about the alphabetical method of classification. Rarely does anyone notice that classification on the basis of structural characteristics is to be preferred to any other, such as classification on the basis of names. When the authors say that the "alphabetical method (of classifying organisms) is not satisfactory," they imply that such a method exists and is worthy of discussion. Neither implication is valid, but in stating the issue in those terms, they focus the reader's attention away from the essential point they are trying to make.

Our point is that the ideal text must cue the reader to think about what the author wants to emphasize. When the author inadvertently diverts the reader's attention, the emphasis is clouded and the reader's thinking becomes confused as to what the author intended. An ideal text guides the reader's understanding by the proper use of emphasis.

■ Unity

Are all the ideas in the text clearly related to the main ideas and major points of the text?

Earlier we discussed the relationship between an author's assumptions and what the reader brings to the text. It is fair to say readers also make assumptions about authors. For example, they assume authors have clear points to make and whatever they say is related to those points. Unfortunately, not all authors are quite so considerate, and most textbooks are subjected to a number of rewrites and editings by different people, a process that sometimes distorts a single vision of the major points and purposes of the text. As a result, you will find that textbooks often contain irrelevancies. Interesting as the occasional sidelight may be, unless the reader is already quite familiar with the topics being discussed in a text, every idea needs to be clearly and explicitly related to the main ideas. Every sentence and every paragraph in a text should clearly contribute to an understanding of a specific topic. One good test for this quality is to ask yourself how easy the paragraphs would be to outline. For example, the main idea of the following paragraph is clearly stated in a topic sentence (the second sentence of the paragraph), and every sentence that follows strengthens the evidence to support the main idea. To demonstrate just how unified the ideas in this paragraph are, try outlining it sentence by sentence. You'll see that every sentence has a place in this very nearly perfect paragraph.

Honeybees

Winter Organization

The honeybee colony, which usually has a population of 30,000 to 40,000 workers, differs from that of the bumblebee and many other social bees or wasps in that it survives the winter. This means that the bees must stay warm despite the cold. Like other bees, the isolated honeybee cannot fly if the temperature is below 7° C. Within the wintering hive, bees maintain their temperature by clustering together in a dense ball; the lower the temperature, the denser the cluster. The clustered bees produce heat by constant muscular movements of their wings, legs, and abdomens. In very cold weather, the bees on the outside of the cluster keep moving toward the center, while those in the core of the cluster move to the colder outside periphery. The entire cluster moves slowly about on the combs, eating the stored honey from the combs as it moves.

The first sentence of this paragraph is a transition from an earlier discussion (or presumed knowledge) of "other social bees or wasps." The sentences following the main idea statement are then all consistent in their relationship to that idea: they tell how honeybees stay warm despite the cold. It may seem obvious to you that any paragraph in a textbook should have the quality of unity, a small matter requiring authors to stick to the point. For the sake of contrast, here are some examples of text with poor unity:

The Pilgrims had many hardships during their first winter at Plymouth. More than half of them died from cold and sickness. The rest of the colonists worked hard to clear the land and build homes. They also made friends with the Indians. One Indian, Squanto, learned to speak English. He taught the Pilgrims to grow corn, to fish, and to trap animals for fur.

This paragraph suffers from the worst disunity. Though it is clearly stated, the main idea is hard to identify because none of the sentences that follow proceed in any logical way. The reader expects a discussion of the many hardships faced by the Pilgrims. Instead, the author briefly mentions death, hard work, and making friends with the Indians before completely digressing to a discussion of one Indian who learned to speak English and taught the Pilgrims some things they somehow didn't know. Now consider another example.

The complex behavior that we can observe in many animals is made possible by their nervous system. Most animals search actively for food. They avoid being killed by fighting fiercely, fleeing, or hiding. Many have evolved special behavior patterns, such as singing, that better enable them to find mates. Some mammals, birds, and fishes migrate long distances. Some animals care for their young. Birds, insects, and other animals may construct complex nests or homes.

Here, the problem is somewhat more subtle than in the prior example. The problem lies in the way the main idea is stated. As it is, one expects to learn something of how the complex behavior of many animals relates to their nervous system, but nowhere is the connection explicitly made. Children reading this selection might find it difficult to see all the things mentioned that animals do as merely examples of complex behavior made possible by their nervous system. And now consider the unity in this example about tornadoes.

> Tornadoes, fortunately, have a small diameter. Their paths of destruction are rarely more than a quarter of a mile wide and average only ten to twelve miles in length. But the destruction within the tornado path is almost total. Buildings are reduced to rubble, large trees are snapped like toothpicks, smaller objects are picked up and smashed, or carried for miles. The funnel cloud may drop down to the ground, travel a short distance, lift up for a while, and then drop to the ground again. The winds may reach 300 to 400 miles an hour but probably average about 200 miles an hour. Updrafts in tornadoes have been estimated to reach the same speed. These wind speeds cannot be measured but are estimated from the damage they cause.

What we seem to have here is a general discussion of tornadoes without any clear unifying topic. The reader is thus left with a collection of facts poorly tied together. The author might have constructed this paragraph in the following fashion, guiding the reader through an organized discussion:

> Anyone who has ever witnessed one knows how terrifying tornadoes can be. Though their diameter is small, the destruction within their path is almost total. Within a path only a quarter of a mile wide and ten to fifteen miles long, buildings are reduced to rubble, large trees are snapped like toothpicks, smaller objects are picked up and smashed or carried for miles.
>
> The characteristic funnel cloud is what we usually picture when we think of a tornado. This cloud may drop down to the ground, travel a short distance, lift up for a while, and then drop to the ground again. The winds within the funnel may reach 300 to 400 miles per hour, probably averaging about 200 miles an hour. (By comparison, winds of 50 miles an hour make driving a car difficult, winds of 75 miles an hour will knock down trees, and winds of 100 miles an hour often accompany destructive hurricanes.) Updrafts in tornadoes, the force which allows the funnel to pick up large objects such as trees and rooftops, are also estimated at 300 to 400 miles per hour. There are no instruments capable of measuring these winds, so estimates must come from the damage they cause.

An ideal text, then, focuses on one topic and all information in the text is related to that topic.

■ **Coherence**

Are the ideas in the text clearly linked in an easy-to-follow, logical way?

Coherence has to do with sticking together, particularly how ideas are related and linked to one another. When text lacks coherence, ideas tend to jump around from detail to detail with no clear relationship to one another. In the following set of sentences, notice that while the ideas are all about bears, the ideas are not clearly related nor do they adequately follow one to another: "The bears live in forests. The bears eat fish and berries. Bears mate in the fall. Bears hibernate in winter. Bears like honey and campgrounds. Young bears are born in the hibernation period of the female."

When a group of sentences flow together, one into the other, where ideas clarify and elaborate one another rather than exist as a mere list of sentences related to the same topic, that text is said to have coherence. Thus, without getting too technical about it, we could make our first two sentences about bears stick together by relegating the second sentence to the status of a participial phrase: "The bears live in forests, eating fish and berries." Now the ideas of these two sentences are not only about bears, they are also linked in a way that enables a reader to see how they relate to one another.

The following paragraph serves as another example of text that is rich in unity but poor in coherence.

> The region called the Far East is a region of great extremes. It contains the highest mountains in the world, the Himalayas, as well as fertile lowland plains. It has one of the world's driest deserts, the Takla-Makan in western China, as well as many areas covered with lush tropical rain forest. It is also the home of some of the most ancient civilizations on earth. The Indus River Valley civilization on the Indian subcontinent developed at almost the same time as the Nile River civilization of Egypt, and the Chinese can claim a civilized culture as far back as 1500 B.C. Yet, there are people living on islands in Indonesia who have remained in the Stone Age right up to the present. The Far East is a region of economic extremes, too, from terrible poverty in parts of India to high prosperity in Japan.

The main idea of this paragraph is clearly stated, setting up a pattern for the discussion that is followed through the next two sentences: highest mountains in contrast to lowland plains and driest desert in contrast to rain forest. But then problems arise. The contrast between ancient civilizations and people still living in the Stone Age is not at all clear; also, the reader is left with the inadvertent implication that Egypt is part of the Far East, which of course it is not. The reader needs to see more clearly that the Far East is the home of civilizations that have flourished for centuries in contrast with neighbors who have never progressed beyond the Stone Age. But in this midsection of the text, the author somehow loses the thread of the argument. The thread is there, but it has no beads or knots that the reader can use to pick his or her way through the discussion.

By contrast, the following paragraph has fairly good coherence, but suffers from poor unity:

> The complex behavior that we can observe in many animals is made possible by their nervous system. Most animals search actively for food. They avoid being killed by fighting fiercely, fleeing, or hiding. Many have evolved special behavior patterns, such as singing, that better enable them to find mates. Some mammals, birds, and fishes migrate long distances. Some animals care for their young. Birds, insects, and other animals may construct complex nests or homes.

The problem with this paragraph, as we noted earlier, lies in the lack of unity around the topic sentence. But there is good coherence in this paragraph, achieved by very good use of pronoun reference tying idea to idea. "Most animals . . ." of sentence two ties to "They . . ." in sentence four and so on through the paragraph. Each sentence begins with a very clear tie to previous ideas.

One way that text may lack coherence is in conceptual relationships. Concepts may be related in a variety of ways, among them relationships such as causality, conditionality, comparison, contrast, and example. As you examine a text, ask yourself whether cause-effect relationships among ideas or events are stated as such, whether the author clearly shows how occurrences depend on one another in a conditional fashion, whether comparisons and contrasts between concepts are explicitly made, and whether, as we said before, examples are clearly identified as examples *and clearly tied to the point* in terms of cause-effect, conditionality, etc.

In the following text, composed of two paragraphs, there is a negative and a positive instance of coherence. The first paragraph is full of examples to substantiate its main idea, but it remains unclear how those examples are the effect of that main idea. By contrast, in the second paragraph the author says explicitly how the examples are connected to their main point.

Adaptations
> Physiological adaptations are involved with the various physical and chemical needs of organisms. The enzymes needed for digestion, clotting of blood, or muscular contractions in animals all have a phys-

iological basis. Secretion of a poison venom by a snake is another example. Protein materials in a spider's web are chemically made. An enzyme released by sperm cells enables them to break down the outer wall of an egg. These are physiological adaptations.

All organisms have many behavioral adaptations. These are adaptations involving reactions to the environment. In general, the number of behavioral patterns depends upon the complexity of the nervous system. The more complex the nervous system, the wider the range of responses. Migration of birds, hunting and storing nuts by squirrels, and tracking abilities of hunting dogs are all behavioral adaptations. They all improve the chances of survival as well as reproduction. Plants, too, have certain behavior although they have no nerves. Their behavior is controlled by hormones. The apparent bending of a plant toward light is an example of plant behavior.

If you did not know before you read this paragraph *why,* for example, chemically made protein material in a spider's web is a physiological adaptation, you don't know now. But in the second paragraph, the author links several examples of behavioral adaptations to improved chances of survival as well as reproduction. Exactly *how* remains somewhat vague, nonetheless.

■ Appropriate Repetition

Does the text discuss new concepts in relation to other concepts previously introduced?

Teachers know at times students need to be reminded of what they already know. But in most academic expository textbooks, the new information flies fast and furiously. A certain amount of repetition helps remind readers what they know and helps them relate new concepts to known ones. A text should hang together in such a way that the reader is given a feeling of interrelated thoughts, interconnected concepts, and ideas that build on one another. Any text can be assessed for these qualities by checking whether the main ideas of the text are explicitly referenced to ideas previously introduced. Look for repetitions of ideas from previous sections or chapters, for use of technical vocabulary previously defined, and for statements such as "Recall that we said before. . . ."

Sometimes texts would be more helpful if only they would refer the reader to previous sections that explain a concept the author assumes the reader now understands. For example, Houghton Mifflin's *Fundamentals of Mathematics,* Chapter 5, beginning p. 132, opens with a section on adding fractions, including fractions with different denominators. The model given for the process is:

ADDING FRACTIONS, DIFFERENT DENOMINATORS

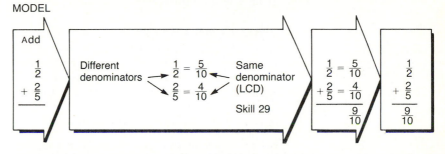

Notice that the concept of LCD is assumed knowledge. However, to make it easier, this author cross-references the skills in the problem-solving models given. Skill 29, referred to in the example, is "writing fractions with the LCD." That skill is in turn referenced to the skill it has to assume, "finding the least common denominator," which is in turn referenced to "finding the least common multiple" and so on back. The student is therefore encouraged and given the necessary help to review each step as the work becomes progressively more complex.

By contrast, the following selection leaves much to be desired in terms of appropriate redundancy.

> *Topography of the Ocean Floor*
> The topography of the ocean basins is different from the topography of the continents. The ocean basins have higher mountains, deeper canyons, and larger, flatter plains than the continents. The ocean basins have more volcanoes than the continents. Earthquakes occur more often under the ocean than on the land. The rock that forms the ocean basins is very different from the rock that forms the continental crust. The crust of the earth is much thinner under the oceans than under the continents.

Several months prior to reading this selection, students explored the topography of the continents. Now the authors are calling on their readers' memories by comparing the general features of oceans and continents. Such aids are more likely to remind students of what they have forgotten than to help them relate new concepts to prior learning.

■ Clarity in Exemplification

Are examples clearly identified as examples?
Certainly one quality of good writing is that abstract concepts are explained by means of concrete examples. Consider the following

selection, an almost perfect structure in which to distinguish abstract ideas from the examples meant to illustrate them.

> **ASSAULT AND BATTERY** An **assault** is a threatening act by one person that leads another person to believe that he or she is about to suffer bodily harm. The victim, as a reasonable person (average individual), must perceive the threat as being real, although the person making the threat may have no intent to carry out the act. Pointing an unloaded gun at an individual and threatening to shoot, for example, is an assault as long as the person being threatened believes that the gun is loaded.
>
> *Palmer, a tenant in an apartment complex, was one month behind on his rent. Beasely, a former professional boxer and now the superintendent of the apartment complex, showed up at Palmer's apartment and rang the bell. When Palmer opened the door and saw who it was, he immediately slammed and locked the door. Beasely then yelled, "Either pay up, or I'll take it out of your hide right now." Beasely's conduct legally was not an assault.*
>
> A **battery** occurs when one person by unlawful physical contact injures another person. Physical contact includes kicking, shoving, or throwing an object that strikes a person. Battery generally includes an assault.
>
> *Lug was at the Senior Ball with his girl friend and left momentarily to make a telephone call. When he returned and discovered that Rund, another senior boy, had insulted his girl friend, he hit Rund and knocked him down. Rund suffered a broken jaw. Lug committed assault and battery.*

In the textbook from which this selection is taken, the examples are printed in different colored ink to set them off even more than we've been able to indicate here. Each subsection of the chapter describes a different kind of deliberate tort followed by a clearly distinguished example. Hence, if one were to outline this text by topic headings, one would have a clear framework of the contents amplified by clear examples. This is by no means always the case; on the contrary, the contents of many textbooks bear slight relation to the outline implied by the subheadings. It is often the case that emphasis and clarity of exemplification work at cross-purposes, as in the following instance.

> Sometimes individuals of two different species are able to form vigorous and fertile offspring in captivity but seldom do so otherwise. In these cases, distinctness of the species is maintained not by lack of ability to interbreed, but by other means. For example, the two species of duck known as mallards and pintails are so different that every duck hunter can tell them apart. Though they are found in the same places

in many parts of North America, birds intermediate between them are rare. Yet when they are put together in the same pen, they readily produce fertile offspring. Apparently wild mallards and wild pintails seldom mate because of differences in their behavior and nesting habits. Alaska brown bears and polar bears provide a somewhat different example. In the Washington Zoo these species have successfully mated and produced vigorous, fertile offspring. However, in the wild no such cross has even been discovered. The reason? Brown bears live in forests, eating berries, small animals, and fish that they catch in streams. Polar bears live on snowfields and ice floes, catching seals for food. Thus brown bears and polar bears rarely, if ever, see each other—except in zoos.

This paragraph occupies just less than one-half page of the text in which it appears. The illustrations surrounding the discussion are of mallard and pintail ducks (the caption says that "females of these two species are much more alike than these [pictured] males"), of a polar bear with a freshly slaughtered seal, and of an Alaskan brown bear with a large fish in its mouth. The authors presumably want to emphasize the "other means" by which "distinctness of the species" is maintained. Those means are behavioral and geographical isolation, one must infer, but his idea is overshadowed by the examples given to illustrate the point. And what do students remember of the paragraph? That brown bears live in the forest eating berries and polar bears live on ice floes eating seals. In our research with this passage, not one student in a hundred remembered the main idea.

Given our present awareness, we could have predicted students would remember the vivid examples of the bears and not recall an implicit, vague main idea. What though would happen if we restated the main idea? We deleted "by other means" and inserted "by behavioral and geographical isolation." The effect was modest. The examples continued to monopolize readers' recall and few students mentioned the main idea of behavioral or geographical isolation.

It is unfortunate that sometimes authors choose to illustrate a major concept with examples that are more interesting and memorable than the major point. In recognition of students' predilection toward interesting information, we have adopted this maxim in examining text: *Beware of overly vivid examples!* They may be hazardous to comprehension.

■ Appropriate Vocabulary

Are ideas expressed with a vocabulary appropriate to the academic level of the students who will be asked to read the book?

In part, it is the function of readability formulas to answer this question since length of word (that is, number of syllables or letters in a word) is highly correlated with how familiar a word is likely to be to a reader. But here the question is whether new ideas are put in familiar as well as technical terms. If the vocabulary in which key ideas are expressed is very technical, then those ideas will escape the reader who is unfamiliar with them. Authors are often in a bind on this issue, though, since the introduction of precise terminology is part of what they are seeking to accomplish. Take note of how the author of the text you are evaluating gets around this paradox. Ideally, all new technical terms would be defined in familiar language, set off in boldface or other highlighting, and introduced gradually to the naive reader. The net effect of this method is to raise the academic level of the students rather than to ignore it. Look again at the discussion of assault and battery. See how the important terms are set off in boldface type and defined precisely. Here is an example that could benefit from a similar approach. Notice how tightly packed are the concepts in this short paragraph.

> The basic nerve cell is called a neuron. Neurons are composed of a cell body, containing the nucleus, with the addition of threadlike projections of the cytoplasm known as nerve fibers. The nerve fibers are of two kinds: dendrites, which conduct impulses *to* the cell body; and axons, which conduct impulses *away from* the cell body. The dendrites of sensory neurons are very different from those of other neurons. They are usually single and they may be very long (as much as 3 feet) or they may be short; but in any case, they do not have the treelike appearance so typical of other dendrites. Each sensory nerve fiber (dendrite) has a special structure called a receptor, or end organ, where the stimulus is received and the sensory impulse begins.

By contrast, here's a paragraph on a related topic that does a fine job of carefully introducing some technical concepts in familiar terms.

> The organs of the nervous system are the brain, the spinal cord, and the numerous nerves of the body. Often the brain and spinal cord together are referred to as the *central nervous system* (CNS)—an appropriate name for them in view of their central location in the body and their central role in the functioning of the nervous system. In contrast, all the nerves of the body together are referred to as the *peripheral nervous sysem* (PNS). Peripheral means outlying. So nerves, reaching out as they do from brain and cord to all parts of the body, seem well named as the peripheral nervous system.

The problem of vocabulary is more than a problem of technical words. Sometimes an author will devote a great deal of text to explaining a concept before attaching an appropriate label. This strategy usually works, but not always. Sometimes the result is a lot of explaining that leads to no definition at all, as in the following discussion of taxes.

> Fire fighters help us. Doctors and nurses give us services. Name some other services that city workers give. All of these workers must be paid.
>
> Cities buy or make goods to use in the work they do for their citizens. The city builds sewers, streets, and playgrounds. The city builds other buildings, too.
>
> The city buys equipment to help keep streets, sewers, and other things in good repair. It buys fire trucks, streetlights, books, and playground swings.
>
> All things that the city buys belong to the people of the city.
>
> The city must have money to pay for all of these goods and services. Where does the money come from?
>
> Citizens of a city pay taxes. Some pay tax money on their businesses. Some pay taxes on their houses and land. Taxes buy the goods and services for the city.

Now if you're in the third grade and don't know what taxes are, you still don't know after reading this. You may remember some of the things taxes pay for, but that's no substitute for a definition.

Sometimes other, more serious problems arise. An author may go into great detail about a concept, only to attach an inappropriate label, or no label at all (as in the text about animal species [p. 44] that refers to "other means" by which speciation is maintained). Worst of all is attaching an incorrect label. If you don't know what manifest destiny is don't be misled by the following extended discussion.

The Fulfillment of Manifest Destiny

> What made the gold fields especially enticing was that many people believed it took little organized effort or capital to become rich. The basic tool could be as simple as a washbasin. The individual prospector, like the one shown at left, scooped up some earth, poured water over it, and sloshed it around to wash dissolved soil away from the heavy particles of gold, which sank to the bottom. Soon men began to use the same method on a larger scale by shoveling earth into wooden boxes (right). This washing, or placer mining process, could make a man rich very quickly, even when he started empty-handed. Many Americans came to believe that it was the Manifest Destiny of the United States to shower wealth on its citizens.

■ **Audience Appropriateness**

Has the author made reasonable assumptions about the prior experiences of the students for whom the text is intended?

Textbooks are inevitably written for a specific audience, usually identifiable by subject area and grade level. Authors of textbooks, then, should avoid including text selections that miss their target. In the following example, *taken from a third-grade textbook,* the author has made some obviously unreasonable assumptions.

How Seeds Are Made

A bee flies from flower to flower. It is getting food. But the hairs on its body pick up pollen from a flower. Some of that pollen sticks to the pistil of the next flower. That flower is pollinated.

When a flower is pollinated, here's what happens. A tiny bit of pollen sticks to the pistil of the flower.

A tube grows from the bit of pollen. The tube goes down into the pistil. It goes into an ovule, one of the tiny round things like beads. The ovule grows into a seed.

The pistil gets bigger and bigger. It becomes a fruit. Inside the fruit are the plant's seed.

There is so much wrong with this text it altogether misses its intended audience. The problem lies partly with the vocabulary. Accompanying the text is a drawing of a flower with some of the internal parts labeled to ease the vocabulary load. (Unfortunately, the pistil is not labeled.) But there is a more serious problem: unless the reader already knows how seeds are made, it is unlikely he or she will understand the process by reading what is said here. The text is little better than a series of statements about bees and flowers and pollination—all of which are related to the main idea of the text but not strung together in any coherent or helpful way. We can't imagine any audience for whom this text is appropriate, much less the third graders for whom it was intended.

Texts may be inappropriate because they contain vocabulary, analogies, metaphors, figurative language, and examples that are unfamiliar to their readers. These problems can often be dealt with in the phase of instruction that precedes the reading. Other problems arise, however, with texts that are inappropriate because the author explains ideas in ways that confuse rather than clarify for the reader. An author must keep clearly in mind what he or she is assuming about the intended audience of a topic under discussion. If the demands made by a text are too great on its readers, then communication will be impeded. As you examine a text, look not just at what the author is saying, but at how it is being said. Knowing your students as you do, would you put ideas to them in ways similar to those chosen by the author? In other words, does the author explicitly link new concepts to prior knowledge and experiences your students might reasonably be assumed to have had?

■ **Format**

Does the format of the text facilitate readers' comprehension?

Comprehension is often aided by italicized type, bold-faced headings, spacing (for example, partitioning of key ideas and examples), and inclusion of clearly related, supportive illustrations, definitions, and references to other parts of the book. The reader should respond favorably to the format, not feel overwhelmed by type size or pages of continuous, unbroken print. Consider the following example, noting especially the embedded question.

> *Special Taxes*. One of the laws passed by Parliament was called the Stamp Act. The Stamp Act was to force the colonists to buy stamps and put them on newspapers, wills, almanacs, playing cards, and many other things. Pictures of some of the stamps are on this page. Which two stamps have the same value?

Students could then examine seven pictures to select the stamps of an identical amount. Such a format feature distracts and confuses learning. Other illustrations have little to do with the main points stressed in the text.

Consider the resources applicable to the selection you assign your students. Does the glossary provide adequate definitions of previously explained concepts? Does the format invite study? We think of format in a theatrical analogy: Does the supporting cast (spacing, figures, charts, illustrations, etc.) clarify and amplify the stars (main ideas) in the show? Or do they detract from an otherwise good performance?

SUMMARIZING JUDGMENTS

■ ■ With the criteria for excellent text and the many examples we've given you, you should be ready to set about practicing on a few texts. We alluded at the beginning of this section to a summary of research published by George Klare (1982). In that essay, Klare points out that "individuals can provide accurate judgments for books (Porter & Popp, 1973) and passages (Carver, 1974; Singer, 1975) *if* the judges are experts or are trained to evaluate texts." (p. 1521) After our lengthy discussion of evaluating texts, you are now very knowledgeable, and the expertise will come with practice. To make the task a little easier, we've summarized the criteria for judging text by reducing them to a series of questions, although we do this with some reluctance. There is danger in reductionistic thinking. It would be a great mistake to exchange qualitative judgment for a quantitative checklist, a rating sheet to derive a numerical score.

Therefore, we'd like to see the following series of questions used strictly in a qualitative way. Keep in mind a singular question as you evaluate a text selection. How appropriate is this selection of text for the students who will use it? Answer that question in a paragraph or two using the criteria for ideal text to frame your main ideas. How does the text you're evaluating stack up against these criteria? What is your evidence? The most important single factor in judging the appropriateness of texts is this: *judge the text from the perspective of the student reader.* We have seen many instances where teachers perceive texts to be appropriate from their own point of view and they are genuinely puzzled when their students have difficulty comprehending the text. Try to forget all you know about the topic and read the material from the perspective of a naive, uninformed reader in your classroom. Pick out a few students, like Marcia, Ronaldo, Freida, Wentworth. Pretend to be one or more of them as you read. Examine each criterion from the students' perspective and your overall rating will be close to the mark even while you are becoming an expert.

One more word of advice about using the questions: If you give the questions to colleagues (for example, members of a textbook section committee), take care that you thoroughly explain each criterion using examples. Do not make the mistake of thinking someone else might be able to understand and use these questions without benefit of at least as much explanation of the criteria as we have given you. Now, with that warning, examine the questions and apply them in evaluating the appropriateness of a text for your students.

REDUCTION OF FRUSTRATION POTENTIAL

Within a transactive framework of reading, as we perceive it, the role of a text is to cause readers to think. Any text, then, has the potential

READABILITY: CRITERIA FOR JUDGING TEXT

The following questions are designed to guide you in your attempts to evaluate the appropriateness of a text for your students. We suggest you consider each of these questions before arriving at a final verdict about the text in question.

Ask yourself which final verdict is most descriptive of the text in question:

EXCELLENT – "Wonderful! I wish every book were this good."

GOOD – "I'd adopt this textbook in a minute."

ACCEPTABLE – "I've seen worse."

FAIR – "I could teach from this text if I *had* to."

POOR – "I'd hate to see any child of mine forced to read this text."

Use these categories and questions to reach your final verdict.

1. *Emphasis*
   a. Are the main ideas clearly stated for the reader?
   b. Do subheadings accurately predict the content that follows them?
   c. Are main ideas for the chapter stated clearly at the beginning of the chapter and repeated at the end?
   d. Are important ideas stated in positive, not negative, terms?
   e. Does the author spend most of the text discussing important ideas?
   f. Are subtopics directly defined or explained apart from examples?

2. *Unity*
   a. Are all the ideas in the text clearly related to the main ideas and major points?
   b. Does the text avoid irrelevancies and stick to the point?
   c. Do the paragraphs of the text lend themselves to easy outline such that each sentence has a place in relation to all the others?
   d. Do you find it easy to pick up the thread of the argument and follow it through the text?

3. *Coherence*
   a. Do the paragraphs that comprise the text lend themselves to easy outline with the effect that each idea in each paragraph has a place in relation to all other ideas in the text?
   b. Do the pronouns all have clear referents?
   c. Are important conceptual relations explicit in the text? Look for clearly stated cause-effect, conditional, comparison, and contrast relationships.

4. *Appropriate repetition*
   a. Are new concepts clarified in relation to related concepts previously discussed in the text?

   b. Are newly introduced concepts restated to reinforce readers' understanding?

   c. Are references to other parts of the text specified to help students locate previously discussed concepts?

   d. Are subtopics discussed in relation to each other and related to the main topics of the selection?

   e. Are important ideas highlighted by repetition?

5. *Clarity in exemplification*
   a. Has the author avoided overly vivid examples?

   b. Are abstract concepts clarified by concrete examples?

   c. Are examples clearly related to the points they are intended to illustrate?

6. *Appropriate vocabulary*
   a. Are new ideas put in familiar rather than technical terms?

   b. Are technical terms defined in familiar language, set off in boldface or other highlighting, and introduced gradually?

   c. Are concepts developed with terms that are understood or defined?

   d. Does the text avoid conceptual explanations for vocabulary that are incorrect or in some other way unsuitable, i.e., vague or imprecise, or too abstract?

7. *Audience appropriateness*
   a. Has the author made reasonable assumptions about the prior experiences of the students for whom the text is intended?

   b. Does the text *relate* new information to appropriate experiences that students might reasonably be assumed to bring from sources external to the text?

   c. Are the vocabulary, analogies, metaphors, figurative language, and examples appropriate to the intended readers?

   d. Are the concepts discussed in the text presented in a context appropriate to the body of knowledge of which they are a part, and is that context likely to be familiar to intended readers?

8. *Format*
   a. Is the layout of the text appealing?

   b. Are graphic aids in the text pertinent to the ideas discussed in the text, illustrative of concepts already introduced in the text?

   c. Is appropriate use made of italicized type, boldface headings, and spacing (for example, partitioning of key ideas and examples)?

   d. Do questions included in the text help readers' thinking?

   e. Does the text provide adequate aids to reading and study such as a good index, glossary, chapter summaries, and the like?

to cue thinking or to confuse thinking. Among the various potential contributors to a reader's success or frustration, the text itself is often a wolf in sheep's clothing. Too often, the text is unequal to its task because it is too difficult or too flawed to cue thinking.

Three methods for assessing a text's appropriateness have been discussed and the one you choose to use on any given occasion must suit your needs. In our view, however, a combination of all three may be the best approach to determining an answer to the critical question: Is the text selection appropriate for the intended purposes and audience? If not, what must be added to the instructional plan to compensate for any deficiencies? The answer to this latter query is one we will pursue for several chapters to come, right after we consider various ways to assess reader comprehension.

3

Assessing Reader Comprehension

SETTING THE STAGE

Reading instruction and instruction that involves reading is most successful when the teacher can make reasonable assumptions about the reader's comprehension. We discussed independent, instructional, and frustration reading levels in chapter 2, and yet there's more to understanding what readers comprehend than ranges or levels of reading.

Consider, for example, what you have comprehended of chapter 2. How well would you do on a test of your understanding of that chapter? Would your comprehension appear different if we used essay questions instead of multiple choice or true-false? Which form of assessment would you prefer, if you had a choice? (How often is there a choice for students?)

What readers comprehend is influenced by the considerateness of the text they read (Alvermann & Boothby, 1983; Steele, 1985). Hence, in your assessment of a reader's comprehension you must account for the effect of the text's considerateness toward a reader's comprehension, as we discussed in chapter 2. In this chapter we extend our discussion of measures of readability to various methods of assessing reader comprehension and to constructing a profile of comprehension that will vary depending upon how you choose to measure it.

However, before we move on, reflect a moment and on a sheet of paper write down everything you can remember about chapter 2, "Textbooks in Classrooms." No, don't look back, just provide an extemporaneous written retelling of what you read. (The name for this is a free retelling, in current literature.)

Now, draw a line at the end of your retelling. Think about the following cues; if the cues remind you of things in chapter 2, add them to the retelling beneath the line you have just drawn. (This is called a cued retelling, to contrast it with free retelling.) Ready? *right stick, formulas, relative readability, reading levels, two years difference, exact replacement, eight elements, unity, polar bears, appropriate repetition, overly vivid examples, reduction of frustration potentials.*

Did the cues make a difference? How much difference? What kind of difference? Examine both of your retellings and analyze the differences. Discuss them with someone else who has done this exercise.

Now, are you ready for some questions?

1. Explain the steps in using the SMOG formula.
2. Why is the exact replacement count important in using the cloze procedure?
3. Why is readability "relative"?
4. Distinguish between emphasis and coherence.
5. Identify and explain the three major approaches to readability analysis.
6. Why might one expect the Fry Graph and the SMOG formula to produce different results?
7. Define "audience appropriateness."
8. What is "inconsiderate" text and what steps might a teacher take to reduce that frustration potential?
9. What are the basic elements that determine whether a student is on an "instructional level"?
10. Why might cloze be a more acceptable readability device than judgment analysis? Why not?

How did you do with these questions? Consider your responses to the three types of assessment. Did you prefer one form over the others? Why? Would you want a multiple-choice test? Would that have provided a better or worse opportunity to show that you understood what you read?

COMPREHENSION ASSESSMENT

■ ■ What readers actually comprehend and what they are able to show about their comprehension may be very different. How often have you felt unable to demonstrate what you know? How did you feel about the exercises to assess your comprehension of chapter 2? While it is important to be able to analyze texts and to anticipate reader comprehension based on such analyses, of even greater importance is an accurate assessment of students' comprehension once they do read the text.

An analysis of a reader's comprehension begins with the device you choose or construct to assess the comprehension. A wide assortment of procedures is available including so-called objective tests such as multiple choice, true-false, fill-in-the-blank, and matching activities. (In point of fact, what is objective is the scoring of the answers, not the test itself.) Other more subjective options include short-answer essay questions and various forms of retellings, or essays. We are more inclined toward the subjective alternatives because they don't force the reader to choose among a series of choices that may, or may not, clearly express the reader's understanding. Multiple-choice, or more aptly multiple-guess, tests do not allow readers to relate their understanding *in their own words*. While such instruments do yield a specific numerical score, the likelihood of that score's accuracy is diminished to the degree the student is forced to respond to someone else's thinking. We prefer options that allow readers to tell what they are thinking. We are, you see, more interested in diagnostic assessment than in testing, per se. Thus, as we examine ways to assess readers' compehension, we'll focus on those procedures enabling us to analyze and probe what readers reveal about what they understand.

The objection might be raised that by asking readers to write in response to their reading, a new variable is introduced—writing—which may interfere with students' showing what they know. This is a legitimate concern that is alleviated by the use of oral retellings, which may be a necessary option for students who have a severe writing problem. The difficulty of oral retellings is that they require either a tape recorder or a one-on-one conference where you write down what the student relates. We prefer the written retelling because it reveals extensive information rather quickly. In fact, if you teach students how to produce written retellings, you will be amazed at how adept they become.

We suggest that a retelling begin with what Rico (1983) calls clustering. (We discuss clustering on pp. 131–133 in chapter 5.) After the clustering, students should then produce a free retelling. When the student has remembered as much as possible, provide cues that will help him or her add to the retelling. Then, as you assess a retelling, don't consider the mechanics; respond only to the content of the student's effort. If the content is insufficient, that's the time to ask the student to elaborate for you orally. In five minutes, a reader can tell more than you would guess, given the chance to show what he or she knows.

■ An Exercise in Comprehension Assessment

Let's begin our examination of comprehension assessment with a familiar task. We want you to read the following selection on alcohol abuse taken from a seventh grade health textbook. As you read, think about some comprehension questions you might ask students after they read it.

THE MOST COMMON PROBLEM DRUGS

Alcohol Is the Most Widely Used Drug

Why is alcohol often called a "social" drug? Its relaxing effects on people who drink it, together with advertising, have made alcohol a "must" for some people at parties and on social occasions. Many people who feel alcohol is a "must" at a party often do not even know that alcohol is a depressant drug.

Alcohol used for drinking is a chemical compound called *ethyl alcohol*—often shortened to *ethanol*. Ethyl alcohol affects the body and mind in ways similar to barbiturates and tranquilizers. The depressant acts on certain parts of the brain, slowing the signals between it and other parts of the body. The more alcohol a person drinks, the less control the brain has over movement, speech, and thinking.

It is the amount of alcohol in the blood that determines when a drinker becomes *intoxicated*, or drunk. If a small amount of alcohol is consumed slowly, the body can remove enough of it from the blood to keep a person from becoming drunk. The average adult body can remove about 1 oz (28 g) of alcohol in the blood each hour. This rate is different for different people. It even changes from time to time in the same person. The rate at which alcohol leaves the blood also depends on a person's weight.

It is dangerous for people to drink any amount of alcohol just before they drive. Alcohol reduces the ability to understand, concentrate, and make judgments. It can also cause blurred vision, dizziness, lack of muscle control, and unconsciousness.

The effects of alcohol also vary with the amount of food in the stomach, the presence of health problems, the drugs or medications a person may be taking, and the feelings and attitudes of the person drinking. This is why no one can ever predict how alcohol will affect the same person at different times.

Because of its effect on the brain and nervous system, drinking even small amounts of alcohol reduces a person's self-control, judgment, and shyness. As people drink more alcohol, they begin to act in ways that may be unusual for them. This is because they begin to lose some control of their emotions. Alcohol can cause crying, fighting, loud laughing, or yelling in people who are normally quiet and calm. This is why some people mistakenly believe that alcohol is a stimulant.

Alcohol slows the brain's activity enough that drinking too much, too quickly, can cause unconsciousness. Mixing alcohol with other drugs is even more dangerous. Alcoholic drinks taken with certain OTC drugs, tranquilizers, barbiturates, or narcotics will dangerously slow down a person's ability to make safe judgments. Combining alcohol with drugs like barbiturates can cause death.

People who consume too much alcohol risk not only their own lives, but also the lives of others. More than 25,000 traffic deaths each year are the direct result of drinking. Even more tragic is the fact that this statistic includes victims who had not consumed any alcohol. They were simply people who were in cars that were hit by drunk drivers.

Alcohol Is the Most Abused Drug

While many people safely drink alcohol to celebrate some social and religious occasions, drinking too much alcohol is a form of drug abuse. This abuse of alcohol is often caused by certain fears in people. It may be that they feel they need alcohol to lose their shyness, to help them feel accepted by others, to feel better about themselves, or to make new friends. Sometimes people fear that they lack certain abilities and skills, and alcohol makes them forget these fears for a while. People who abuse alcohol to escape problems later learn that when the effects of the alcohol disappear, the problems are still there. Sometimes new problems are added.

Many people develop a tolerance for alcohol. They need more and more alcohol to feel its calming effects. Abusing alcohol is the most common form of drug abuse today. It is also a serious health problem. It can result in permanent heart, liver, and brain damage. Since people who abuse alcohol often lose their appetite for food, it can also lead to *malnutrition*. Their bodies are not receiving the food nutrients they need. Alcohol abuse may also cause damage to nerves and high blood pressure.

Alcoholism

Alcoholism is a disease in which a person's body becomes dependent on alcohol. This physical dependence soon leads to psychological dependence, as well. People who suffer from alcoholism are called *alcoholics*. Alcoholics and their families often are not aware of the disease in its early stages. The alcoholic is simple thought to be a "heavy" drinker or a "problem" drinker. The "heavy" drinker's body has built up a tolerance for alcohol. Such a person may drink several times a day, but then stop short of really being drunk. The "problem" drinker probably has developed a psychological dependence on alcohol. This person might get drunk often, believing that he or she must drink in order to get through the day. "Problem" drinkers often become aware of their problem and stop drinking. However, for many alcoholics, leaving alcohol alone completely is too difficult to do without help.

In addition to health problems, alcoholics usually suffer serious social and family problems. Outbursts of anger, along with periods of depression and despair, are common problems of alcoholics. Families and friends often find the alcoholic's changed behavior frightening and embarrassing. The alcoholic's employer and co-workers are angered by the poor quality of the alcoholic's work. They also become fearful that the alcoholic may create a safety risk for everyone in the office or factory. Unless alcoholics seek help in curing their disease, they often lose their families, their friends, their jobs and their self-respect.

Teenagers and Alcohol

The National Institute on Alcohol Abuse and Alcoholism reports that approximately 1.3 million people between the ages of twelve and seventeen have serious problems with alcohol abuse. This is alarming because research studies prove that the younger the people are when they begin drinking, the more likely they are to become alcoholics. Because young people are still growing physically and intellectually, alcohol reduces the chance that they can attain the best health possible for them.

Some young people look to alcohol and other drugs as a way to escape from the pressures of school and of growing up. Drugs do not solve problems. They do help to destroy the energy people need to cope with and solve their problems. Educational and job opportunities are usually closed to the young person with a drinking problem. Goals of becoming skilled in sports or other activities may vanish as the body and mind are damaged by alcohol.

Alcohol does not seem to be a problem or danger to everyone. For example, most people of legal drinking age seem to be able to drink small amounts without harming their health. Some doctors believe that small amounts of alcohol may even be helpful to some adults. They believe that when taken with food, a small amount of alcohol seems to aid the process of digestion.

Many young people and adults choose not to drink alcoholic beverages. Some simply do not like the way alcohol tastes or how it makes them feel. Others choose not to drink because they want to avoid the safety and health risks caused by alcohol. Many people also decide not to drink alcohol because of family custom, background, or religion. Laws have been passed so that most young people do not need to make decisions about alcohol until they are older and know more about the hazards involved. These laws make it a crime for people to sell alcohol to anyone under a certain age. This legal age varies from state to state. (Barnes, 1983, pp. 208–212)

Now, design ten questions you would use in a comprehension assessment for this selection. When you finish, work with a partner and discuss why you chose the questions you did.

The next part of this exercise will require you to classify the *answers* to the questions. To do this, label each question according to the following test:

Is the *answer* to your question

    a. information that extends across the entire selection *and* is important to understanding the main topic(s)? *or*

    b. information about a major subtopic *or* information *essential* to understanding a major subtopic? *or*

    c. information *not essential* to understanding the main topic(s) or any major subtopic?

When you complete that classification, there is another set of criteria on which your questions can be classified. Re-examine your questions and classify them according to this test:

Is the *answer* to your question

    a. explicitly stated in the text? *or*

    b. implied by the text? *or*

    c. in the reader's head *before* he or she reads this selection?

After completing this exercise, compare your classifications with your partner. Discuss why each question is classified as it is and whether it is a good question. (We'll leave it to you to decide what is meant by good.)

TWO PERSPECTIVES ON COMPREHENSION

We want this exercise to demonstrate how questions can be designed to elicit specific kinds of responses. You were asked to classify your questions according to two perspectives on comprehension. The first test determined the hierarchical level of the information solicited. The second test identified the source of the information relative to the reader and the text. These two perspectives are critical to assessing comprehension and require further study.

■ Hierarchical Levels

As you may now realize, the statements in a text can be arranged hierarchically according to importance. Thus, the most important concepts are included at the highest level, the subtopics and elaboration of them are next highest, and the extraneous, nonessential information is grouped at the bottom of the scale. This becomes important in comprehension assessment when you realize that students sometimes recall more of the higher level information and lower level information at the expense of the mid-level information (Vaughan, 1981). In other words, if students generally tend to see the forest and the individual trees but not the groves into which the trees might be arranged, a teacher would want to know that for instructional purposes. Thus, assessing the conceptual levels students are comprehending enables a teacher to determine where to concentrate instruction.

The research on what levels of information students tend to recall is inconclusive, but we consider this approach helpful for instructional purposes. If students tend to recall main ideas only, instruction must focus on the major subtopics. If, however, as some research indicates, students recall nonessential information at the expense of major subtopics or even main ideas, a different instructional approach will be necessary. Instead of making assumptions about what levels of information your students remember, you can use this perspective on comprehension to determine where your instructional attention should be focused.

Our discussion of hierarchical levels has been in general terms up to now. Below you will find the technical terms and more technical definitions for these levels, which will aid our discussion of them.

Superordinate Concepts: Within the context of a specific reading selection, superordinate concepts extend across the entire topic of the selection; such concepts are usually identified as those that express the main idea(s) of the selection.

Subordinate Concepts: Within the context of a specific reading selection, subordinate concepts either specify a major subtopic or provide information essential to understanding the essence of a major subtopic.

Nonessential Details: Within the context of a specific reading selection, nonessential details are those concepts not essential to understanding the essence of the main topic(s) or any major subtopics, but are included in the text as "dressing" for the first- and second-order concepts.

You should note the restrictive clause in each of the definitions that limits the classification to the context of a specific reading selection. Presumably any concept can be a main idea, a major subtopic, or a nonessential detail, depending upon its context. John Wilkes Booth could be the main idea in a biography of him, or a major subtopic in a selection about Lincoln, or a nonessential detail in a passage describing successful actors in the Baltimore-Washington area from 1820–1860. Hence, as you classify information hierarchically, the context will determine the importance of any given concept.

■ Informational Source

Our second perspective on reader comprehension is the source of the information. Does the information come from the text, the reader, or an interaction between the reader and the text? If students can answer questions that require regurgitation of textual statements but have difficulty answering questions that draw directly from their prior experience, it may mean they have not had the experiences an author or even a teacher assumes they have had. Students will tend to reveal better comprehension with text-based statements than with questions that require inferencing. By examining students' comprehension according to its source, you can better understand how much literal information students retain, how well they infer ideas from the text, and how much prior knowledge they can relate to a given reading assignment.

The technical labels for the various classifications and their definitions, as we have adapted them from Pearson & Johnson (1978), are as follows:

Text Explicit: Information stated directly in the text is text explicit information, sometimes referred to as factual or literal information.

Text Implicit: When the reader must make inferences or deductions using information stated or implied in the text to arrive at certain conclusions, the information for such conclusions is text implicit.

Scriptal: Scriptal information derives from a reader's background knowledge or experiences prior to reading the selection.

Teachers occasionally have difficulty distinguishing between the scriptal and text implicit categories. The most helpful distinction we have discovered is to classify a question as scriptal if the information must come from the reader's *prior* knowledge, not from any inference to be drawn from the text. If the essence of a response is information drawn from the text, albeit not explicit, then we would classify that question as text implicit.

Perhaps you have noticed our emphasis on classifying answers and not questions. Classification is based on information according to various perspectives such as hierarchical levels and informational source. Questions are not classifiable because they do not contain information, per se; questions elicit information. Questions, then, can only be classified according to anticipated responses because it is in the response one finds the information that can be classified. Let us caution you, however: students do provide unexpected responses, as we all know. Thus, if readers' responses deviate from what you expected, you may need to re-classify an item for your comprehension analysis. So classify questions according to anticipated answers and be prepared to revise your classification when students' responses surprise you.

ASSESSMENT PROCEDURES TO CONSIDER

We want to elaborate now on procedures for various assessments of reading comprehension. Each has its advantages and disadvantages, but all three can provide opportunities to understand what readers comprehend. The three approaches, which we have already introduced, are (1) free retellings, (2) cued retellings, and (3) cued comprehension questions. For readers beyond the primary grades, we recommend using these approaches in situations where students write their responses, or in unusual cases, give oral responses. For younger readers, and very poor readers, inexperience with writing may interfere with an accurate assessment of their comprehension, but for more mature students, and even marginally good readers, the advantages of written responses seem to outweigh the disadvantages, at least for classroom purposes. The advantages we refer to are (1) students have an opportunity to reflect and revise their thoughts, and (2) teachers have a record of students' thoughts without having to infer from right or wrong choices on an alternative kind of test. Thus, as we consider these procedures, we will discuss them as written protocols.

Free Retelling

A free retelling allows a reader to structure his or her demonstration of comprehension without the constraints often imposed by a testing situation. Popular in the late nineteenth and early twentieth centuries, the free retelling re-emerged as a viable comprehension assessment procedure in the past twenty years, notably due to research conducted by Kenneth Goodman (1965; 1967).

Directions often used with free retellings are "Write down everything you can remember about the selection you just read." Such a format allows readers to structure their comprehension in any appropriate fashion. This means readers are free to reveal whatever they can (or desire) about what was remembered. The value of the free retelling format is perhaps best expressed by Sharon Smith (1979) when she noted, ". . . if the objective of the assessment is to find out *how* the student is thinking about the content rather than *how much* he can demonstrate that he knows, the unprobed [free] retelling is . . . the best response." (p. 90)

Researchers find the free written retelling to be an invaluable tool as they explore issues relating to reading comprehension. In providing a response from readers, free retellings allow analysis of the link between the response and the original source (the text). In many cases these analyses had been done with complex linguistic analysis systems that sought to compare a description of the text and the retelling. For reasons related to this complexity, free retellings have not found their way into many classroom situations. Teachers have also been rather skeptical of free retellings because they do not lend themselves easily to a scoring system. If you feel that the free retelling has potential, we may be able to help with the scoring. But first consider some related topics.

Cued Retelling

In a variation of retellings, readers are given cues to facilitate their recall. In the exercise at the beginning of this chapter, you were asked to produce a free retelling and then given some reminders to help jog your memory of some things that did not come to mind during the free retelling. As we all know, understanding and remembering are not synonymous, and numerous examples of research exist to verify the value of retrieval cues as an aid to comprehension (Bransford, 1979).

Meyer (1977) was among the first to combine word cues with a free written retelling format. The emerging value of the cued written retelling procedure is that it offers the reader freedom to indicate his or her comprehension according to personal dictates while simultaneously providing bits of text to help dissolve the confusion between what is understood and what is remembered. The free retelling offers more freedom to the reader. Comprehension questions designed by a teacher, however, limit the reader to those questions. Cued retellings may be a best-of-both-worlds device. The directions for a cued written retelling are similar to those for a free retelling, as an example of instructions for the alcohol passage will illustrate.

> Retell everything you can about the selection you just read. Use the following cues to help you remember. But tell as much as you can, not just what you know about these cues.
>
> alcohol
> widely used
> social drug
> depressant
> ethanol
> less control
> effects of use
> abused drug
> traffic deaths
> alcoholism
> "problem" drinker
> embarrassing behavior
> cirrhosis
> teenage drinking
> aids digestion

Even with the directions page set up like this example, some students will try to approach the cues as discrete questions. You may need to practice with this format before you and your students become comfortable with it. Students not familiar with the procedure for formal retelling will need some experience before using it to provide valid information about their comprehension. We encourage students to produce a free retelling and then to look back at the cues when they get stumped. The cues can get them going again.

■ Cued Response Questions

If it is cued comprehension questions you want to use, your assessment procedure should be designed with a plan in mind. Consider the questions you developed for the alcohol passage. Did you have a plan as you designed your questions? If not, think about the perspectives on comprehension we discussed earlier—hierarchical level and informational source. Examine the following grid that links those two perspectives on compehension:

| | Informational Source | | |
Hierarchical Level	Text Explicit	Text Implicit	Scriptal
Superordinate			
Subordinate			
Nonessential Details			

You can design questions that simultaneously provide information from each of the two perspectives. Of course, you wouldn't need to ask questions in every category, but if you re-examine the questions you developed for the alcohol passage, you can chart them according to this grid. Do you have a lot of text explicit—nonessential detail questions? Let's hope not, but regardless of how your chart looks you can determine the kinds of information you are eliciting from students by the questions you tend to ask.

Using the alcohol passage, we can examine questions designed to fit each of the various categories in this dual classification scheme. First, look at the following questions designed to elicit information from the superordinate level:

1. Name three things that support the argument that alcohol is a widely used drug.
2. Although alcohol is a widely used drug, why is it less a problem for some than others?
3. If you wanted to reduce the wide use of alcohol, what might you do?
4. Alcohol is considered a social drug. How does that contribute to its wide use?
5. What is a drug?
6. What are some examples of alcohol?

Each of these questions seeks to elicit from readers information that extends across the entire passage. If students understand the essence of this passage, they will be able to provide reasonable responses to these questions. Hence, to assess readers' understanding of information at the superordinate level of a selection, you would want to design questions like these.

What about the subordinate level, the "groves"? If you want to assess student comprehension of the major subtopics and information essential to understanding the major subtopics, you would begin by identifying information at the subordinate level and then you'd design questions to elicit responses that included subordinate level information. Some sample questions for the alcohol passage are:

1. What does it mean to have a psychological dependence on something?
2. What is meant by the term "abused drug"?
3. Identify three ways alcohol can cause death.
4. Why is it often difficult for an alcoholic to quit drinking?
5. What is the difference between a "heavy" drinker and a "problem" drinker?
6. Why is it difficult to predict how alcohol will affect a drinker?

To assess reader comprehension of nonessential details, you would design questions to elicit responses such as these:

1. According to this selection, how many traffic deaths a year are the direct result of drinking?
2. Explain how alcohol is digested.
3. Why is cirrhosis dangerous?
4. Why might an alcoholic be suffering from malnutrition?
5. What are OTC drugs?
6. Define barbiturates.

Before you challenge us about the nonessential nature of these questions, let us remind you about the definition of nonessential. We do not mean to imply that the information associated with these questions is not important or interesting. However, knowledge of barbiturates or OTC drugs is not essential to an understanding of either the main ideas of this selection or the major subtopics. Hence, if students recall many nonessential details but cannot explain the main idea or major subtopics, then either the text is misdirecting students, as is too often the case, or the readers are misdirecting their search for information. Unless you assess students' comprehension with the intent to learn what students do and do not remember, you can only speculate about their comprehension and subsequently the appropriateness of your instructional focus.

Now, then, what about the area of informational source? How might you design questions to assess that perspective? We suspect you already have; re-examine the questions you developed earlier for the alcohol passage. Then consider the arrangement of our questions into the three classifications that follow:

Text Explicit Questions:

1. Name three things that support the argument that alcohol is a widely used drug.
2. Although alcohol is a widely used drug, why is it less a problem for some than others?
3. Identify three ways alcohol can cause death.
4. What is the difference between a "heavy" drinker and a "problem" drinker?
5. According to this selection, how many traffic deaths a year are the direct result of drinking?
6. Explain how alcohol is digested.

Text Implicit Questions:

1. If you wanted to reduce the wide use of alcohol, what might you do?
2. Alcohol is considered a social drug. How does that contribute to its wide use?
3. Why is it often difficult for an alcoholic to quit drinking?
4. Why is it difficult to predict how alcohol will affect a drinker?
5. Why is cirrhosis dangerous?
6. Why might an alcoholic be suffering from malnutrition?

If you're wondering how these questions are classified, examine the passage and determine reasonable, expected responses to the questions. Remember, the questions are classified according to the anticipated responses.

Scriptal Questions:

1. What is a drug?
2. What are some examples of alcohol?
3. What is meant by the term "abused drug"?
4. What does it mean to have a psychological dependence on something?
5. Define barbiturates.
6. What are OTC drugs?

Notice that these scriptal questions are primarily vocabulary questions that ask students for meanings of ideas *not defined in the selection*. In our experience texts often include terms that are not explained, presumably because the author assumes that students know the terms.

By including scriptal questions in our comprehension assessment, we can determine to what degree the author's assumption is valid.

A LEVELS-BY-SOURCE ANALYSIS

■ ■ You undoubtedly noticed that the questions we used in the informational source categories were identical to those used in the hierarchical level categories. You might now return to the grid on p. 67 where we first linked these two perspectives. If you were to pigeonhole these questions into their respective slots on that grid, you'd realize we designed two questions for each of the nine categories. That is, there are two superordinate text-explicit questions, two subordinate text-implicit questions, and so forth. Our purpose was to elicit responses in each category, hierarchical level and informational source, using as few questions as possible while including enough items to allow students multiple opportunities to indicate comprehension in each category. This approach allows one to analyze comprehension according to hierarchical level and informational source simultaneously. We used two questions in each of the nine subcategories to increase the students' chances to reveal comprehension in each category. (Two questions reduces the chance of testing error.) This use of cued comprehension questions to assess reading comprehension is called a levels by source analysis.

In a recent study (N. Vaughan, 1984) using this approach with the questions on the alcohol passage you read earlier, we were able to compare students' comprehension across the three hierarchical levels and the three informational sources. We scored each item on a scale of 0–10 and interpreted the mean scores according to the criteria for independent (90–100 percent), instructional (70–90 percent), and frustration (below 50 percent) reading levels. The mean scores in each category indicate these students are frustrated in their comprehension within each of the six categories, as Table 3.1 will reveal:

TABLE 3.1   Mean Scores of Cued Comprehension Questions

Hierarchical Level		Informational Source	
Superordinate	$\overline{X} = 48.0$ ·	Text Explicit	$\overline{X} = 45.1$
Subordinate	$\overline{X} = 46.7$	Text Implicit	$\overline{X} = 48.6$
Nonessential	$\overline{X} = 44.6$	Scriptal	$\overline{X} = 45.7$

Substantial instructional assistance will have to occur before successful learning can be expected for the students who read this material.

If you intend to use cued comprehension questions as your primary mode of assessing reader comprehension, you might want to use this levels-by-source analysis scheme. But don't neglect to examine individual responses by category in determining the strengths and weaknesses in an individual's comprehension.

SCORING AND INTERPRETING RETELLINGS

Understanding reader comprehension is among the most important issues in reading instruction because sound instructional decisions must be based on an awareness of what students do or do not comprehend as they read. As a means of text analysis, the measurement-analysis techniques we've been discussing may be preferable to prediction or judgment analysis since they involve readers engaged in a reading task. When analyzing reader comprehension, the profile you get may be influenced by the assessment device you choose to use.

In her study comparing the profiles derived by free written retelling, cued written retelling, and cued questions, Nancy Vaughan (1984) found striking differences among the three profiles. That is not to conclude one procedure is better than any other, but simply that each tends to reveal different pictures of what readers recall. Keep in mind this study reflects only one reading situation and the profiles with other selections and other students may vary. With that in mind, look at the following profiles based on the alcohol passage.

Free Retelling Profile

Students who read the alcohol passage and responded to the free retelling tended to include an equal amount of information across the three hierarchical levels. They tended to report information explicitly stated in the text and only occasionally inserted information that could be considered text implicit. One quarter of the information included in the free retellings was scriptal, usually of a personal nature. The following examples (from seventh graders) illustrate what these retellings revealed.

Free Retelling by Rick:

> Alcohol is a depress made from ethanol (ethyl alcohol). May people think it is a stimulant because it causes rapid and slurred

speech, loud talking. It's the world most commonly abused drug. After a period of time the body will build up a tolerance for it. When a tolerance is built up, more and more is needed to get intoxicated, or drunk. Some people feel like they need it to make friends, or to not be shy.

Alcoholism is a disease where a person feels they have to have a drink. This disease can be cured.

Mixing alcohol with other drugs is dangerous. In fact, mixed with barbituates it can kill.

A lage majority of high way accidents are caused by drunk drivers. There are laws against drunk driving, but people still do it.

Free Retelling by Bernadine:

Alchol is bad for your health. It is the most used drug in the State. Also it is a number one kill. Last year 25,000 people were kill by alchol. Many people were not even driving just hit by another drive that was. Alchol is a depressant. Many people think that it is a stimulant because it makes people forget things but it is not. Many people use it because they think it will solve their problems, but when the alchol effects wear off they find out that the problems are still there. Some doctors think alchol is ok to drink with food because it helps the food digest quicker. Alchol may cause permanent brain liver, and kidney damage. Not only adults have problems with alchol teenages drink it to. Many teenagers drink alchol to forget or get over school and family problems. Some start to drink as young as twelve-years of age. some even younger. Most people don't drink because they either do not like the way it taste or the after effects it has on many people.

Free Retelling by Ramona:

The selection was on alachol. Alachol can be hazardous to your health, it can cause brain damage, dizziness, it can cause you to see things blurry. You should not mix alachol with drugs. It can cause death. About 25,000 people who were drinking alachol had car accidents, sometimes drunk drivers hit other people's cars and endangered them. People who depend upon alachol are called alacholics. They depend on alachol to hide their promblems. Some people use OTC drugs while drinking. OTC drugs means over the counter, these drugs can be found on the counter, you do not need prescriptions for these drugs, one drug for example, the most common one is asprins. Some people drink alachol for special occasions, to celebrate things, some people drink to hide their promblems, for other people it is a custom. Teenagers between the ages 12 and 17 drink too, some even younger. It is very dangerous for children to drink, it can cause your growth to stop. Some children who drink are most likely to become alacholics. They have passed a law that alachol can be sold to children, unless they are a certain age. When alacholics are drunk they are to do crazy things, like yell at people for no reason, get in their cars and drive. Some people can control their drinking and stop whenever they want to and others can't. Sometimes you may lose your job or can't find one, and you may lose your family and your friends, because of your drinking promblem. Some people drink to digest their food better. They may give it to their children for toothache medicine.

Notice the tendency in these retellings to present explicit information and to deal with ideas across all three hierarchical levels. Although these samples do not indicate the tendency to insert scriptal information, many students, such as Daisy Sue, did bring in their own experiences.

Free Retelling by Daisy Sue:

Alchol can hurt your health very badly. Drinking alchol makes you grumpy, and very mad. Mixing drinks can hurt you just as bad or worse. If you start drinking while your young, you will most likely be an alcholic. You can easily stop, yes it may be hard, but if you stick with it you can stop. Even your family or friends will help you. Even though you drink a little or a lot it will hurt you, and your health.

The article I read tells me that drinking is very bad, or worse as smoking. If you tell yourself that you can't stop then most likely you can't and won't. If you tell yourself that you can, well do it.

Do not listen to people, if they won't you to drink. Just walk away and ignore them. The selection I read told me, or taught me to *never* drink even though I wouldn't. If your nerves keep on telling you to get something to drink, just read, or watch television.

Drinking can make you never to get to do activities and have fun. If your drunk, do not get into a car and drive. That is how people get killed everyday. Most likely if you drink all the time, people wil not trust you. So if you have a problem get help. Don't ignore the situation. If little kids see a person drinking, then they may want to start doing the same thing. If you quit, and haven't drank in a long time, then you just had to have another swallow, most likely you will start all over again. So stop and stay stopped. That is what I learned in the article I read.

Daisy Sue and others like her who clearly had emotional involvement with the topic tended to reveal their emotions as they tried to recall what they had read. The blend of cognitive and affective responses were both interesting and revealing. It is difficult to believe that such information could have been revealed by any other form of assessment besides the retelling format.

■ **Cued Retelling Profile**

Students who responded to the cued retelling procedure tended to report information about the topic that could be traced to the text and they tended to add very little information from their prior experience. (This proved quite different from the free retelling format, which produced some instances of considerable additions of scriptal information.) The cued retellings consisted of important ideas, those at the superordinate or subordinate levels, far more often than nonessential information. In this circumstance, students tended to generalize and synthesize ideas more than retell statements directly from the text. Perhaps most importantly, they included almost 50 percent more information than did students who used the free retelling. The following examples will illustrate these tendencies.

Cued Retelling by Sidney:

Alcohol is a depressant. It can cause cirrhosis and kidney diseases. It slows down your judgement of reaility. It causes less control over what you have. Sometimes its not that bad as a social drink if you don't consume very much. OTC drugs and alcohol can cause death. Most accidents that happen are caused by drunken drivers. Some are caused just by a drunk hitting his car. There are two types of drinkers, a Problem drinker and a Social drinker. A Social drinker can drink and hardly get drunk but a Problem drinker always gets drunk and depends on it through the day. Drunkeness can cause embassing behavior like yelling or screaming when he/her is usually calm. Sometimes its not bad because it helps aid digestion.

1.3 million teenagers drink in the United States. In the past few years its become an abused drug. People abuse it so no one can use it. Ethelonal is called Ethel. Ethel is short for the other name so its called Ethel Alcohol. Its the most widely used drug besides maryawana or solid drug. The effects of it are always different. Signs of anger or funnyness or different kinds of behavior.

Cued Retelling by Marcia:

In the selection I read it told me that alcohol is a drug that is widely used by people. It is call a "social drug" because people drink at parties and things. Alcohol is a depressant drug and if you drink to much you become less controlable of you movements. Alot of people die because people lose control of their car or truck while their drunk. Alcoholism is a disease caused by alcohol. Alot of people drink to get away from their problems they call this person a problem drinker. When people drink they do things that they wouldn't do if they were sober. They do thing to embarrass people. Alot of teenages drink just because their friends do or because they think it cool. Doctors say that some alcohal is good for digestion.

Before we continue with more examples of cued written retellings, we want you to notice that Marcia has basically responded to the cues as questions, although she has imbedded her responses into an essay format. Re-examine Marcia's retelling with the cues in mind: alcohol, widely used, social drug, depressant, ethanol, less control, effects of use, abused drug, traffic deaths, alcoholism, "problem" drinker, embarrassing behavior, cirrhosis, teenage drinking, and aids digestion. This is a potential problem with cued written retellings. Marcia may not have been able to recall much without the cues *or* she may have felt so tied to the cues she was unable to go beyond them. This potential problem can be resolved by having students practice providing a free retelling and relying on the cues only when they need the crutch cues provide.

Cued Retelling by Diane:

Alcohol is a big problem in todays lifestyle. Alcohol can mean serious health or other harmful problems to many people.

One thing mostly about alcohol is its widely used. Many people start drinking with one and just keep on and keep on.

About half of todays deaths are caused by heavy drinkers or by heavy drinkers who drive.

What most people don't know is alcohol is a depresent. People think alcohol helps them relax or forget their problems. That is not true. If you drink alot in one night you can become dizzy, lose control of your speech and muscles, or you can pass out. Alcohol stops oxygen to the brain and it also stops the blood. This is why your dizzy or lose control.

One thing about alcohol is if a person drinks too much it can cause embarrassing moments to family or friends.

Many people are not aware that drinking can cause death. If a person mixed a drug with alcohol it can cause death. In some cases alcohol can give you such diseses as cirrhosis of the liver.

When people drink it causes them to lose their apitight. This can result in malnutrition.

Many teenagers are becoming alcoholics as well. It is starting at the ages of 12 to 17. Many teenagers do it for kicks or to forget school or family problems. 3.1% of the teenagers drink. Instead of forgetting their problems it can cause even more.

Over half the teenagers that drink at an early age make chances of living healthy lives slight. Most teenagers grow up to be alcoholics and can't stop with one drink it takes two or three.

Cued Retelling by Harvey:

Alcohol is a very abused drug, it contains a substance called ethanol. When abusing the drug his behavior becomes embarrassing to his or her family and friends and even to himself when he's sober. The disease of alcohol is called alcoholism. Most people think alcohol is a stimulant however it is a depressant. Too much alcohol can result in a disease called cirrhosis of the liver. Teenage drinking is another very serious problem among teenagers, there is a legal age limit for the selling of alcohol, but it hasn't helped much.

Alcohol can be helpful in some ways, such as in adults alcohol aids in digestion. Alcohol can be fatal when mixed with such drugs such as barbituates. A "problem" drinker is a person who knows his drinking is getting out of control and he usually gets help. Alcohol is a widely used drug not just in one state but in several. Some people have less control of their drinking than others. The people who lose control normally turn into alcoholics.

In some people having a few drinks never hurts, but in others their weight and size does not allow them to drink very much.

Cued Retelling by Marcus:

Alcohol is a real bad drug. It can cause problems in your life and if it is widely used it can cause heart problems and real bad problems. Social drugs are real bad drugs. They can be taken with barbiturates and maybe can cause problems. Social drugs can be used as depressants and can cause dizziness. With use of alcohol it can cause less control of your muscles and of your nerves. The effects of the use of drugs is dizziness, lack of sleep and other bad things. Traffic deaths are leading cause of death because of drunk drivers. More than 25,000 people have died in car wrecks because of driving when intoxicated. Alcohol can help digestion of food.

From your initial reading of these cued retellings, you may not be able to distinguish between them and the free retellings. Perhaps, though, you did notice that the cued retellings included more information than the free retellings and less scriptal information. Other differences may become apparent as you analyze these samples more closely to become sensitive to a way of scoring them.

◼ Scoring Retellings

If either the free retelling or the cued retelling format appeals to you, the issue of scoring remains to be considered. For grading purposes, we suggest a subjective view, sometimes known as wholistic scoring.

In the grading of essay tests or English themes, wholistic scoring is traditional.

In reading comprehension assesssment, we seek to determine if and how much a reader is comprehending. For wholistic scoring purposes a four point scale would seem appropriate to indicate a potential range of comprehension. The scale would need to reflect degrees of comprehension, maybe answers to the question, "Does the reader comprehend?" Appropriate answers might be something like, "Yes," "Kinda," "A Little," or "No." Other descriptors or different ranges would be equally fitting. The appeal of wholistic scoring is in its flexibility. Of course, you could even use traditional letter or numerical grades if you felt they were more appropriate. The key to wholistic scoring lies in evaluating the response, or retelling, as a whole and then describing your evaluation in a nutshell.

For diagnostic or evaluative purposes of greater significance than a grade, you will want to tally the amount of information and the kinds of information included in the retelling. Again, you will seek to answer the overall question, "Is this student comprehending this selection?" If the answer is not "Yes!", you will want to examine the retelling to classify the retold information according to hierarchical levels and informational sources. We'll begin with Rick's retelling and examine the responses to the free retellings to give you some practice at this.

Your first step in analyzing a retelling should be to identify meaning units within the retelling itself. By "meaning unit" we mean a statement that makes sense and is a complete statement. To demonstrate what we mean we will divide Rick's retelling into meaning units. To help keep track of the meaning units, we will insert numbers at the beginning of each new unit.

(1) Alcohol is a depress / (2) made from ethanol (ethyl alcohol). / (3) May people think it is a stimulant / (4) because it causes rapid and slurred speech, / (5) loud talking. / (6) It's the world most commonly abused drug. / (7) After a period of time the body will build up a tolerance for it. / (8) When a tolerance is built up, more and more is needed to get intoxicated, or drunk. / (9) Some people feel like they need it to make friends or / (10) to not be shy. /

(11) Alcoholism is a disease where a person feels they have to have a drink. / (12) This disease can be cured. /

(13) Mixing alcohol with other drugs is dangerous. / (14) In fact, mixed with barbituates it can kill. /

(15) A lage majority a high way accidents are caused by drunk drivers. / (16) There are laws against drunk driving / (17) but people still do it.

Rick, then, has included 17 meaning units that can be examined for their hierarchical level and informational source. Notice that most of these meaning units are independent clauses but sometimes the subject or verb applies to more than one meaning unit. For example, meaning unit 2, "made from ethanol ..." has as its subject "alcohol" from meaning unit 1. Likewise, "loud talking", meaning unit 5, has as its subject and verb the same as meaning unit 4, "because it causes . . . ". If you are familiar with other methods of identifying meaning units, you may prefer them to our approach. Whatever method you choose to use should allow you to break down a retelling into elements that can be described; then the description can be analyzed.

The second step in analyzing Rick's retelling is to classify each of the seventeen statements according to hierarchical level and informational source. This can be done informally, that is, by "eyeballing" his retelling, or more methodically by listing the units by number and their corresponding classifications as we have done.

The following abbreviations will be used in this classification chart:

Levels	*Source*
Sup = Superordinate	TE = Text Explicit
Sub = Subordinate	TI = Text Implicit
Non = Nonessential Detail	S = Scriptal

Meaning Unit	*Level*	*Source*
1	Sub	TE
2	Non	TE
3	Sub	TE
4	Non	TI
5	Non	TE
6	Sup	TE
7	Sub	TE
8	Sub	TE
9	Non	TE
10	Non	TE
11	Sub	TI
12	—	S
13	Sub	TE
14	Sub	TE
15	Non	TE
16	—	S
17	—	S

You've noticed that scriptal information has not been classified according to hierarchical levels. Since scriptal information is extra-textual, any hierarchical ranking of such information would be highly subjective. On the other hand, scriptal information must be carefully examined to determine whether it meaningfully elaborates or strays from the topic.

Rick includes three scriptal statements in his retelling. "This disease can be cured" is evidence he knows more about the topic than is included in the article and his statement elaborates the topic. The same holds true with his other two scriptal statements. Thus, Rick's scriptal information can be considered valuable contributions to his retelling.

To continue our evaluation, we would tally the classification from his retelling according to the grid discussed earlier. This would help us see the pattern in his statements. Such a tally would look like this:

Hierarchical Level	Informational Source		
	Text Explicit	Text Implicit	Scriptal
Superordinate	1	0	(3)
Subordinate	7	1	
Nonessential Details	4	1	

Now that we have described Rick's retelling, how would you evaluate his comprehension? We'd rate it modest at best. Rick seems to have remembered more "important" information (determined by adding the superordinate and subordinate categories together) than nonessential details. His ideas, however, generally skip around and it is not clear he has a secure understanding of the topic. Although Rick is not frustrated by this text, he would benefit from additional instruction with this information.

Now, let's describe Bernadine's retelling. First, you should return to the original on page 72 and attempt to divide the text into meaning units. Then compare your effort with ours that follows:

(1) Alchol is bad for your health. / (2) It is the most used drug in the State. / (3) Also it is a number one kill. / (4) Last year 25,000 people were kill by alchol. / (5) Many people were not even driving just hit by another drive that was. / (6) Alchol is a depressant. / (7) Many think that it is a stimulant because it makes people forget things but it is

not. / (8) Many people use it because they think it will solve their problems, / (9) but when the alchol effects wear off they find out that the problems are still there. / (10) Some doctors think alchol is ok to drink with food because it helps the food digest quicker. / (11) Alchol may cause permanent brain / (12) liver, and / (13) kidney damage. / (14) Not only adults have problems with alchol / (15) teenagers drink it to. / (16) Many teenagers drink alchol to forget or get over school and family problems. / (17) Some start to drink as young as twelve-years of age, some even younger. / (18) Most people don't drink because they either do not like the way it taste or / (19) the after effects it has on many people.

You may disagree with some of our divisions; there is no iron-clad rule on how ideas in text should be divided. Even those of us who have lots of practice at parsing text cannot agree in every case. We recognize that parsing is somewhat subjective and arbitrary, even with guidelines. The issue, then, is not absolute agreement, but identification of meaning units. If you have a good reason why you divided in places other than where we did, that is sufficient. However, you may find it helpful to discuss your divisions with others; often, differences can be resolved through discussion. Understand that the object is to provide a description and analysis of a reader's comprehension; the subjectivity that accompanies retellings seems to become less of a problem as teachers come to appreciate the potential of retellings to reveal what a reader comprehends.

Now, examine a tally of Bernadine's responses.

Hierarchical Level	Informational Source		
	Text Explicit	Text Implicit	Scriptal
Superordinate	1	0	(1)
Subordinate	7	2	
Nonessential Details	8	0	

On the whole, Bernadine has a fair understanding of this selection although, like Rick, she could benefit from further instruction. The text is not frustrating for her and yet she tends to list details somewhat haphazardly. Bernadine can learn from this material, particularly with instruction that helps her relate details to major superordinate and subordinate concepts.

Now, what about Ramona and Daisy Sue? We suggest you try to analyze those on your own and compare your description and analysis with colleagues. We have offered our own brief analysis to help you determine if you're on the right track. In our estimation, Ramona comprehended quite well even though a few errors popped up in her retelling. For example, we believe she meant to indicate a law has been passed that "alachol can *not* be sold to children" although she wrote "can be sold . . .". Ramona has a tendency to use run-on sentences which can be a problem for meaning-unit division if you have been relying on proper punctuation to guide your parsing. We feel Ramona has remembered both important information and interesting nonessential details, indicating a thorough understanding of this passage. We identified 34 meaning units, of which 7 were scriptal. The scriptal statements, except for the incorrect ". . . it can cause your growth to *stop* . . ." (emphasis ours), all elaborate the topic rather than stray from it. Of the remaining meaning units (27), all but two statements were text explicit and they were almost equally representative of important and nonessential information. Does that seem to fit your description?

As for Daisy Sue, she provides 27 meaning units of which 19 are scriptal. Do her scriptal comments elaborate the text or stray from the meaning of the text? Do you agree that she has a sense of the selection, but needs instructional help and more experience with this kind of reading material at this level of difficulty? Daisy Sue's retelling may help you realize the importance of not being fooled by the amount of information included. Her retelling would indicate she hasn't really remembered much about the selection. Look carefully, now, and determine what kind of information she does include that is not scriptal. Does she have the gist? Or does she include more nonessential details than important information? Compare your judgment with a colleague.

As we mentioned earlier, the free written retellings tend to produce a comprehension profile that is different from the cued written retellings. We hope you kept this in mind as you analyzed the examples we included. Now, continue your practice in the description and analysis of retellings by evaluating each of the five cued retelling samples included on pages 74–76. Discuss your evaluations with others and hone your descriptive and analytical skills. You'll get better with practice and really improve as you conduct an assessment of your students using the textbook(s) you have in your classroom.

INSTRUCTIONAL ASSESSMENT

■ ■   Of all that we might say about assessing reader comprehension, one idea stands above the rest: *Assessment should occur in the context of instruction, preferably in the process of guiding comprehension.* If instruction is successful, students will learn; as students learn, they provide continuous opportunities to assess how they learn and what help they need.

Yetta Goodman encourages teachers to be "kidwatchers." So do we. When we attend to what students mean by what they say and do, we can find ways to help them be successful. In the chapters that follow we will share with you instructional activities that are perfect for kidwatching opportunities; where you can watch what kids are doing and how they respond to various instructional activities. What we mean to say here is that you might think of assessment as an ongoing process rather than a momentary occasion.

If you engage in kidwatching, you might find it helpful to do what many coaches do as they work with their team. Get a clipboard or a notebook. Carry it around with you during class. As you notice learners in action, or inaction, jot down what you see and what you think. Make notes about what students do as they try to learn. And record things you do too; things that work and things that don't. One teacher commented to us that she jots down messages and reminders to herself, even such mundane things as pick up milk on the way home. She claims this helps free her mind of clutter, leaving her better able to concentrate on the important job at hand—teaching children!

UNDERSTANDING AND REMEMBERING

■ ■   One final issue remains for us to consider. We cannot be convinced that assessment with recall instruments of any kind (multiple choice, cued questions, or free retellings) is an equitable measure of reader comprehension. At best we measure readers' recall of what they have read and recall is not necessarily the same as comprehension.

We'd like to suggest a way to get past remembering to understanding. This is important in classroom settings and can be accomplished rather easily, especially after the students have a little practice with it. Mind you, however, it won't work with objective tests, but it works well with retellings and even cued questions.

After a student has done all he or she can do with a retelling or with responses to cued questions, allow five minutes to return to the selection. You'll need to have the student distinguish between the remembering and the understanding phases of this assessment, but that's easy to do. If you use cued questions, students will have to change from pen to pencil, and we suggest pens for remembering and pencils for understanding. That way the remembering can't easily be altered, providing a clear distinction between what was remembered and what was understood but not recalled. This is important because the instructional implications of remembering are different from those for understanding.

During the five minutes (or whatever time limit you prefer), students can add anything to their retelling *but they can't copy.* They can only paraphrase ("put it in your own words"). The object is to provide students with an opportunity to reveal more about what they comprehended; after all, we want to understand as much as we can about readers' understandings as well as their rememberings.

SUMMARY

The assessment of reading comprehension is crucial to effective comprehension instruction. To determine with confidence the appropriateness or considerateness of any text, you must know what readers comprehend of that text. Decisions about where to focus instructional attention and time can only come from an awareness of what students understand.

Assessment can be accomplished by various approaches. We prefer what might be considered more subjective approaches because they allow students greater opportunity to reveal what they understand and remember as opposed to the more confining procedures found in objective tests. We prefer the cued retelling format because it seems to offer the best of the free retelling coupled with some text-based reminders. Another option is cued comprehension questions. If you choose to use this format, we suggest you design questions geared to assessing comprehension according to hierarchical level and informational source.

We began this chapter by asking you to demonstrate your comprehension of chapter 2. First you had to produce a free retelling, followed by additions based on cues, and finally you were given a few questions to answer. Given our research findings about the variations in comprehension profiles that can emerge from different procedures, it would be wise to use all three formats when assessing reader comprehension. This requires approximately ten or fifteen extra minutes in most assessment situations, but the payoff is enormous.

4

The Content Reading Lesson: A Design for Anticipation, Realization, & Contemplation

SETTING THE STAGE

One of our primary aims in this book is to equip you with strategies and activities that can improve the reading comprehension of your students. Toward this aim, we are going to encourage you to employ a basic instructional program that is firmly rooted in learning theory.

Learning is an evolutionary activity that progresses from awareness, through understanding, to remembering. In this chapter we examine how such learning is facilitated. The framework for our discussion is the basic scientific model of inquiry: (1) identification of the problem and potential solutions, (2) exploration of evidence, and (3) evaluation and explanation of the data in the context of the problem. Think for a moment about how you learn and about some of the reasons why learning can be difficult. Do you recall our potential contributors to comprehension frustration (p. 13)? What follows is a framework to reduce the potential of such difficulties.

FACILITATING READER COMPREHENSION

■ ■ As we have discussed throughout previous chapters, reading comprehension does not always come easily; for many students in school, it seems to come with extreme difficulty. However, reading can and should be more enjoyable and rewarding for students than it often is, and we want to share a plan with that in mind. Let's consider what's involved.

1. *Anticipation*. Readers' knowledge, feelings, and inclinations serve as the foundation for all learning. In the same way that perception is governed by expectation, comprehension is governed by anticipation. It is important that readers anticipate what they are going to read by first becoming aware of what they know, believe, and feel about the topic. Thus, reading with an attitude of anticipation is one of the most important reading skills. Inquisitiveness is intelligence, in the case of reading.

   Another important component of the pre-reading or anticipation stage of reading is the setting of purposes for reading (for example, "Why am I reading?" "What will I learn?"). To set purposes for reading, readers consider the text in relation to their prior knowledge, needs, and interests. Our plan to improve reader comprehension, then, begins with anticipations based on prior experiences.

2. *Realization*. Comprehension is the realization of meaning in text. Realization (that is, *real-ization,* "the act of making real") is accomplished by the reader interacting with cues in the text. On the basis of anticipations, the reader asks questions like, "Does the text confirm or deny my expectations?" "What new and interesting information is contained in the text?" During the realization process, the reader seeks to understand ideas that emerge from the interaction between anticipations and discoveries.

   Readers need to know that they play a crucial role in the process of comprehension and that what they comprehend from text depends on their prior understandings and experiences. As readers associate prior experiences with the ideas in the text and blend the new with the known, they begin to take charge of their reading and reasoning and thereby take a more active stance in their learning.

3. *Contemplation*. Following reading, an activity we call contemplation insures that readers will make new realizations

on their own. During the contemplation stage, anticipations and realizations are compared and new understandings are integrated with prior understandings, beliefs, and feelings. Here is where remembering occurs, and it is built on understandings that emerged during the realization process. In the classroom, contemplation activities often center on group discussion, but remembering may be facilitated by a variety of post-reading activities, which are themselves part of the entire process of reading.

ARC: ANTICIPATION, REALIZATION, CONTEMPLATION

Learning through reading occurs as readers weave their way through overlapping and interconnected stages we call anticipation, realization, and contemplation, or ARC as we abbreviate it. We devote a chapter to each of these stages, but our object here is to provide an overview of ARC as a teaching format. Within the basic framework of ARC, a teacher can orchestrate a wide variety of activities appropriate to successful reading and understanding. Here are just a few.

To foster an anticipatory frame of mind in the students, activities are chosen to arouse interest and to jog students' memories relative to the topic at hand. During this stage, the teacher asks questions such as the following:

- What is this selection going to be about?
- What do you know about this topic?
- What would you like to learn about this topic?
- Why might you want to learn that?
- What do you expect the selection will tell you?

To guide realization, the teacher might assign a task that will promote active involvement with the reading. The task should vary with the content of the selection and the purposes for which the students are reading. For example, a student might be instructed to:

- Make a check in the margin beside information that confirms previous understandings, or
- Put an "X" sign in the margin beside information that contradicts previous understandings, or
- Put a question mark in the margin beside anything that is puzzling or confusing.

Alternatively, students might be asked to fill in the missing parts of a partial outline of the reading selection.

To encourage contemplation, post-reading discussions might be initiated with such broad questions as:

- What did you find in the text?
- How did the information in the text fit with your expectations?
- If you were to explain what you've just read to someone who hasn't read it, what would you be sure to say?

Notice that these contemplation questions are intended to focus discussion on the main point and other important ideas in the reading, rather than on nonessential details.

The Content Reading Lesson

One way to implement the ARC format is through the content reading lesson, a plan teachers can use to guide students' understanding of content. Modeled after the directed reading-thinking activity described by Russell Stauffer (1969), the content reading lesson is designed for use primarily with expository texts. It can, however, be used with any type of material when the focus of the lesson is on content; hence the name, the content reading lesson.

As a demonstration of the ARC format, the content reading lesson can be modified to fit specific instructional purposes without losing its essential shape. To demonstrate what we mean, we have adapted a content reading lesson from one designed by Sonja Bolton for her seventh grade science class. Notice how Ms. Bolton arouses students' anticipation, has them read a segment of text to seek answers to questions they themselves have suggested, and then engages them in reflection and contemplation about what they have learned.

Content Reading Lesson: The Eye as a Camera

With students seated, turn off the lights and get the room as dark as possible. Get out a fluorescent green glow-stick. Move it around making different streaks of light including circles. Have a student take a picture of the streaks of light, using an instant, self-developing camera. After the picture is taken, wave the glow-stick around a bit longer. Tell them to watch carefully and then quickly hide the glow-stick behind your back. Turn the lights back on and begin discussion while the photo develops.

Teacher: What did you see when the glow stick was being waved in the air?

Juan: It was like the circles that sparklers make.

Theresa: You could see the light after the stick was hidden.

Teacher: Yes, you could! How long could you see the light after I put it behind my back?

Theresa: Just a second.

Marvin: I couldn't see the light after you hid it.

Kelley: I could, but then the light started to disappear.

Teacher: Actually, our eyes can see an image for about 1/10 of a second before the image begins to fade. What about the photo? (Hold it up and let students see the developed picture.) Will the photo fade?

Angie: No.

Jeff: It might, but not for a long time.

Teacher: Maybe it will, maybe it won't. What about the picture we have in our mind's "eye"? Think about that today while we compare a camera to our eye. What do you know about cameras? Let's list what you know on the board.

Marvin: Cameras make pictures.

Oscar: Light goes through the opening in the camera.

Meg: The opening is controlled by a setting on the camera.

Josh: Cameras use film to record the picture.

Teacher: OK, now how is an eye like a camera?

Oscar: The eye lets light into the brain.

Kelley: It has an opening right in the middle where the light comes in.

Teacher: OK, we have some things on our list, and we are going to read a selection about how the eye is like a camera. What do you think you'll learn about the eye as a camera?

Warren: How the eye is like a camera.

Tina: How we see pictures.

Teacher: Let's read the first part of this selection. Read the first two paragraphs and stop. As you read, think about what you already know about the eye and the camera. Do these two things: (Write on board)

(1) Put a plus sign in the margin whenever you come to information which is new to you.
(2) Put a question mark in the margin beside anything which is puzzling or confusing. When you finish, close the book but keep a marker in your place.

Ms. Bolton has introduced the lesson with something that the students are familiar with and encouraged them to predict what they will learn. She is helping them make some connections between what they know and what they are about to learn. Now let us turn our attention to the first part of our readers' assignment. The text is taken from the MacMillan Science Series (1966).

The Eye as Camera

The human eye is a kind of camera—a very special kind. The part of the eye called the retina (RET-ih-nuh) serves the same purpose as the film in the camera. The image of the object we are looking at appears there.

The retina is made of the ends of nerves which are connected to the brain. It is thought that light striking the retina affects certain chemicals in those nerve endings. A message then moves along the nerves to the brain. The eye not only "takes" the picture, but "develops" it and sends the final "print" to the brain. It does all this instantly. Much of the evidence we collect about the world comes to us in various ways as a series of pictures taken by our eyes. (p. 164)

Teacher: Now that most of you are finished, what new information did you find?

Howie: The retina is like the film and chemical things make a picture in the brain.

Meg: The retina is connected to the brain by a bunch of nerves.

Marci: The retina causes chemical changes in the brain.

Bob: Nope, that's not it. The light on the retina causes some kind of chemical reactions that send messages to the brain.

Teacher: Why is the retina like film?

Marvin: That's where the light goes. It goes through the lens in the eye to the retina. That's the same as the film in a camera.

Teacher: Good, Marvin. Who can tell us what kind of chemical changes might be happening? Do cameras or film go through chemical changes?

Alicia: They sure do. My mom takes pictures all the time and she has a darkroom where she develops pictures. There are chemicals all over the place.

Teacher: Now, how's that like an eye?

Teacher: Nobody? Bob, you were talking about it a few minutes ago. Well, let's look back at the book to that part. Look at the middle of the second paragraph. Read it to yourself.

[It is thought that light striking the retina affects certain chemicals in these nerve endings. A message then moves along the nerves to the brain.]

Teacher: What does all that mean?

Tom: It doesn't tell us how the chemicals work. It just says that light makes a chemical reaction begin.

Teacher: Right. What kind of chemical reaction might it be? (No response.) Well, we'll look for the answers to that as we go. Now, though, let's read about the lens. What do you think you'll find out about lenses in the eye?

Freida: Where they are.

Alicia: How they are adjusted like when there's too much or too little light, like when I adjust the shutter on my camera.

Oscar: How the lens filters the light.
Teacher: OK, let's read the next two paragraphs. When you're finished, close the book and think about what you found out.

At this point, let us direct your attention to a couple of things. After the first reading, Ms. Bolton elicited the gist of the selection and whatever else came to students' minds about what they had read. She then pursued their responses with follow-up questions. She found trouble with the matter of chemical changes, but that was because the text introduced the topic but never really explained what it meant. The teacher was wise at this point to let it slide, but she will come back to it later. So, with a slight shift in the discussion, she got some predictions about lenses. We can now rejoin the students as they read these paragraphs:

> In a pinhole camera you cannot change the focus. But in many cameras the lens can be moved back and forward. With each change, such cameras can shoot a sharp picture at a different distance.
>
> Compare the lens in the eye with the lens in the camera. The eye cannot move its lens toward the retina or away from it. But it can change the shape of the lens by means of a set of muscles. These help the eye focus automatically and receive clear images of objects far and near. (MacMillan Science Series, p. 164)

Teacher: What did you find out?
Mark: The lens in the eye moves like the one in a camera but the one in the eye moves when muscles move.
Meg: And when the muscles move, it causes the lens to take a different shape. That's what makes things clear or fuzzy.
Teacher: Anything else? No? OK, what was not included in the passage that you want to find out besides how the chemical elements work?
Bill: How the muscles expand and contract to change the shape of the lens.
Teacher: Do you think you'll find out?
Bill: I doubt it.
Teacher: Maybe you'll be surprised. What else do you want to know?
Angie: How the light gets to the brain. But that's about chemicals, isn't it?
Teacher: Yes, but it also involves the pupil. Do you know what the pupil is?
Jeff: It's the big dark part, right in the middle.
Kris: That's where the hole is for the light.
Tom: They get bigger in the dark, too, to let in more light.
Teacher: Good. What do you think you'll find out about the pupil?
Fred: How it's like a camera.

Alicia: How it helps us see.
Teacher: OK, let's read the next two paragraphs and finish this section about the eye as a camera.

> The pupil of your eye is really a small opening through which light enters. It looks black for the same reason that a window in an unlit house looks black. The interior is not as brightly lighted as the outside. The pupil of your eye can be adjusted to let in more or less light. The opening in a camera may be adjusted to do this, too.
> The pupil becomes smaller when a bright light hits the eye. The part of the eye which closes the pupil is called the iris (EYE-ris). It is the colored part of the eye. The iris is really a small muscle. If someone wakes you from sleep at night and turns on a bright light, the pain or discomfort you feel in your eyes is caused by this muscle being made to work more quickly than usual. The part of the camera which controls the amount of light entering the lens is called an iris, too. Look for it on a camera. (pp. 164–165)

Teacher: What did you learn?
Frank: Light enters the eye through the pupil and it adjusts to let in more or less light.
Wanda: And the iris opens the pupil. It decides whether more light is needed.
Teacher: How is this like a camera?
Kelley: A camera has an iris that can be adjusted to let in more light if it is dark or less light if it is bright.
Teacher: What do we still need to know?
Bob: About the chemicals. How does the chemical change and how does the image get to the brain?
Tom: What is an image?
Marcia: How all the parts of the eye go together.
Teacher: Those are good questions. And some of them are answered in the next section of the text. But let's first pull our information together about what we do know. In fact, let's go over what we have on the board and review.

We'll leave Ms. Bolton's class here but suggest you examine Figure 4.1 to see what she was going to review on the chalkboard. The students' learning was developing as they explored the relationship between the eye and a camera. They were led to seek associations between what they knew and what they were discovering. They were guided to ask questions and to remain aware of information that was still lacking. In effect, Ms. Bolton led the students through an exploration and a discussion of what they found. If there is one guideline we can offer that best captures the spirit of the content reading lesson it is this: *lead the class in a conversation about what is being studied.* Look again. That is what Sonja Bolton did.

FIGURE 4.1   Example of View of Chalkboard during a CRL.

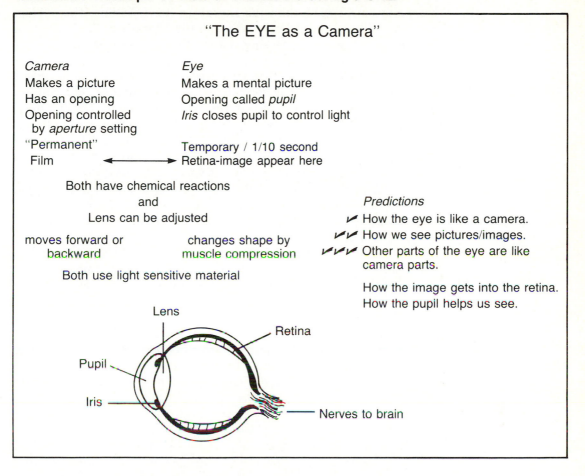

"The EYE as a Camera"

Camera	Eye
Makes a picture	Makes a mental picture
Has an opening	Opening called *pupil*
Opening controlled by *aperture* setting	*Iris* closes pupil to control light
"Permanent"	Temporary / 1/10 second
Film ⟷	Retina-image appear here

Both have chemical reactions
and
Lens can be adjusted

moves forward or backward   changes shape by muscle compression

Both use light sensitive material

Predictions
↙ How the eye is like a camera.
↙↙ How we see pictures/images.
↙↙↙ Other parts of the eye are like camera parts.

How the image gets into the retina.
How the pupil helps us see.

Lens
Retina
Pupil
Iris
Nerves to brain

Such is the nature of a content reading lesson. It is an exploration surrounded by a discussion; a continuous cycle of anticipations, realizations, and contemplations. The responsibility of the student is to seek realizations; your role as teacher is to facilitate and encourage students' efforts.

■ **The Content Reading Lesson with Literature**

Narrative, poetic, and dramatic material comprise the subject material of literature classes, but that material is often approached as content information. The result is that in many literature classes there is an acceptable, "correct" interpretation for whatever is read, and acceptable interpretations, rather than the literature itself, become the subject of study. But, we would ask, what of the literature? Isn't there a dangerous paradox in bypassing the reading of literature in favor of study of its interpretation?

This issue reminds us of an instance where a twelfth-grade student and her honors English teacher ran afoul of one another. The conflict arose during a discussion of the interpretation of a poem, "Ozymandias" by Percy Shelley. When called upon to explain the poem, Laura suggested that it was about the conflict between man and nature and that in such instances nature will, in the long run, win out. It was a reasonable interpretation and in fact was one discussed in a creative writing class several months before. Her teacher, however, disagreed. After several other students were unable to provide the desired response, the teacher announced, "Can't you see it? Shelley is speaking out against the despotic rulers in Europe during the 1840s."

Such may be the literary interpretation this teacher learned in a graduate English course, but the likelihood that any student, other than a Shelley scholar, would or even could arrive at such an interpretation on his or her own is remote at best. Here again is an outrageous example of the teacher as surrogate author. (Shelley would probably turn over in his grave at the thought.) This teacher "knew" the "correct" interpretation and insisted on her students knowing it as well as she did.

After hearing her teacher's interpretation, Laura proceeded to say, "But, aren't I entitled to my own interpretation?" To which her teacher retorted, "Of course you are Laura, but don't put it on the test or it will be counted wrong."

We find ourselves rather sympathetic to both teacher and student in this instance. Laura is entitled to her personal interpretation and without considerable background knowledge she cannot be expected to arrive at the interpretation acclaimed by Shelley scholars. Concomitantly, however, her teacher has a right, even a responsibility to communicate *the* meaning derived by literary critics. That is, after all, the content of this British literature course. How to resolve the dilemma?

We suggest that this teacher could have heeded the words of our young friend Jeff (p. 13) who thought the teacher should ask him what *he* thought the story was about before asking what the author meant (or what the teacher thought the author meant). In such a case, Laura's English teacher might have responded to Laura's interpretation somewhat differently, such as: "That is an interesting view, Laura. Can you tell us what clues in the poem led you to that interpretation?" After Laura elaborates her opinion, other students might be asked to join in with their opinions. Subsequently, the teacher might then have said, "Now, let me share with you the standard interpretation of literary critics." The teacher could then share the "content" and even point out how the critics had arrived at their interpretation. Later, when Laura asked, "But aren't I entitled to my interpretation?" her teacher could have replied, "Yes, of course you are, but on the test I may ask you for the interpretation of literary critics as well as your personal interpretation."

A similar approach can be taken by any teacher with any narrative, poetic, or dramatic selection. The issue need not be whether literary critics have determined the "authoritative" interpretation; the teacher is likely to have greater insights into a poem or story than the students. The teacher can, however, withhold the "correct" view until students have had an opportunity to share their views, regardless of how non-conformist their views happen to be. After all, isn't it the *process* of interpretation that we want to teach rather than the interpretations of others? Then, too, it should be both.

ARC Guides

Another way to use the ARC format is an activity that guides students through the various elements of ARC. Since this activity engages students in anticipations, realizations, and contemplations, we call this activity an *ARC guide*. The multiple options in each stage of this activity make it attractive to teachers and challenging for students. Before we say more, however, let us show you an example designed by Sharon Harper for her fourth grade students. The text selection comes from *Science for a Changing World* (p. 78). Work through this example yourself to get a sense of the potential of these guides.

ARC GUIDE FOR "SOURCES OF HEAT"

ANTICIPATION

1. When you think of the word heat, what ideas come to your mind?

   _____

   _____

   _____

2. List any heat-giving sources (things) that you can think of:

   _____

   _____

   _____

3. Why do you think we need sources of heat?

_____

_____

_____

REALIZATION

Read the passage. As you read, try to figure out which heat source is the most important one to us.

Sources of Heat

Without heat energy, our world would be a frozen place without life. Plants and animals could not live and grow. Nothing would move without heat energy.

Heat comes to us from many things. However, the sun is our biggest source of heat as well as light. We call heat and light from the sun *solar energy*.

You have learned that energy can change form. We produce *chemical energy* when we burn fuels. This energy was once heat from the sun. Wood is sometimes used as a fuel. It comes from trees that could not have grown without the sun. Oil and gas were formed from plants and animals that lived many years ago. The sun made them grow.

Electrical energy is often produced by burning fuel. Therefore, the solar energy was changed first to chemical energy and then to electrical energy. If electricity comes from mechanical energy of falling water, that also was once solar energy. Heat from the sun makes water evaporate. Then it falls to earth again and runs into the rivers. The water in rivers can be used to turn a turbine to create electricity. A *turbine* is a machine that has blades turned by water, steam, or air.

Rubbing your hand on your desk makes your hand feel hot. This rubbing together of objects is called *friction*. Friction causes the heat on your hand.

CONTEMPLATION

1. Which heat source is the most important to us? Why do you think this is true?

_____

_____

_____

_____

2. Now that you have read the passage, write down as many facts about heat sources as you can. (Do not look back at the passage.)

_____

_____

_____

_____

3. Now look back at the passage and check to see if your information is complete and correct. Change anything that is wrong or incomplete.

4. Paragraph 5 deals with the source of heat called friction. Can you name other examples of friction?

_____

_____

_____

_____

Of course you noticed the similarity between this ARC guide and a content reading lesson. We suggest you encourage group discussion or even paired discussion of responses to the contemplation questions. As the framework for learning, ARC is probably the most valuable feature of teaching we can share with you. In subsequent chapters, we discuss various ways to stimulate anticipation, realization, and contemplation, and all of those additional strategies can be integrated into ARC guides. To demonstrate some of the possibilities, we have included several other guides developed by teachers we know; notice the variety of activities they have chosen to use.

ARC GUIDE FOR "THE BALD EAGLE"

ANTICIPATION

1. Imagine for a minute that you are a bald eagle soaring high above the canyons looking down on the small world. Describe what your life is like while flying high above the world.

_____

_____

_____

_____

_____

_____

2. While flying above the land there must be many dangers that threaten your life. Describe these dangers and tell how you would protect yourself against them.

_____

_____

_____

_____

_____

_____

3. Describe your life style when you're not flying and searching for prey for your dinner. Let your imagination soar!

_____

_____

_____

_____

_____

_____

_____

REALIZATION

Read the article silently. As you read, place a (+) beside the things that you did not know about the eagle. Place a check (√) next to things you did know and then place an (!) next to things you found interesting in the article.

The Bald Eagle

The very emblem of the United States—the bald eagle—is among those animals now threatened with extinction. As with so many other creatures, the eagle is becoming another victim of man's science and weapons. The National Audubon Society has been a leading influence in wildlife preservation over the years. Audubon officials estimate that there are no more than one thousand breeding pairs of bald eagles to be found in the entire continental United States. In spite of the fact that the bald eagle, as well as golden eagles, are protected by federal laws, forty-eight were recently found dead within a six-week period.

These were birds which found the sun-baked cliffs of Jackson Canyon in Wyoming ideal for their winter home. Here, near the trout-filled North Platte River, the huge birds nested from November through March. With warming weather, they flew north to Canada and Alaska with the help of their seven-foot wings.

Their deaths came from several causes, but the main one seems to have been from poisoning. The poison, thallium sulfate, was set out to help protect sheep flocks from such suspected killers as coyotes. It was placed in the bodies of dead antelope left along a dirt road to attract and kill predators. Instead of coyotes, eagles ate the poisoned meat, and now even fewer of the majestic white-headed birds remain. Birds are frequently victims of insecticides, pesticides, and poisoned bait intended for other animals, not only in the United States, but the world over. Reports of eagle deaths from deliberate shooting and from accidental electric shock on power lines continue to be received. It may soon be that the only time anyone can see an eagle will be in a museum or on the Nation's money.

CONTEMPLATION

1. What has caused the eagle to become extinct in the U.S.?

_____

_____

_____

_____

2. What could you do to help preserve the bird that is the national emblem?

_____

_____

_____

_____

3. What did you learn about where eagles live?

_____

_____

_____

_____

4. What did you think was the most interesting thing you found out as you read this article?

_____

_____

_____

_____

The previous guide was adapted from one designed by Jill Von Edwin for seventh grade readers. The text is from *It's Our Choice,* (pp. 72–73).

One further example was designed for middle grade students in a reading class. Notice how it stresses figurative language within the context of a reading activity.

ARC GUIDE FOR "SKYDIVING"

ANTICIPATION

Have you ever thought you would like to try skydiving, or parachute jumping? Why or why not?

_____

_____

REALIZATION

In this selection, the author shares with you the experience of skydiving by using words which appeal to your senses. Underline each word or phrase which appeals to one or more of your senses as you read.

SKYDIVING

You are plummeting toward earth at 80 miles per hour. Your altitude is 5000 feet. You have free-fallen for 10,000 feet. In 42 seconds your body will slam against the ground! The only thing between you and certain death is the small pack on your back. It holds a small colorful chute. The rip cord is yanked. "Old Faithful" blossoms! You are down safely again—for the 700th time in the past two years. Every weekend, Saturday and Sunday, you have jumped, jumped, jumped. Jumping is in your blood. It has been worth the time and the effort because. . . .

You are now an accomplished jumper. You team up with other members of your club and practice what is referred to as RW. This is a series of routines involving aerial acrobatics and hookups. Competition on a national level may be in the offing, if your group really gets good.

Skydiving is a recreational activity which requires a fair amount of money. A jumping outfit, for example, can cost up to $2000. Add seven dollars per jump and you readily understand the cost factor. So if you have the cash and the time, skydiving may be your thing. If you get past the first few jumps, say the enthusiasts, you will find the time and the cash. Then, they say, you will be hooked!

CONTEMPLATION

1. Each of the three paragraphs in this selection has a different topic related to skydiving. For each paragraph, write a sentence to state the topic:

   Paragraph 1 _____
   _____

   Paragraph 2 _____

   Paragraph 3 _____
   _____

2. In this type of writing, colorful language helps give the feeling of excitement. For example, if, instead of saying ". . . your body will slam against the ground," the author had written "your body will hit the ground," the effect would not have been quite as terrifying. Many of the colorful expressions used here should be the ones you underlined as you read. They are the words and phrases which appeal to your senses.

   What did the author mean by each of the following expressions:
   a. plummeting toward earth _____
   b. The only thing between you and *certain death* _____
   _____
   c. The rip cord is yanked . . . _____
   d. "Old Faithful" blossoms! _____
   e. Jumping is in your blood _____

ARC AND READING ABILITY

■ ■ Perhaps it is apparent that the content reading lesson and ARC guides can help facilitate a reader's comprehension of a specific selection. What, though, about improving a more generalized ability to read? Many authorities in reading maintain that improvement in reading comes from reading; hence one learns to read by reading. We agree, up to a point. What about the reader who continues to practice bad habits and gets better at reading poorly? What kind of practice is that?

Consider an analogy with learning a sport, tennis for example. Can one get better at tennis just by playing? Yes, but only up to a point and, in most cases, only very gradually. What happens when the novice gets good coaching? Improvement becomes apparent more rapidly. Now consider the flip side of the scenario. Can you improve as a tennis player only with good coaching? Yes, again, but only up to a point. Our point is that learning to read better is like learning to play tennis better: it requires good coaching *and* lots of practice.

The content reading lesson provides the opportunity for good coaching, especially when students work with their teacher in small groups. The ARC guides offer practice time whereby "the coach" can be sure students are practicing the fundamental skills that lead to improved reading ability as well as increased comprehension of the specific selection being read. Thus, an adequate dose of content reading lessons with substantive practice through ARC guides should result in better reading and better readers.

There is one last ingredient essential to efficient practice and good comprehension: students must discuss what they are doing and you must lead that discussion. After a content reading lesson or the completion of an ARC guide, a brief period should be devoted to considering the kinds of anticipations that occurred, the ways various students approached the selection, what sorts of problems with comprehension arose and what was done to solve the problems, what realizations emerged, and what kinds of contemplations were memorable. We want to stress that *students must understand the process they are using,* and for them to integrate the learning format of ARC into their independent reading and reasoning activities, they must assimilate the plan into their framework for study. Such assimilation will rarely occur serendipitously; it must be planned and integrated into the instructional lesson.

ARC AND THE CYCLE OF READING

■ ■ Our major purpose in this chapter has been to offer practical suggestions about how to help students with their reading in ways that affect their immediate understanding and their general reading abilities. To this end, we have introduced you to a basic instructional format, ARC, and two instructional activities derived from ARC, namely the content reading lesson and ARC guides. To conclude our discussion, we offer some theoretical perspective to support what we have suggested. As we elaborate upon the learning theory underlying ARC, we ask that you reflect upon these ideas in relation to both ARC and your own experiences as a reader.

Ulric Neisser is one of the founders of cognitive psychology, the subdiscipline representing psychology's big break from behaviorism. Neisser (1976) proposed a model of perception called the perceptual cycle. We believe his model goes a long way toward helping clarify the process of reading comprehension, which we perceive as a cycle of reading. Before we elaborate upon this cycle of reading, let us restate our view that reading is thinking cued by print and it is an event that involves a reader, a text, and a context. None of those elements, however, explain anything of what happens during a reading event. The cycle of reading, an extension of Neisser's perceptual cycle, does provide some indications of the cognitive processes involved in reading.

The procedural model upon which we rest all of our pedagogical suggestions comprises three parts (see Figure 4.2) but they are inseparable, except for purposes of description and definition. That is, the process of reading is cyclic, as we will explain, but it is also synergistic. The latter term is borrowed from biology, where it refers to the action of two or more organs to achieve an effect that is beyond the capability of either organ individually. It is the interaction among these so-called parts of the reading process that enables comprehension to emerge; the whole is greater than the sum of its parts.

The idea of the cycle is also important. Consider your own reading. Your knowledge, feelings, and inclinations determine what you expect to gain from the reading and they direct what you do when you read. The composite of your experiences (knowledge, feelings, and inclinations)—your cognitive structure—enables you to "see" certain things in a text, as with the poem about Columbus in chapter 1. Thus, when you examine a text, you see things you expected to see. Further, what you do see has the effect of modifying what you know, feel, and are inclined to do, all of which changes what you are capable of expecting, and so forth continuously and simultaneously, as we have depicted in Figure 4.2.

Within this cycle you can, of course, find anticipation, realization, and contemplation. Your cognitive structure establishes expectations from which emerge anticipations; your purpose for reading and your

FIGURE 4.2   A Cyclic Model of Reading Behavior (after Neisser, 1976).

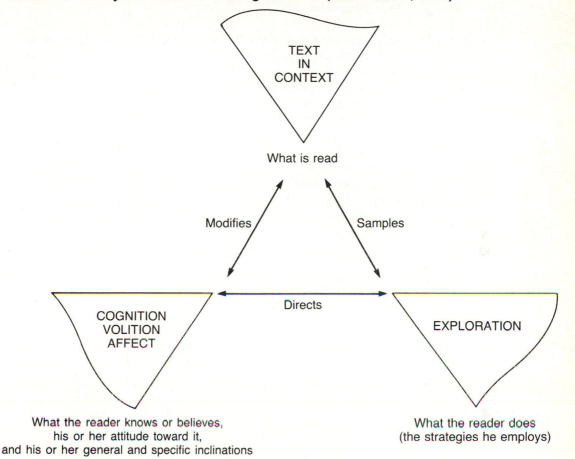

anticipations direct the choice of strategies (for example, skimming, scanning, studying, or casual reading); then you use the chosen strategies to realize meaning as you read; subsequently, you alter your cognitive structure through contemplations; and so the cycle goes.

As you may recall from chapter 1, Louise Rosenblatt (1978) takes up the cycle idea in an analogy with an electric circuit. As she puts it, what one understands from reading

comes into being in the live circuit set up between the reader and the text. As with the elements of an electric circuit, each component of the reading process functions by virtue of the presence of the others. *A specific reader and a specific text at a specific time and place; change any of these, and there occurs a different circuit, a different event. . . .* (p. 11, emphasis ours)

We might extend this analogy by suggesting that each of the elements in an electric circuit must be functional and must operate harmoniously with all the other elements or there will be a break in the circuit. In fact, there can be no circuit without cyclic synergy.

Reading as a learning activity is hardly simple to understand or explain. Keep in mind that the reading act is dynamic and everything in the model happens all at once and continuously during the reading event. Notice, too, that the arrows in our diagram go both ways; all the parts influence all other parts and are separable only in a diagram. During reading, anticipations, realizations, and contemplations synergistically interact to enable the emergence of comprehension. ARC, then, embodies the cycle of reading and the content reading lesson and ARC guides facilitate this synergistic cycle.

5

Anticipation

SETTING THE STAGE

"Hey, kids, don't forget your assignment for tomorrow, pages 44–52. And there will be a test on Friday." How often have you had a reading assignment introduced in just such a way as you rushed from a class? One student we recently talked to said he had quit reading textbook assignments since the teacher was going to cover it all the next day anyway. Or at least, what was likely to be on the test.

The problem with this scenario is that the cycle of reading is short-circuited because anticipation is bypassed. Comprehension emerges from an integration of new understandings with prior awarenesses, as we have stated previously, and thus anticipation sets the stage for new learning. When the anticipation phase of the cycle is omitted, especially when the newly known connection is likely to be strained by the amount of new information to be absorbed, is it any wonder that students find it difficult to make new understandings their own?

All reading and virtually all learning depend on what the learner brings to the task of learning. In the same way that perception is governed by expectation, comprehension is governed by anticipation. Thus, reading with an attitude of expectation is one of the most important facets of reading comprehension. The psychologist David Ausubel (1978), one of the pioneers of cognitive psychology, stressed the importance of prior knowledge in this way: "If we had to reduce all of educational psychology to just one principle, we would say this: The most important single factor influencing new learning is what the learner already knows. Ascertain this and teach him accordingly." (p. 163)

We'd like to extend the framework of ARC and the content reading lesson. In this chapter, we'll suggest a number of ways one might "ascertain this and teach him accordingly."

We believe spending a full half of instructional time helping readers anticipate what they will understand can increase readers' understandings *and* rememberings. Time invested before reading will, as an extra dividend, reduce the amount of time required after reading to explain to students what they didn't understand. Let us, then, consider further the rationale of anticipation and some additional ways to help readers anticipate what they will learn.

PRIOR KNOWLEDGE AND COMPREHENSION

■ ■ Read the following paragraph:

> Always begin from the left. Accomplishment requires balance, as well as the ability to stand on one foot cross-legged. You should, of course, hold on. The steps are these: push your left leg down on the left pedal, picking the right one up and over and down in one smooth movement. The propulsion which is caused will complicate the matter, so be careful!

If you are like most readers, you found the paragraph incomprehensible. Why? Because there is nothing in the paragraph or in the context of your reading that allows you to relate the content of the paragraph to anything you know. That is, the text does not cue you to any prior knowledge. If only we had said, "We're going to tell you how to mount a bicycle," your comprehension would have been near perfect; ah, it all becomes so clear because you *do* know about riding a bicycle. Hence, when either the teacher or the text provides a cue to existing knowledge, the reader is ready to realize meaning from the text.

Marvin Minsky (1975) puts this in slightly different terms with his notion of "frames." Whenever we try to understand anything, he proposes, we do so by trying to relate it to a framework we have previously constructed from our experiences. Thus, if you had known before you began reading our earlier paragraph that it was about getting on a bicycle, you would have "pictured" certain expectancies of what the paragraph was to be about, and your "frame of reference" would have guided you to realize immediately what was being described. As it was, you had no way to picture what was being described and so you failed to understand. Your frame for getting on a bicycle was buried somewhere, and we weren't doing much to help you access that knowledge or bring it into focus. A well-written paragraph, by contrast, is a help to the reader, and a successful reader is constantly modifying or adjusting his or her frame of reference on the basis of continually flowing information provided by the text. Such is the nature of the intact circuit, the cycle of reading.

Our point is this: Successful comprehension depends upon one's ability to relate prior knowledge to the information in a reading selection. In fact, comprehension of anything, books included, occurs because the reader can relate concepts to one another, particularly known concepts to new concepts. One factor that may cause a text to confuse rather than cue thinking is a reader's lack of prior knowledge about the topic being studied, which is why we include insufficient prior experience among our frustration potentials. Our bicycle example enables us to extend this idea to include situations where, even when prior knowledge exists, it is not adequately accessed by the reader.

We confess our bicycle mounting directions were written to prevent comprehension, done in fun and only to demonstrate our point that students often need help relating what they are trying to learn to what they already know. For students in school, though, reading incomprehensible paragraphs is not such fun. Unfortunately, what you experienced in reading the bicycle example happens frequently to them. Too often, when students are reading, either their experiences have not enabled them to build the frame of reference needed to understand the assigned selection, or they are not properly oriented to the appropriate frame of reference. In either case, they don't understand what they read because there is no way to relate the message of what they are reading to what they already know.

As one more example of what we're driving at here, we have included a favorite passage from a journal article by Bransford and Johnson:

> If the balloons popped the sound wouldn't be able to carry since everything would be too far away from the correct floor. A closed window would also prevent the sound from carrying, since most buildings tend to be well insulated. Since the whole operation depends upon a steady flow of electricity, a break in the middle of the wire would also cause problems. Of course, the fellow could shout, but the human voice is not loud enough to carry that far. An additional problem is that a string could break on the instrument. Then there could be no accompaniment to the message. It is clear that the best situation would involve less distance. Then there would be fewer potential problems. With face to face contact, the least number of things could go wrong. (Bransford & Johnson, 1979, p. 205)

If you fail to understand what's going on here, look at Figure 5.1 on the facing page. This illustration should accompany the story. This is an experimental passage, not real text, but it does show that readers need somehow to "get the picture" of what they're reading; even if they know all the words, they may fail to comprehend. Most texts do a better job than this one or our bicycle mounting directions, but we reiterate: Any time a reader, despite the best of efforts, fails to comprehend something being read, he or she has somehow failed to get the picture. It is possible that the text has failed in its role to cue the reader in any of several ways we've already discussed in chapter 2. It is also possible that the reader didn't get the essential help needed to relate the new information to prior experiences. Part of the help we are referring to here is the responsibility of authors. But part of the responsibility also lies with the teacher to help students relate what they are trying to learn to what they already know. (And part must come from the student, as we will discuss in chapter 11.) The teacher's options are varied, but they begin with anticipating students' needs.

ANTICIPATING STUDENTS' NEEDS

■ ■ Teachers must, we maintain, read each assignment they make to determine its appropriateness and to anticipate potential difficulties it may pose for readers. To accomplish this successfully often requires that you read the assignment as if you were Susan, Rosalind, Hiram, Miguel or others in the class. We have found that when we fail to take our students' perspective, we often overlook potential hurdles because the material is so familiar to us. By perceiving assignments from the students' point of view, you should be able to anticipate what prior knowledge and frames of reference students must possess if they are to understand as they read. Let's elaborate what we mean with several examples.

A popular story by Edgar Allen Poe, "The Masque of the Red Death," describes a medieval party that extends over several days during which time a plague infests the occasion. Poe assumes that his reader knows that a masque is a medieval ball held as a celebration where guests come from miles around and join in extended festivities. What, though, do junior or senior high school students know of such occasions? Precious little; nor do they associate "the red death" with a plague. A teacher who can anticipate students' lack of knowledge about masques and plagues can provide them with information enabling

FIGURE 5.1 Appropriate Context for the Balloon Passage

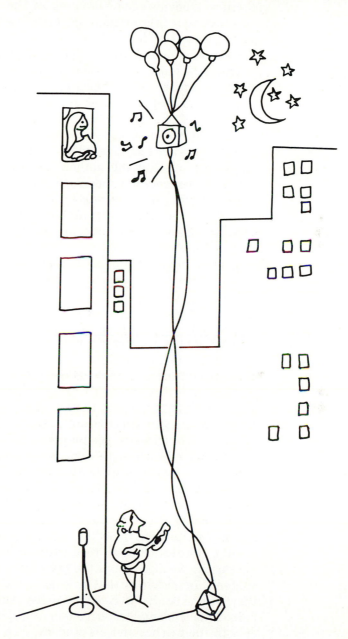

(Bransford and Johnson, 1972, "The Balloon Study")

them to realize the events of the story as Poe describes them and can facilitate students' understanding of the story by simply providing the contextual information and historical background that students need to understand.

On other occasions, anticipation instruction isn't quite so simple. Recently we observed a group of students groping to understand a science selection on the topography of the ocean floor. (We used an excerpt from this text in chapter 2 as an example of appropriate repetition.) The selection was of interest to the students and they approached it with considerable diligence. They were, unfortunately, thwarted by the fact that the text never explained the concept of topography; instead the authors assumed that the students would remember the concept of topography because they had studied it several months before. The students also encountered difficulty because 53 percent of the ideas included in the selection were nonessential details. What we observed was students attempting, with little success, to relate all the bits and pieces of information they found in the text to their prior knowledge of oceans and features of the earth's surface; they also tried to organize the bits and pieces relative to one another in hopes they could understand how the concepts and details fit together.

The irony of this example is that when the students were able to "see" the whole, the bits and pieces became clear. The teacher, by his own admission, had not read the selection before he assigned it; thus he had neither anticipated students' needs nor had he developed with the students a conceptual framework they could use in exploring the new information. And yet, had this teacher read the text from the perspective of a naive, uninformed student, he would have probably recognized the problems that the students did in fact encounter; further, in a matter of minutes, the teacher could have prepared the students to read the selection with considerable ease.

While inconsiderate textbooks abound in classrooms, we believe that considerate teachers can do much to reduce the potential difficulties of such texts. The example we just shared does, by the way, have a happy ending. This teacher now recognizes that the text he is using has a potential for impeding students' learning, and he now takes twenty minutes or so to read every selection before assigning it to his classes. He also spends the last part of every class period engaging students in activities that help give them an overview of the topic they will be studying. Needless to say, such considerate teaching has helped his students overcome potential problems, and the frustration of both the teacher and his students has been substantially reduced.

We have one final example that will amplify what we mean by helping students prepare to learn from their reading. This example illustrates a different sort of problem, namely one where students possess the requisite knowledge for learning but they either fail to realize that they know or they fail to use their knowledge appropriately. We refer to situations where students seem to approach their learning in a vacuum. They memorize details and definitions instead of seeking to understand new dimensions of concepts with which they already have prior experiences. This tendency to isolate learning from prior knowledge can often create problems for students and frustration for teachers. Let us share the example and then we'll briefly speculate upon its causes.

The instructional setting is a class in United States history. The students have recently learned that manifest destiny was a compelling force in the westward movement, or at least as perceived by historians. The students have learned that Senator Thomas Hart Benton proclaimed that settlement of the Columbia River valley in Oregon was a momentous goal for the emerging nation because settlement of the West was an actualization of a divine plan to improve the condition of the world through the civilization of all parts of the continent, including its remote areas. Needless to say, the concept of manifest destiny is more complex than one simply associated with settlement of the western United States, but that's what these eighth graders had learned. Let there be no mistake that they had learned it either, for they had explained it accordingly on a test just two days before reading the following paragraph in a selection entitled "The Fulfillment of Manifest Destiny."

> What made the gold fields especially enticing was that many people believed it took little organized effort or capital to become rich. The basic tool could be as simple as a washbasin. The individual prospector scooped up some earth, poured water over it, and sloshed it around to wash dissolved soil away from the heavy particles of gold, which sank to the bottom. Soon men began to use the same method on a larger scale by shoveling earth into wooden boxes. This washing, or placer mining process, could make a man rich very quickly, even when he started empty-handed. Many Americans came to believe that it was the Manifest Destiny of the United States to shower wealth on its citizens.

Disregard now, if you can, the inaccuracy of this section and its clear confusion of manifest destiny with the gospel of wealth. Consider instead how these students reacted to the sentence, "Many Americans came to believe that it was the Manifest Destiny of the United States to shower wealth on its citizens." Remember that just two days previously they had learned a very different concept of manifest destiny. And how did they react two pages later to these sentences: "The era of

Manifest Destiny closed in a frenzy of business activity. In time Americans even came to believe that the man who got rich was helping his country as much as the soldier or the explorer." How did these students react? They simply absorbed this most recent information about manifest destiny into a conceptual frame that completely ignored their prior learning.

While we are concerned that the students were given inaccurate information, we are more concerned with the phenomenon that the students never considered the inconsistency of the information. How could they do this? From their viewpoint, it was both easy and understandable. They had already passed one test with one answer; now they had to pass a different test with another answer. Their prior knowledge was useless, for it had been used; the new information, inconsistent though it may have been, was what would be called for on the next test. How, then, we might well ask, do these students *now* conceptualize manifest destiny?

Much of this type of learning is common across grades and content subjects (Baker, 1979; Petrosky, 1982) and fits the information gleaned from adolescents about their tendency to memorize details and definitions when reading "because that's what teachers test." Students seem to learn in a vacuum that keeps all information unrelated because that is how they perceive the game of school. We believe the anticipation phase of ARC can be used to focus students' attention away from details and memorized definitions and more toward the gist of a selection. Such considerate teaching would prepare students to recognize inconsistencies like those posed by the passage on manifest destiny and would encourage students to broaden their perspective by relating new learning to prior knowledge.

We are hopeful that you recognize prior knowledge as an important factor in learning. Let us offer one caution before we describe some activities you may find useful. In several recent studies (for example, Langer, 1984; Rothwell, 1983; Vaughan & Vaughan, 1983), researchers have found that what teachers identify as being familiar for students does not correspond with what the students themselves identify as being familiar. To avoid such miscalculations, we encourage teachers to engage in discussions with students about topics to be studied. The strategies we are about to share have proven to be effective, but in every instance the critical factor contributing to that effectiveness is the dynamic interaction that must occur between teacher and students or students and students while these strategies are being used. It is the give-and-take that occurs in the process of these activities that leads to increased learning. During these activities, the students' role is one of considering what they already know about the topic and generating some expectations about what they will learn. The teacher's role is in guiding students' realization of what they know and their use of previously accumulated experiences to facilitate new learning.

BUILDING ANTICIPATION: THE TEACHER'S ROLE

Any pre-reading activity must be based on what the students will be studying (for example, what information is in the text and how is it structured) and on what the students know about the topic. It is appropriate, therefore, to devote the initial part of any lesson to determination of students' prior knowledge. Once you know what prior knowledge the students possess, you must decide whether it is sufficient for them to succeed with the assignment *if* you have also helped them establish a purpose and a desire for learning. If you believe the students lack certain requisite information, then provide that for them. We want to emphasize, however, that it is important not to *give* students a lot of new information. There is always a risk of preceding one difficult learning task with another while actually facilitating neither. Notice that in each of the techniques we describe, the focus is on *what the reader knows*. If you find that the readers know little or nothing relative to the content of what they're about to read, you can take that as good evidence that the reading is likely to be difficult, perhaps even frustrating, and may well be inappropriate. What should you do to make the assignment more appropriate before requiring it of your students? As you will realize, you have plenty of options for anticipation activities. We begin with a strategy that is unrivaled in its sophistication, although deceptively simple to use once its subtleties are understood.

A Pre-reading Plan (PReP)

As we have tried to emphasize, successful pre-reading instruction begins with identification of what students already know about a topic to be studied. Judith Langer (1981) has recognized this problem from first-hand experience and has developed a strategy, PReP, that combines both an assessment feature and an instructional component. Her intent is to provide teachers with a way to avoid making ". . . instructional decisions *based on assumptions* about students' knowledge," for when teachers plan pre-reading activities based on inaccurate assumptions, ineffectual teaching is almost certain to result. As Langer says, "PReP is a very straightforward teaching strategy [and] an understanding of why it works is essential to implementing it successfully."

PReP addresses two issues, namely: (1) how knowledge is stored and accessed and (2) how new knowledge can be added to memory. Needless to say, these issues are rather complex. Let us explore the basics, without, we hope, oversimplifying them too much.

Factual, informational knowledge seems to be stored as ideas that are connected by links in much the same way that cities and towns are connected by roads. Presumably, a person's memory is composed of ideas and links. The ideas are interconnected by their association or relationships to one another, some directly (for example, government—president), others indirectly (computers—manuscripts). Hence, when a learner is exposed to new ideas, the learner searches for a place in the network of ideas to fit the new idea. PReP is a technique that prepares the reader to anticipate what prior knowledge will be useful for understanding new ideas.

PReP consists of three stages built upon one another. In the first stage, the teacher seeks students' initial association with the topic. In the second stage, the students explain why they made those associations. In the third stage, the students reformulate their conceptualizations by adding associations that did not initially occur to them. As the students are proceeding through these stages, the teacher seeks to assess (1) the amount of prior information the readers have about the topic *and* how this information is organized; (2) the language students use to express their knowledge of the topic (language used to express conceptual understandings can indicate sophistication of knowledge); and (3) how much additional information and vocabulary students might need before they can successfully comprehend the text.

To initiate a PReP discussion, give the students a cue that will elicit their associations with the topic. If students are to read about banks and the federal reserve system, you might begin by asking them, "Tell anything that comes to mind when you hear the word *banks*." You might also use a phrase or, in some cases, a picture, or have students read the first paragraph of the selection if the text will cue the kinds of responses you are looking for. As students provide you with their associations, you can then add another cue; for example, how do banks send money to one another? One caution is in order at this point: *Avoid using terms that you suspect the students do not already know*. In this instance, if you used "federal reserve system" as a cue, you would probably inhibit responses rather than encourage them. If students themselves mention the federal reserve system in response to your cues, then you get a sense of their knowledge, but your cues must be chosen to stimulate responses, not restrict them. Recognize, too, that one student's response will trigger another student to say something he or she did not originally think of. Encourage students to expand on each other's ideas.

Remember that you are trying to assess how much students know and how it can help them learn new ideas they will study. After you obtain a list of initial responses to your cues (and we recommend that you write the responses on the board for reference and easy access), have the students reflect on and elaborate the reasons for their responses. Ask students to explain "what made you think of that." So, if a student mentions home loans in response to banks, explore that response to find out why he or she thought of home loans. Your purpose here is to help students develop an awareness of the network that connects their associations.

Students also have a chance to listen to each other's explanations, to interact, and to become aware of their developing ideas. They can consider, reject, accept, revise, and integrate old and new ideas. When asked what made him think of Christmas in response to banks, Chris replied, "I get a check every December from my Christmas Club account." When Becky, who had mentioned monthly statements, was asked about her response, she said, "I have a checking account at First National and every month I get a list of my checks and my balance." While Becky probably knows more about banks than Chris and certainly more than Franklin, who never said a word, both Chris and Franklin are given the opportunity to make associations with what others say and hence may come to realize they know more about banks than they thought they did.

The second phase of PReP begins only when you have elicited a good sample of students' prior knowledge and reasonings. The important diagnostic question here is why students thought of the ideas they have shared, the associations they have for the topic. If you have been listing students' responses on the board, you can ask them to examine the information and suggest ways to cluster and classify it. If they seem to need help, suggest categories such as services, types of accounts, functions, and the like, depending of course on the information the students have provided. We're adding this feature to Langer's PReP because we think it is important to help students recognize ways of organizing the information they have. Such organization will help students perceive a framework for what they know; it will also help those who have learned about banks during the discussion to codify and arrange their new learning. In either case, students will have a frame of reference to guide their reading. We will later discuss the importance of establishing this frame of reference in the context of a discussion of a pre-reading technique we call categorical overview.

You should not proceed to the final stage of PReP until after the organizational categories have been established. Because you have helped the students organize their knowledge during phase two, they will now be likely to clarify and elaborate their initial responses. Encourage them with comments like, "Based on the way we've organized our knowledge about banks and banking, do you have any other ideas to add, anything that comes to mind about types of accounts? bank services? the way banks work?" Ask them about each category one at a time. You want to encourage students to verbalize associations and relationships. Because you provide an opportunity for students to elaborate and because the categories have been specified, responses during this phase will often be much more refined than the original responses during phase one.

The real value of PReP is that it encourages students to think beyond their initial response that too often typifies a mere word-association task. When you observe students providing more refined responses during the third phase of PReP, you will immediately realize why it is rarely enough to ask only phase one, brainstorming kinds of questions. As a case in point, during this third phase, Franklin managed to offer, "I don't quite get it yet but I see that a bank can help me in lots of ways if I have money or if I need money."

When a PReP activity is completed and all the information and impressions that have been shared are pulled together, they will represent a good working sketch of the topic at least to the degree students are able to anticipate it. It certainly provides them with a clear framework of reference to use as they learn about banks. Some lines of association will fade as students read and others will become stronger, but you can be sure the students will understand far more of what they read than if they had approached the text without thinking about the topic. In fact, Langer (1980) and Langer & Nicolich (1981) have reported that the kind of prior knowledge we're talking about is more important than IQ in determining how much a student recalls from reading. Wetmore (1984) has reached similar conclusions.

Langer has extended our understanding of how to make pre-reading instruction more effective and, although it is not absolutely essential to your use of PReP, her diagnostic perspective gives PReP its most sophisticated feature. Once you understand this perspective, you can apply it to any diagnostic-instructional activity you might use, be it for pre-reading purposes or an assessment of what readers have accomplished at any stage of learning.

Langer distinguishes three levels of responses that could emerge during a PReP activity. In effect, she makes qualitative categorizations of readers' knowledge that can help you understand the sophistication of students' understanding of concepts. The categories are not necessarily labeled, but can be described.

At the first and lowest level of sophistication, the students' knowledge is superficial and associations are often irrelevant. Asked "what comes to mind when you think of banks?" the student says, "people" or "big buildings" or "offices" or "drive-in windows." In some cases students might respond with a word that merely rhymes with the stimulus or has some structural feature in common, as in "penance—a necklace" or "binary—bicycle" or "despot—depot." Knowledge at this level also includes tangentially related experiential associations, as "My sister used to work at a bank."

Many responses at this level of information should serve as a warning that students' prior knowledge may be insufficient for the reading task ahead of them. Such is not always the case; the key determiner will often be how well the text explains new ideas and concepts and if the new ideas are well organized. That is why we say such superficial knowledge *may* indicate that the reading will be difficult. If students know nothing about cellular structure and read a selection about the importance of nutrition for cellular growth, they will be in for a tough time. It is, of course, always possible that at a succeeding phase of discussion, such as during the third phase of PReP, the students will display a higher level of awareness and thinking. This is particularly true when students are simply unaccustomed to thinking about what they know in this way and really have more knowledge than they can indicate during an initial discussion.

At the second and middle level of sophistication, students' awareness of a topic generally takes the form of examples, attributes, or features that are relevant to the topic. To a question about Congress, students might say "makes laws" or "representatives" or "House and Senate." To a question about banks, students might say "deposit money" or "make loans." These kinds of responses are quite good during the first phase of PReP or any other initial, off-the-top-of-the-head discussion because they indicate knowledge that can easily be elaborated in a guided discussion.

The third and highest level of sophistication of knowledge is characterized by associations with more general concepts, more abstract ideas, complete and accurate definitions, analogies, or elaborations that include various components of a concept. "Congress is like Parliament in that . . ," or "Banks serve the public in various ways well beyond the checking and savings departments; for example, they serve as the economic base for a community," or "Holograms are three-dimensional representations of a whole where every part is capable of reproducing the whole." This is the level you are working toward, especially *after* the students have studied the topic. If possible, bring the students to this level before the reading so their thinking can stretch well beyond the level of simple associations, memorization, and definitions. The object, then, is to mobilize students' maximum reasoning skills as well as to provide them with a frame of reference relative to the topic.

As you judge the level of prior knowledge your students possess, on-the-spot instructional decisions can be made. Is there enough prior knowledge to permit comprehension? How should I try to channel their thinking? What sorts of expectations are they capable of? The knowledge you draw from them during any pre-reading discussion is your best clue to their potential success or frustration. Every learner has some knowledge that can be related to a new topic, since all knowledge is connected and interconnected. Students can be led to see how their knowledge can be applied to what they learn, although at times the relationship may not be obvious. As students do learn the new ideas, they will discover that these concepts are all interrelated.

Applicability of prior knowledge in a specific learning situation varies from person to person within any given task. The specific knowledge, the potential of that knowledge to be accessed, the way it is stored, the degree of its sophistication, and the strength of the links that bind associations all contribute differentially to each person's ability to associate new learning to prior knowledge. The goal is not, nor can it realistically be, to create a common, convergent frame of reference for all members of a class. Instead, the goal is to help individuals in a group recognize the prior knowledge they have, evaluate it, organize it, to construct their own frame of reference, and then use it actively to seek new learning.

CATEGORIZING STRATEGIES

Among the most helpful aspects of PReP is the obvious notion that students' experiences, individually and collectively, vary from topic to topic. Traditionally, however, strategies do not account for this differentiation in students' prior knowledge, and, too often, activities are used as anticipatory strategies irrespective of students' background. Our thanks, again, to Judy Langer for calling this to our attention. We will, therefore, follow her lead and suggest that of the various strategies we discuss, some will work better than others depending upon the amount of prior experiences you might predict that students will have had with the topic to be assigned. Our simple categorization scheme is based on whether students are likely to know a little, some, or a lot.

■ Anticipation Strategies When Students Know Little

We have included three strategies in this category and all are framed on the assumption that students will have to stretch their awarenesses to find connections with the topic to be studied. Our three strategies are (1) ReQuest, (2) scavenger hunts (of a special kind), and (3) brainstorming.

☐ *ReQuest*

Any discussion of pre-reading strategies would be incomplete without inclusion of Anthony Manzo's ReQuest technique (Manzo, 1969). Like many similar techniques, ReQuest encourages students to base their purpose for reading on anticipatory questions. Of additional importance is the motivation that can emerge from discussion and questioning during the initial stages of a reading assignment. Unlike many strategies, ReQuest has a built-in feedback and modeling feature that gives the reader needed information.

ReQuest is an acronym for reciprocal questioning, and its name comes from the questioning that the students and the teacher engage in together. This strategy involves the following steps.

1. Both teacher and students read the first sentence in the first paragraph of a selection. (With older students, segments longer than one sentence are often appropriate.)
2. The teacher closes the book; the students keep their books open. The students may ask the teacher any question they wish relating to that first sentence. The teacher must answer as accurately and completely as possible. Then, without threat or negativism, the teacher gives feedback to the students on the quality of the types of questions being asked.
3. The students then close their books and the teacher asks any questions that come to mind. These questions purposefully include (a) any that will help the students realize what knowledge they have relative to the topic, and (b) the kinds of questions students might try to ask when their turn comes again.

4. The procedure is continued through a paragraph or two until students can be expected to project answers to the classic purpose question: "What do you think you will find out in the rest of the selection?"

ReQuest has been validated as a strategy that helps students relate prior experiences to new learning with both narrative and expository material. It is best used in small groups to encourage each student's participation, but it can also be effective with large groups when combined with the interaction similar to that included in PReP and other activities we will discuss such as LINK and categorical overview.

With younger students, especially when they are just beginning to engage in this activity, we suggest you follow the steps as we described them. With older students, you may find it more valuable to extend the amount of text that is read between each questioning session. How much text to read at a time depends on its complexity, how much prior experiences with the topic students have had, and their sophistication with questioning techniques. As you can imagine, one sentence often isn't enough to engage all learners in a meaningful question/discussion session.

Your object here is not to evaluate students' comprehension; instead, you are seeking to stimulate critical thinking and reasoning skills by modeling questioning techniques. Recall, though, that this activity is included under the category of "little known information." This is because you direct students to become engaged in the topic and to ask questions that will provide some introductory information about the topic. Too, it will often generate interest and curiosity that might not otherwise emerge.

☐ *Scavenger Hunt*

Like ReQuest, this strategy is best suited for students who have little, if any, background knowledge about a topic you will soon be studying. Teachers and students both have found this strategy to be an enjoyable, motivational activity as well as a way to develop an initial awareness about a new topic. As designed by Cunningham, Crawley, & Lee (1983), this form of scavenger hunt exposes students to vocabulary related to the subject and helps them build appropriate experiences with unfamiliar concepts before the study of the unit begins. Using these guidelines, students then get a head start on the unit.

1. A few days before a new unit begins, announce the unit topic to the class and tell them some of the key vocabulary and

concepts they will encounter. For example, a unit on weather might include terms like Celsius, cirrus clouds, barometer, and so forth.

2. Divide the class into teams and have each team select a captain.
3. Give each team identical lists of terms for the scavenger hunt. Allow the teams a limited number of days to gather all the information they can about each word. Encourage students to produce all kinds of information from varied sources, such as pictures, photographs, written descriptions, tape recordings (if sounds aid in description), and even an object itself.
4. The team captain will divide the terms among team members so each person has certain words on which to concentrate. Team members will be cautioned to keep the information they discover secret from other teams who are searching for the same things.
5. On the designated day, presumably the first day of the new unit, each team shares what they found in their hunting. This allows every class member the opportunity to be exposed to varied informational sources as it is unlikely any two teams will have identical data about the respective words and concepts.
6. The teacher can devise multiple ways to award points and credit for participation or successful completion of assigned hunting tasks.

Our initial reaction to this activity was skepticism until we saw it work. We don't mean to limit its use to situations where prior knowledge is minimal, but we feel it works best in such situations. If students already know a lot about a new topic, a scavenger hunt won't require much scavenging. The real bait in this is the competitive spirit with a twist of novelty and physical activity. The payoff comes in the motivation, which new, unfamiliar topics rarely stimulate in students. Then, too, it may not work with some "high-brows," like eighth graders, so use scavenger hunts with a measure of discretion.

☐ *Brainstorming*
The basic "what-comes-to-your-mind-when-I-say" brainstorming activity is the cornerstone of many anticipation activities. We include brainstorming in its most basic form in the "students know little about the topic" category because more sophisticated versions generally require extensive information and manipulation. As you examine the various strategies for anticipation, notice how often they begin with or center on a brainstorming activity; we refer to PReP, categorical overview, clustering, cubing, and LINK (discussed later in this chapter).

When using brainstorming as an anticipation activity, your object is to access information related to the topic of study. So, if you are to study taxes in third grade, you might begin by asking how much students know about money. Were you to ask them to brainstorm about taxes, you'd not be likely to get much response. Similarly, if you are about to study verbals in English class, low-level associations can be expected irrespective of the frequency with which students use verbals. Our point is that brainstorming should be used to maximize access to students' prior knowledge. The initial cue must be a term related to the new topic of study but also it must be known to the students.

As a final suggestion regarding brainstorming, we want to mention that our greatest successes have come when we asked students to write out on scratch paper their individual responses to brainstorming cues. While oral activities work too, we have found when students generate written responses, it (1) helps students remember their ideas as we write responses on the board, (2) enables us to determine individually what students associate with the cues, and (3) tends to stimulate better discussion because the students think before they react. We allow about a minute or two for students to write down their reactions and then extend the discussion about their responses as long as it is valuable. Of course, a final advantage of brainstorming as a "students-know-little" activity is that you can move from it into PReP or other strategies if you determine they know more than you expected.

■ **Anticipation Strategies When Students Know Some**

When students know more than a little about a topic to be studied, the strategies to initiate discussion can be more sophisticated. Likewise, the discussion itself will be more involved. To facilitate anticipation discussions when students know something about what they will study, we offer three strategies: LINK, cubing, and imaging.

☐ *LINK*
This activity evolved from Langer's PReP and the similarity is apparent. We designed it to help students make a link between existing prior knowledge and information they will be studying. An acronym, LINK represents list, inquire, note, and know, the basic steps and processes involved in this strategy. Here is how the procedure works.

1. On an overhead transparency, expose a key cue word for a brainstorming activity. Be sure it is a word that will trigger

some response among most, if not all, students. Instruct the students to *list* on a piece of paper all associations they have with the cue word. Allow three minutes for their responses.

2. After the time limit, solicit responses from the students and list them on the overhead transparency. (Try to limit the list to one transparency to simplify subsequent parts of the strategy.) We like to obtain only one response per student until every student has had an opportunity to include something on the list. To aid in this, we tend to call on less active participants at the beginning of the listing to increase chances of their involvement. We then allow students to offer a second idea until everyone has a chance, then a third, and so forth. Our object is to maximize participation.

3. When the transparency is filled or students' ideas depleted, encourage students to *inquire* about the items on the list. They may ask for clarification or elaboration; they may ask for examples or definitions. During this questioning period, students ask students about the items they included. The teacher's role is largely passive and neutral; if students ask direct questions of the teacher, a direct response is appropriate. Remember, though, that the purpose here is to have students share and elaborate their understandings. The students have compiled the list they are viewing on the transparency; let them discover their errors and difficulties. The inquiry time is often exciting and fraught with controversy, but it also brings to the surface prior awarenesses that students may have forgotten.

4. Once the inquiring is done and all questions have been considered, turn off the overhead projector. Instruct students to turn their paper over and to write down everything that comes to mind in response to the exact same cue as used before. This time, however, limit their brainstorming to one minute. Have them *note* all that they *know* about the word based on prior experience and the class discussion.

It is our experience that LINK engages students in shared anticipation and association largely due to the inquiry phase of the strategy. We have also found that sophistication in both quantity and quality of responses during the second brainstorming is significantly greater in a shorter timespan. We marvel at students' awareness of their burgeoning knowledge and their motivation to study more carefully when the assignment is given. Students find that as a result of using LINK, they know some basic information about the term or topic because they have established a *link* to their prior knowledge.

☐ *Cubing*

We have found that most anticipation activities are enhanced when they begin with a writing component, and we found this strategy among others proposed for writing by Cowan & Cowan (1980). There are two advantages offered by writing: (1) writing allows time for reflection and a chance to gather one's thoughts about a topic and, (2) writing offers a record of ideas so that during discussions, students can refer to their written version of brainstorming.

Cubing is most effective in those situations where you suspect your students have some prior knowledge of the topic at hand. Cubing employs a cube, as you might have guessed—a cube of foam rubber 6 to 8 inches on a side although a cubical box of almost any size will do. Cover the cube with paper or contact paper that you can write on. On each side of the cube is written a direction to stimulate students to write briefly on certain aspects of the topic. According to Cowan & Cowan (1980), the six directions on the cube are:

Describe it: Look at the subject closely (perhaps with your mind) and describe what you see. Colors, shapes, sizes, and so forth.

Compare it: What is it similar to? What is it different from?

Associate it: What does it make you think of? What comes into your mind? It can be similar things or different things, places, people. Just let your mind go and see what associations you have for this subject.

Analyze it: Tell how it is made. (You don't have to know; make it up.)

Apply it: Tell what you can do with it. How can it be used?

Argue for or against it: Go ahead and take a stand. Use any kind of reasons you want—logical, silly, or anywhere in between.

If the topic is whales, students could, for example, be directed to the side of the cube that says, "Describe it." Students would then be allowed a set amount of time (usually 2 to 4 minutes) to write all they can describing whales, making rough notes of associations and not worrying about complete sentences, spelling, or other mechanics. Another turn of the cube would ask students to "Compare it," and students could compare whales to other animals they know. When using cubing, you can use all six sides of the cube at one time, or you may choose to limit the writing to two or three sides only.

Following the writing period, ask students to share their responses to each direction on the cube. This sharing is vital because students with limited background will learn from those with a richer base of information on the topic. We have also found that teachers should write along with their students during each of the writing times. Then, during the sharing times, teachers should join in with their responses. As a footnote, though, we prefer to add our "two cents" at the end of the sharing session or occasionally at the beginning to get the ball rolling. Of course, our participation is intended as sharing, and not meant to be overbearing. It is important that the teacher model an interest in writing, sharing, and learning by participating alongside his or her students. It enhances the teacher-student relationship as well as the discussion.

Cubing works well with a variety of subjects. Not only can students be asked to write about topics of information, they can also "cube" on people from history or characters in stories and novels. If cubing on Henry VIII, for example, the directions on the cube would be modified appropriately. "Describe it" could become "Describe him" and "Analyze it" would be changed to "Analyze his character."

Students have shown enthusiasm in cubing activities we have directed. The cube itself is often novel enough to generate interest the first few trials. A clever teacher can find countless ways to adapt the basic format. We like cubing because it encourages students to call forth their prior experiences and fosters creative imaginings. It also gives students practice with various types of writing, something many students need desperately. As an extension of cubing, you might consider alternative labels for the various sides of the cube such as argument, persuasion, factual description, analytical reasoning, comparison, contrast, point of view, and logical deductions. For teachers who work with less sophisticated students, the following labels for cube sides might be appealing:

1. Tell how big it is
2. Tell what colors it is
3. Tell what it can do
4. Tell what's good or bad about it
5. Tell where it comes from and where you can find it
6. Tell what it's like
7. Tell where it's kept
8. Tell what it's made of
9. Tell what we'd do without one
10. Tell why it's important

As a final thought about cubing, remember that the important feature is the discussion. Making associations between new learning and prior experiences is only the beginning; students' awareness of essential concepts and their links to one another comes through the sharing of perspectives. Make it fun; make it crazy. Engage kids in the freshness of exciting interchange.

☐ *Imaging*

Do you remember the Shadow? Big John and Sparkey? Fibber McGee and Molly? All those old radio shows that sparked our imagination also allowed us to practice the valuable skill of creating a picture in our head, or imaging. In this age of television, children have been deprived of opportunities to create their own images and have come to rely on media for visualizations. However, children can still learn to image and visualize. In fact, because Gambrell (1982) has found that imaging helps students access prior knowledge, we recommend it as an anticipation activity.

Imaging is another strategy that can be used when students have some prior knowledge of a topic. It is especially valuable when you are seeking to establish a certain mood or a particular context for a topic, primarily because it is a "right-brain" activity that tends to foster sensations rather than logical responses.

Imaging is similar to guided fantasies. The teacher acts as the guide and verbally leads students to create a series of mental images. It is important to use your voice effectively if imaging is to be successful. Talk slowly and in quiet, low, restful tones so that the verbal directions do not interfere with the creation of mental scenes. Remember that talking slowly and soothingly encourages students to relax, whereas talking quickly and loudly creates an intense mood and response. Some teachers choose to lower the lights and provide appropriate background music for an imaging activity. Such aids may be helpful on certain occasions, but are certainly not necessary. And slumber is not what we are seeking to induce!

Guided imaging activities should begin with the direction that students close their eyes and concentrate on a key cue word, for example, "a car's engine" or "a small town in America at the end of the Revolutionary War" or "a dingy, cramped cell in the center of a Polish ghetto." Direct students to help them get a general sense of where they are, to notice who else is there, what it smells like, what is happening, and then *give them plenty of time to follow the lead*. Do not rush them! Add various senses as you go so that eventually all five senses are included. The more senses involved, the more effective and impressionable the activity will be for students.

Allow plenty of time for visualizations. To serve as a check on yourself, do the activity along with the students. You are trying to help learners access experiences that will facilitate understanding and recall. Let their images rise to consciousness. Keep the class quiet.

After a reasonable time, softly announce that they are to begin to return their attention to the classroom. Warn them the activity is coming to an end and to capture a lasting picture of what they have seen, felt, heard, tasted, and touched as they depart their experience. Caution students to open their eyes slowly and not talk for you don't want them to distort or forget their images and sensations. Keep the classroom quiet, even as students start to look around and exchange knowing looks. Then, ask students to write down images and sensations that came to them during the activity.

After allowing a short period for writing, which provides a record as well as allows a more complete re-focus of attention, time should be allowed for oral discussion. Students may profit best from sharing and discussing their images with each other in small groups although large group discussions can also be provocative. As with all anticipation activities, the intent is to allow students the chance to gather their thoughts and senses about a topic and to share what emerges. The sharing allows increased awareness for everyone and establishes a base from which predictions can be made about the topic to be studied.

It may seem that imaging is best for fiction; we disagree. It does work for stories, even poetry, but we have become excited by the heightened awareness when imaging is used prior to reading expository text. For those of you who remain skeptical, Gene Cramer (1982) has empirically validated imaging with expository texts, but the most appropriate validation would be for you to use it yourself. Try it before you read the next section of this text. Close your eyes. Get comfortable. Think about students who know a lot about what they will study. Imagine who they are. What do they look like? What do they act like? What kinds of things do they say during a discussion? Drift off to your own mental images of kids who know a lot about a topic. What are they like?

Come back to the page slowly. Record your thoughts, images, sensations. Share them with others when you can.

With the proper cues as a basis for imaging, this activity can also work in situations where students know just enough to get them started. As a prelude to the study of slavery, for example, an imaging exercise about being a slave in chains on a slave ship or being separated from loved ones can trigger a lively discussion about slavery.

Imaging stimulates the affect and the volition as well as cognition, so give it due consideration.

■ **Anticipation Activities When Students Know a Lot**

As we have emphasized, the role of prior knowledge and previous experiences is without question among the most significant contributors to new learning. Unfortunately for many students in school, they know little or, at best, only some about the topics they are studying in school. Of course, school is designed that way, for it goes without saying that students are in school to learn new things, not "old" things. With careful planning and a sense of students' awarenesses, however, anticipation activities can maximize the old while highlighting the new. With that perspective in mind, then, let's consider two strategies that work particularly well when we can tap into a virtual wealth of students' knowledge.

☐ *Categorical Overview*
More a process than a strategy that we can actually specify, the categorical overview involves students in the construction of a framework for understanding what they read. This framework is constructed of students' prior ideas about what they are going to learn from a particular reading. Keep in mind as we discuss the strategy that it is the process, not the product, that makes this strategy most valuable.

A categorical overview is a four-step process—brainstorming, categorization, reading, and revision. Initiating the categorical overview by a brainstorming exercise, the teacher either tells the students the topic to be studied or, if the text lends itself to this, lets them read just far enough to get the gist of the selection. Then the teacher encourages students to share whatever bits of information, feelings, or inclinations they may have about the topic. Here the whole class can participate at once, groups of two or three students can brainstorm together and then share with the rest of the class, or individuals can free-write or cluster the topic of the reading selection (clustering will be discussed in the next section of this chapter). To show you what we mean, we'd like you now to initiate a categorical overview for yourself. Get a blank sheet of paper and make as many notes and associations as you can for the topic "crocodiles." Later we will have you read a newspaper article on crocodiles, so this exercise will serve the dual purpose of enhancing your anticipation while giving you a feel for the technique we call categorical overview.

If you were in a class we would now ask you and the others to tell us what came to mind. The written record would serve as a reminder for you but the discussion would focus on oral responses. As ideas, concepts, and facts were suggested about crocodiles, we would write them on the chalkboard, ignoring for the moment whether all the information was strictly accurate. The possibility of making a written record of inaccurate information will disturb some people, we know. But the reading will make all the necessary corrections, or at the very least leave questions to be answered by other reading. After the reading, the last step will be to look again at the categorical overview to see what possible additions, deletions, or corrections the text has suggested to the readers. If questions remain in anyone's mind, they can be so indicated with a "?" next to each problematic idea.

We're getting ahead of ourselves, though. Before the reading the board might look like Figure 5.2:

FIGURE 5.2 Responses to "Crocodile" Cue

alligators	swamp	live long time
fish-eating	see in zoo	bogs
vicious	Florida	lizards
sharp teeth	marshlands	lay eggs
long mouth	Louisiana	smiles
green	hinged jaw	man-eating
reptile	water	crocodile tears
long tail	Africa	Captain Cook
gator traps	belts	shoes
tail dangerous	handbags	stay in water
rough skin	big eyes	a long time
slimy	amphibians	4 legs

Notice that what we have on the board is lots of information, randomly presented and recorded. Our next step would be to lead you to categorize all this information, asking you to "tell us how all this information is related; do some of these ideas seem to go together or relate to a more general idea?" Look now at the ideas you had about crocodiles. Does it seem to you that there are categories for the information you wrote down?

This categorization step is vital to the process of a categorical overview since it is at this step that the framework for understanding emerges. The key to the categorical overview is this: The organization of prior understanding provides a framework for new understandings. And just as the information to compose the categorical overview has to come from the students rather than from the teacher, so the categories for that information must come from them also. This will help insure that all the learners have a vested interest in the learning.

Look again at the items included in Figure 5.2 that we recently collected during an in-service workshop. How would you categorize this information?

Five categories emerged for the workshop participants. They were (1) geography (where to find crocodiles) (2) physical appearance (3) behaviors (4) uses and (5) miscellaneous (only because no agreement could be reached about where to categorize "Captain Hook"). As the categories were identified, each idea was linked with its appropriate category.

Think of this process in the following way, and you will see more clearly what we are getting at: *The categories that emerge for a categorical overview are concepts; ideas and information for the category are features of their associated concept.*

The linking of categories with features is the most important step in the process of constructing a categorical overview. We have found two effective ways to do the linking with students. One way is to place the labels across the top of the chalkboard or an overhead transparency. Write the features under each label as they fit, but let the students make the decisions about matching feature to category label. Sometimes the group will discover they have to alter their categories as the activity proceeds. Discussion and debate ensues that fosters understanding and awareness on which to build new understandings. Were we to have completed the categorization and listing activity in this manner, using the ideas in Figure 5.2, it would have looked like Figure 5.3.

A second approach to the linking of categories and information is to list and number the categories on the chalkboard. Then place the number for each category beside any appropriate feature in the list. The disadvantage to this second alternative is that students do not see the category and its features in a neatly constructed package.

We have one final comment about the categorical overview. What we have described is the way we have seen it work in many classrooms. The emphasis is on student involvement that emerges from teacher guidance. The intent is to create an overview in which students can see a framework of prior knowledge upon which to build new learning. For you to become comfortable with this activity, practice and experience will be required. We suggest that you develop, and implement if possible, several lesson activities to incorporate the categorical overview using your own materials. Remember, you are trying to build a bridge between what the students know and what the text says.

FIGURE 5.3   Categorical Overview to "Crocodile" Cue

Geography

Florida

Africa

Louisiana

zoos

swamp

bog

marshland

water

Behavior

lays eggs

reptilian

smiles

amphibian

hinged jaw

fish-eating

man-eating

stays in water
   a long time

lives a long time

Physical Appearance

vicious

sharp teeth

long tail

tail dangerous

slimy

crocodile tears

big eyes

alligators

long mouths

4 legs

rough skin

green

lizards

Uses

belts

handbags

shoes

gator traps

Miscellaneous

Captain Hook

☐ *Clustering*
We have often suggested that writing is an important element in the learning process. We discovered clustering as a writing exercise described by Gabriele Rico (1983). She explains clustering as "a nonlinear brainstorming process akin to free association." (p. 28) While clustering was designed as a writing activity, it also offers a way to evoke a global perspective on a topic in a manner akin to the categorical

overview. By way of introduction, let's ask you to participate in a clustering exercise.

On a sheet of paper about a third of the way down, write the word PEACE. Now circle the word.

Now, free-associate with the word PEACE. As a word comes to mind, write it near the nucleus word. Circle it and draw a line to the nucleus word to indicate the association. Do you now think of associations with the second word you have circled? For example, we first associated "brotherhood" with PEACE. With brotherhood uppermost in our minds, we thought of races, caring, sharing, breaking down barriers. Our "cluster" then looked like Figure 5.4:

FIGURE 5.4 Cluster for "Peace"

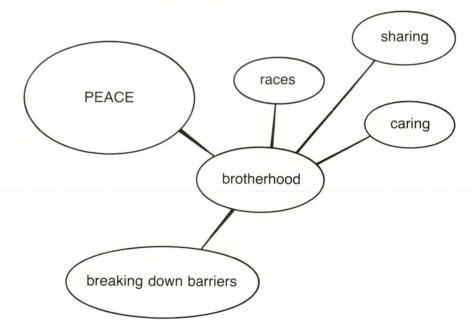

Get the drift? What did you think of? Add it to ours and keep going. When you are finished, discuss with others what you included and why. For now, just finish the cluster.

Want to try another one? This time center the word ANTICI-PATION about a third of the way down a blank sheet of paper. Build your cluster as far as you can. (See Figure 5.5.)

Share your cluster with others. Compare it to the one we have done.

FIGURE 5.5 Cluster for "Anticipation"

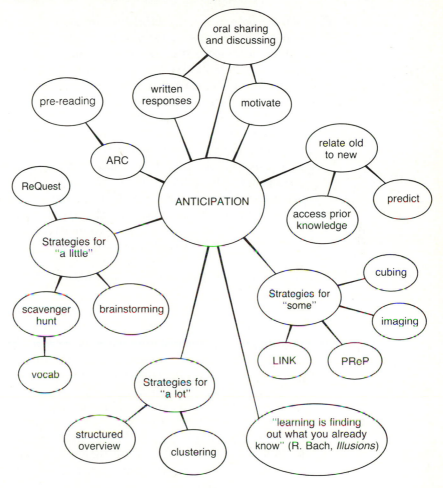

The steps we suggest for clustering are (1) identifying a key nucleus word, (2) allowing time for brainstorming and clustering of ideas on paper, (3) sharing and discussing among students, perhaps even in small groups or pairs, and (4) constructing a group cluster on the board if it seems appropriate. Follow your own best instincts with clustering, but remember there is no correct way to create any cluster. Each one will be unique to its creator. The purpose is to allow students to structure a lot of information so they can use it as a foundation for new learning.

REDUCTION OF FRUSTRATION POTENTIAL

■ ■ Among potential frustrations for readers is the lack of essential prior experiences necessary for new learning. In the words of Richard Bach (1977), "learning is finding out what you already know." (p. 46) Learning can *only* occur in the context of what you already know; hence, anticipation is the cornerstone of new learning.

During any anticipation activity students seek to determine what it is they already know that is related to the topic under scrutiny. An awareness of related knowledge, feelings, and inclinations serves as a hierarchical foundation and scaffolding for new learning as well as a sense of security that what is to be learned is not altogether unfamiliar. The student who is aware of the value of anticipation activities and who can activate anticipations and predictions is well on his or her way to mastering the art of study.

The teacher's role in anticipation activities is to assist the student in activating prior experiences and using the prior associations to lay the foundation for new learning. This is simplified by various strategies such as PReP, ReQuest, LINK, cubing, clustering, and categorical overview, each of which seems to work best when chosen with regard to students' familiarity with the topic to be studied. The student's role is to evoke all relevant subsuming information and associations and then to predict new learning based on existing awareness. We believe many students engage in anticipation activities on their own, especially since we maintain anticipation is an essential feature of the reading cycle. The degree to which students become masters of study may depend on how cognizant they are of ways to anticipate consciously. In sum, the object of anticipatory activities prior to reading is to access relevant information, to discuss it with others, to predict what will be learned, and to motivate an interest in the topic.

Before you proceed to our next topic, the R in ARC—realization of meaning—you may wish to peruse the various student-oriented anticipation strategies we have included in our final chapter, "The Art of Study." If that is your preference, first stop and think about what you might include in a list of things you might do to anticipate before you read. Write out your list on a piece of paper, discuss it with others, and then compare your list with the one we include in chapter 11.

6

Realization of Meaning

SETTING THE STAGE

As Alvin Toffler (1980) and Marilyn Ferguson (1980) describe their vision of a new age into which we seem to be rapidly moving, they forewarn of the growing need for people to learn how to manipulate information. This is not to suggest that information per se will be less important in the future, but rather there will be a greater need to handle vast amounts of information literally at our fingertips, through computers. Edward de Bono (1983) notes that "information is no substitute for thinking, and thinking is no substitute for information. The dilemma is that there is never enough time to teach all the information that could usefully be taught. We may have to reduce the time we spend teaching information in order to focus instead on the direct teaching of thinking skills." (p. 704) It is this preparation of students for the twenty-first century that we have in mind as we describe various strategies that tend to develop independent learners.

READING AS MAKING CONNECTIONS

■ ■ Understanding and remembering are not identical, but they do bear an interesting relationship to one another—they both depend on connections between what is being understood or remembered and something else the learner already knows. Mnemonic devices work because they help learners associate new information with something easier to remember—Roy G. Biv is no one's name, but remembering it does make remembering the colors of the rainbow easier: red, orange, yellow, green, blue, indigo, and violet. But mnemonics (literally, devices to aid the memory, so named after the Greek goddess of memory, Mnemosyne) are themselves meaningless and thus can be cumbersome. The alternative and preferable aid to memory is understanding. It is within the nature of understanding to aid memory; to understand is to connect what is being understood to some previous understanding, as when a child who can count four pennies realizes that 2 + 2 is like counting two pennies and then counting two more. Later, this same sort of understanding helps the child understand (and remember) that 20 + 20 = 40. Nothing, from simple addition to complex calculus, is remembered so well as when it is understood.

Now we ask, what is understanding? How does comprehension happen? What is meaning? These are not imponderables. We find it helpful to start with meaning and define it as the connection readers make between what they already know and what they are trying to comprehend. When comprehension happens, when understanding is achieved, the reader will say or think, "Oh, I see!" See what? How things go together. Or often the reader will say, "I get it!" Get what? The *meaning* as a *connection* or fit between what he or she knows and the information in the text. Understanding what you read means taking possession of ideas, making them your own *uniquely* by connecting new to known ideas. Readers need to know that they themselves are crucial to the process of comprehension. As we have already discussed in chapters 4 and 5, an understanding of text depends on what readers bring to their reading in the form of prior understandings and anticipations. Accomplished readers know this; others must be informed. Likewise, what readers do during and after reading to control their understanding and remembering is as important to comprehension as is their prior understandings.

A crucial and fundamental idea about reading that we'd like all readers to know is this: If you read to understand, you probably will remember; if you read to remember, you probably will forget. Understanding leads to remembering. Meaningful connections make memory possible. With these ideas in mind we offer a variety of teaching techniques and learning strategies to help students understand in ways that make them remember.

■ An Interactive Notation System for Effective Reading and Thinking (INSERT)

Accomplished readers react to ideas that occur to them as they encounter cues in text. INSERT is a formalized activity often used unconsciously by accomplished readers to clarify their thinking as they read. Its success lies in getting readers involved in making decisions as they read, asking them to consider text in terms like these: text confirms their beliefs, text contradicts, text raises questions, and so on. But this is easier to show than to tell. We want you to read a passage and in the process to experience the decision making we have included in INSERT. The idea is that you will "insert" your ideas and decisions into those proposed by the text.

The essay we want you to read begins: "This is a story about power, sex, predation, and violence in Africa. It's about crocodiles."

STOP right there! You'll recall our earlier discussion of crocodiles in chapter 5 when we used this topic for our example of a categorical overview. If you have not participated in that activity recently, we want you now to consider carefully and deliberately everything you know about crocodiles. On a sheet of paper, list what you know about the characteristics of crocodiles, about their habits and habitat, anything you can recall or think or feel about these fearsome reptiles.

Having given some thought to your present understandings, either now or during your recent reading of chapter 5, your anticipation is raised and you should now be ready to read. As you read, we want you to make some decisions about the ideas expressed in the text. The kinds of decisions we want you to make include "I knew that," "I disagree," "That's new to me," "I wonder about that," and "I don't understand." Use the following notations to indicate your responses and place the notations in the margin of the selection as you read.

If an idea:	*Put this notation in the margin:*
1. confirms what you thought (makes you say "I knew that")	√
2. contradicts what you thought (makes you say "I disagree" or "I thought differently")	×
3. is new to you and is interesting (makes you say, "Hey, I didn't know that")	+
4. intrigues you (makes you say, "WOW! that's really neat!")	!
5. puzzles you (makes you say, "I wonder about that")	?
6. confuses you or leaves something unclear (makes you say, "I just don't understand")	??
7. strikes you as very important (makes you say, "That's really worth remembering")	*

We're asking you to do consciously what you might normally do without making marks in the margin or without really giving it much thought. We've reproduced the notation system here at the beginning of the selection and again at the end so you won't have to memorize the code or be flipping back and forth. Oh yes, you might want to use more than one notation for the same idea, like "+!*" to mark an idea you find new, intriguing, and important. Go ahead now and read the essay (Kronholz, 1980, p. 1) before we say more.

NOTATION REMINDER	
I agree = √	WOW = !
I disagree = X	I wonder = ?
That's new = +	I don't under-stand = ??
That's important = *	

SHED NO MORE TEARS OVER THE CROCODILE: IT HAS SNAPPED BACK

Zambezi River, Zimbabwe — This is a story about power, sex, predation, and violence in Africa.

It's about crocodiles.

Under cover of Zimbabwe's seven-year guerrilla war, armed poachers did a land-office business in crocodile skins here. With the poachers slaughtering the adults and with natural predators of the unarmed variety making off with the young, the Zambezi River was being drained of its crocodiles.

Crocodylus niloticus had become an endangered species.

But with peace restored to Zimbabwe, game wardens can safely begin their poacher patrols again, and Zimbabwe is enjoying something of a crocodile comeback. In light of that news, here are some observations about crocodiles.

First, the power. A crocodile can grow to a length of 20 feet, weigh half a ton and tackle a 900-pound buffalo that wanders past at lunchtime. A crocodile can stay under water for 2 1/2 hours without a breath of air by slowing his heartbeat and going into semihibernation. He can outrun a man in a 100-yard dash, although there is no record here of any such footrace.

A crocodile has 66 teeth that he tends to lose like mittens in the hurly-burly of hunt, so he grows up to 45 sets in a lifetime. For all those teeth, a crocodile can't chew. When a 900-pound buffalo strolls too near the river bank, a crocodile snaps onto its leg and drags the buffalo under water, holding it there until it joins the choir invisible. Then the crocodile wedges the buffalo between some underwater roots and rips into its hide, swallowing whole a chop here, a rib roast there.

A 364-Day Cycle

A crocodile usually needs two or three good feeds like this a month, although one crocodile under study by a Victoria Falls naturalist went for a year without eating. That crocodile then starved to death, however, so it would appear a crocodile needs to feed at least once every 364 days.

Now for the sex. A crocodile reaches maturity when he is 2 1/2 feet long, which can take anywhere from 10 to 20 years, depending on how well he has been eating. When a male crocodile is at last mature, he claims a territory—the size depends on how well stocked it is with food—and also claims all the females in it. A mature female who doesn't like the housekeeping arrangements can move on.

Crocodiles mate in the water, where the buoyancy is all that keeps them from crushing each other to death. They are sweetly gentle in the passion. Two months after the assignation, the female lays 50 leathery white eggs in a hole on land, while a dozen or so crocodiles from the neighborhood gather round. Perhaps they are there to protect the mother; then again, perhaps they're just curious. At any rate, the mothering female fills in the hole and pats down the soil, and everyone slinks off for a swim.

Ninety-six days later, when the embryos can tell from the trembling of the earth that mother is overhead, one begins to squeak. The others take up the cry—which is as close to crocodile tears as they ever come—and the female rushes to dig out the hole. As the baby crocodiles chew through their eggshells with their egg teeth (set No. 1), the female pops them into a satchel in her mouth and totes them down to the river. They quickly get down to the vital business of snapping for bugs.

The Predation Angle

Here's where the predation comes in. An adult crocodile has only one predator: A man with a rifle (a Soviet-designed AK-47 is preferred in these parts). But all the world seems to be after the little crocodile: bigger crocodiles, mongooses, snakes, jungle cats, big birds and the elements themselves. Most of the crocodile nests along the Zambezi are destroyed by predators or floods, and only 2 percent of the crocodiles that hatch ever rumble into adulthood. For those that make it, however, there are many rewards, including a 100-year life span and sexual potency right up to the end.

Now, finally, the violence. Given a choice between a man and a buffalo, a crocodile almost always will opt for a fish. But occasionally a man will happen along the river bank and look for all the world like groceries on the shelf. Zimbabwe game wardens estimate that along the Zambezi, 40 or 50 people are demoted to dinner in this way every year.

But Zimbabwe doesn't know how many people it has, so it's hard to believe it knows how many are missing. For that matter, it doesn't know how many crocodiles it has either, so there isn't any way to figure how many are missing because of poachers.

There are two differences between a crocodile and an alligator, aside from the fact that crocodiles live in Africa and alligators live in the U.S. and China. The first difference is temperament: There are Everglades Indians who make a living wrestling alligators, but no one wrestles a crocodile. The second difference is the jaw: An alligator's teeth don't show when its mouth is closed; a crocodile's do. That gives the crocodile an unctuous, toothy simper that Alice in Wonderland found herself commenting upon:

> How cheerful he seems to grin,
> How neatly spreads his claws.
> And welcomes little fishes in
> With gently smiling jaws.

NOTATION REMINDER

I agree = √	WOW = !
I disagree = X	I wonder = ?
That's new = +	I don't under-stand = ??
That's important = *	

Well, what do you think? Did you find yourself more active than you might have been without the notations? Were you more critical as a reader? We suspect you were, and that is what we are seeking to encourage in your students. The seven specific decisions we have included in INSERT represent a variety of ways a text can be understood; because the decisions are overt and conscious, they are open to discussion, examination, justification, and modification. Such decision making forms the basis for critical reasoning by clarifying what one thinks of the ideas encountered during reading.

You might be thinking that the notation system represents what most people do when they underline, so let's consider underlining for a moment. Many students in public schools don't underline in their books because they can't—they aren't allowed to. Worse still, when people do underline in books, especially when they are studying in an academic course, the nature of the underlining is often less than helpful. Often underlining is too indiscriminate to be of much use. Why do people underline? The reasons given are that something strikes them as important or familiar or curious (you know, like INSERT), but when they look back over their own underlining, they can't tell at a glance *why* something is underlined. The problem, then, is that it is not the underlining but the reason for it that is important. Thus, research on underlining as a study skill suggests that when it works it does so "because of the amount of processing required to make the decision about what to underline" (Anderson, Armbruster, & Kantor, 1980). Unfortunately, too many developing reader/learners are not very clear about what and why to underline, and they make decisions with little conscious judgment. INSERT forces students to make conscious decisions because until a decision is made about any given idea, the student is uncertain about what notation to make. It is for this reason that we have found INSERT to be more valuable than underlining as a study strategy. Further, students in public schools can use INSERT by placing a strip of paper along the margin of the text to avoid breaking the rule against writing in books.

We do not suggest you introduce this notation system to students all at once. As you were reading about crocodiles, we asked you to use any or all of the codes because we are reasonably certain they represent responses you have made to ideas over years of practice. We're not willing to make such assumptions about your students' experiences. We propose INSERT as a strategy that can help students become critical reasoners and recommend that you introduce the strategy to your students *gradually,* perhaps in the context of content reading lessons or ARC guides. For very young or immature readers, the "√" and "X" may be quite enough to use for a while. When they become comfortable with these ideas, introduce them to "*." Explain what they are to do; they must understand why and when to use any notation. The object is not to have them place markers in the margin of a text; the object is to get students to consider critically ideas they find in texts.

DECISIONS VARIOUS READERS CAN MAKE

■ ■ We've been doing some research over the last few years to determine what it is that readers at various levels of accomplishment do or don't do when they read. One interesting finding is that accomplished readers, those in control of the activity of reading, have little difficulty spotting important ideas as they read; furthermore, they tend to recall those ideas they consider important. What they generally real-ize (make real) about text is what you, or we, or the author might expect.

In the case of tenth graders the story is different. While tenth graders, on the average, do agree fairly well with more mature readers in terms of what is important in a reading selection, they tend to recall what they find to be familiar in the text. Thus, their recall centers far more on what they find familiar than what they consider important. Perhaps they do this because familiar information in a text reinforces their understandings and, more importantly, the connections that make memory possible are already established. Unfortunately, what tenth graders find to be familiar are often not the central ideas. The central ideas are usually the new information, and the familiar ideas are often the scaffolding from which the author builds. So when tenth graders recall the familiar background information from their reading, they miss the importance of the new, central ideas.

For seventh graders, the picture is worse still. They seem to think that what is familiar in text is what is important. Seventh graders tend to "recall" information they already knew before they read. In part, this may be saying something about what it means to be twelve or thirteen years of age. It may also suggest something about how students are taught to read texts up to that age. Many accomplished readers seem to develop their abilities for themselves, out of their own experiences. It is hard to imagine that less experienced, less motivated students in lower grades could, on their own, develop abilities required for understanding and remembering.

Before moving on, let's re-examine an issue raised in chapter 2. Part of the problem that readers face when dealing with texts in a critical and thoughtful manner is that textbooks don't always lend themselves well to the realization of their meanings. That is, the cues in many textbooks tend to obscure rather than promote the realization of meaning. Here's a selection of text we've used in our research to determine what readers do and don't do when they read.

> The iron horse now came puffing and snorting onto the scene. Both English and American inventors had developed workable locomotives by 1825. In the United States the first railroad promoters were the businessmen of the growing cities. They wanted a transportation system that would bring farm produce from the nearby countryside to their warehouses, and then carry the manufactured goods they sold back to the farmers. Between 1828 and 1835 the merchants of Baltimore, Boston, Charleston, New York, and Philadelphia had sponsored short rail lines.
>
> Between 1830 and 1850 the railroad-building boom overtook the canal boom. In 1830 there were 1,277 miles of canals and only 73 miles of railroad tracks. By 1850 there were 3,698 miles of canals and 8,879 miles of rails. The next 10 years saw a huge growth of railroads marking the end of the canal-building boom.
>
> Early locomotives were clumsy-looking things. But *Tom Thumb*, built in 1830 for the Baltimore and Ohio, excited the top-hatted gentlemen who were taken on a trial run. When *Tom Thumb* was tearing along at better than ten miles an hour, some of them took out pens and

notebooks and wrote their names just to prove that "even at that great velocity (speed) it was possible to do so."

What would you pick out to underline as the central idea of this excerpt? Most teachers, when asked this question, agree that the central idea is "They wanted a transportation system that would bring farm produce from the nearby countryside to their warehouses, and then carry the manufactured goods they sold back to the farmers." What, though, does the text emphasize? Numbers! The miles of track and canals and the dates clearly dominate this passage. Note, too, the specificity of the numbers: 1,277 and 3,698 miles of canals as compared to 73 and 8,879 miles of rails. Of course, no section about the early days of railroads is complete without students' learning about "Tom Thumb." It is little wonder students tend to memorize details and definitions rather than trying to reason their way to an understanding of the ideas they find in texts.

We are not saying that texts like these are impossible to understand. On the contrary, we believe efficient learning from these texts requires readers to make some sophisticated decisions about the ideas they encounter. We also believe students need considerable help in developing strategies that will aid them in making sophisticated decisions. If students can shift their focus of attention as reader/learners away from memorization to understanding, they will learn considerably more than they do now. It is for this reason that we emphasize the notion of a learning strategies curriculum, one in which students develop a sophisticated sense of how to learn. Toward this end, let's consider several other effective learning strategies that facilitate readers' realizations.

■ A Self-Monitoring Approach to Reading and Thinking (SMART)

Confucius is reputed to have said, "It is a wise man who knows what he knows and knows what he doesn't know." SMART is built on the premise that learning begins with an identification of what one understands and what one does not understand from reading. It has several simple steps and one condition for its use. We'll deal first with the steps.

1. While you read, do these two things:
    a. Place a "√" in the margin if you understand what you are reading, and
    b. Place a "?" in the margin if you *don't* understand what you are reading.

2. After each section of the assignment explain to yourself *in your own words* what you *do* understand. (Yes, you can look back at the text while you do this.)

3. Next, after each section, examine those ideas that you did *not* understand and do these things:

   a. Read again the parts that you did not understand. (Does the extra reading help? If you now understand something that was previously unclear, change your "?" to a "√.")

   b. If the idea remains unclear, try to specify what is causing the problem. Is it a word? A phrase? A relationship?

   c. Try to think of something you might do to help yourself understand, and if you can think of something (like, use the glossary, examine pictures or diagrams in the text, review another part of the text), try it out. (Again, if your strategy works, change your "?" to a "√.")

   d. Finally, try to explain to yourself those ideas that you still do not understand (for example, "I still don't understand how seeds grow into plants" or "I don't see how heat causes water to boil").

4. Study the entire assignment using these three steps. (You might find it helpful to divide your study into sections of the assignment, but that is up to you.) After you have finished studying each section or the entire assignment, you should do the following things:

   a. Close the book and explain to yourself what you do understand. (Some people like to do this by talking aloud to themselves.)

   b. Look back at the book and refresh your memory for anything you left out. (Don't worry about what you didn't remember; you'll remember it later.)

   c. Now, re-examine those ideas you still do *not* understand. Think about those ideas. What could they possibly mean? Is there anything else you could do to help you understand (except ask someone else)? Don't worry about what you don't understand. You can ask someone later. Just be sure that before you ask someone else (1) you have done your very best to figure it out for yourself, and (2) you can tell someone else exactly what you don't understand. (Most people are willing to help you if you have tried your best and if they know exactly what you don't understand.)

   d. Close the book one last time and explain to yourself again what you *do* understand.

These, then, are the steps one uses with SMART. Its effectiveness requires a willingness to forego any effort to memorize. The condition for its use that we mentioned earlier is that as you introduce SMART to your students, tell them they must *think* rather than try to memorize what they read. We find students to be very receptive to SMART, and after only a couple of trials most realize that their understanding and remembering increase substantially. Soon students accept the idea that rote memorization is not as efficient as understanding, which leads to remembering. The details and definitions students have been trying to memorize even begin to make sense. Of course, review and reinforcement are sometimes helpful, but students learn that after new learning makes sense, the "re" in review takes on new meaning too.

Teachers, too, are quick to respond favorably to SMART. In addition to the heightened awareness expressed by students who use this strategy, teachers discover that students become more adept at asking questions about what they do not understand. This enables teachers to establish a student-centered framework for discussion in that ideas requiring clarification and elaboration are noted by students.

We offer one note of caution. Some students tend to ask for help a bit too quickly, without seeking a solution for themselves even though we emphasize it in the description of SMART. At the same time, we have sometimes found it difficult to distinguish between the student who is hasty or even a bit lazy, and one who has made an effort but has difficulty explaining the effort. (Have we not all encountered at some point the feeling of not understanding enough to ask a question?) Therefore, we suggest you require two things of students as they ask for help after using SMART. First, students should be able to specify the source of the difficulty (for example, a word, phrase, clause, or a relationship). Second, they should be able to explain what they have done to try to unravel the puzzle. Ideally, of course, we would like students to explain *why* they don't understand (for example, the text doesn't elaborate on this, the text doesn't explain what the main idea is, the author assumes I know these words but I don't), but the answer to why they don't understand may only become clear to them *after* they realize the solution to their problem.

■ Look-backs and Talk Alouds

Imbedded into SMART are two commonsensical strategies used by accomplished readers everywhere. The first of these is look-backs, an activity validated as a valuable study aid (Garner, 1982). We encourage readers to focus their attention during reading on understanding, rather than remembering, and if it is helpful or necessary to re-examine text several times to clarify understandings, so be it. Accomplished readers do! The irony of look-backs is that it is such a commonsensical thing rarely does anyone think to tell students to do it. Some students may discover it on their own but too many seem to believe it is cheating to look back. (Can we imagine where they got that idea?) To look back is often to make connections among several new ideas.

We want also to mention "talk alouds" as an activity for students when reviewing what they did or did not understand during SMART. Talk alouds reinforce understanding and aid recall by allowing the learner to apply new learning as he or she rehearses a retelling to another student. The act of talking aloud clarifies for the student what has been understood and what remains unclear.

■ Paired Readings

Don Dansereau and his colleagues at Texas Christian University have for several years been developing a learning strategies program that has as its central feature the idea that two heads are, indeed, better than one. That is to say, when students work together they learn more and retain more of what they have learned. Most of the strategies Dansereau has developed in his latest work involves readers in two types of activities as they discuss relatively short segments of text (usually 600 words or so). Dansereau calls his strategy "paired readings," and the following is a basic outline of the procedures.

1. Two students read silently a segment of an assignment; one student is a designated "Recaller" while the other student is a designated "Listener."
2. After reading, both students put the material out of sight. If one finishes the segment before the other, he or she goes back and reads the segment again until the partner finishes.
3. When both have finished reading, the Recaller orally retells what has been read without referring to the text.
4. During the retelling, the Listener should only interrupt to get clarification.
5. *After* the retelling, the Listener should proceed to do two things: (a) point out and correct any ideas that were summarized incorrectly, and (b) add any ideas that were not included in the retelling but which he or she thinks should have been.

The Reteller can help the Listener during this clarification and elaboration; in fact, the two partners should work together as they seek to reconstruct as much as possible of what they read.

6. Students should alternate roles after reading each segment. This form of cooperative discussion seems to help both learners understand and recall more of what they read than if they study alone.

From our view, several other encouraging features are included in this cooperative learning approach. First, students make a "social contract" to work together so each is more likely to attend to the task and together they are less likely to be distracted. A second bonus for cooperative learning is that students learn from one another about ways to work through problems of comprehension and study together. A third advantage is an increase in the amount of understanding of ideas; with two people studying a text, the chances are that one of them will understand something that confuses the other. Hence, we find again in Dansereau's idea of cooperative learning that the object of study is understanding. Rarely, outside of school settings, does one find solitary attempts at understanding; usually people invite others to share in their discoveries and to engage in cooperative learning activities. This is true for erudite scientists and casual readers alike.

Paired Reading with SMART

Paired readings and SMART go together like toast and jam. If you like paired readings and can identify ways to use it to help students learn in your classroom, we offer some further elaboration.

1. Two students are identified to work together.
2. The students survey the assignment and together agree on how to segment the selection into manageable parts, segments of appropriately short length to make reading easiest.
3. Each student carefully reads each section of the assignment *silently,* one segment at a time. As they read, students note, by using "√" and "?," what they do and do not understand.
4. After studying each section, one student orally retells what he or she understood, referring to the text where necessary.
5. After Reader A completes a retelling, Reader B adds anything omitted by Reader A and asks questions for clarification.
6. Reader B continues the discussion by noting anything not

understood. (Again, the student may refer to the text during this discussion.)

7. Reader A helps Reader B if possible with those ideas that were not clear and adds other items that were not clear.
8. Both readers now discuss ideas that they did not understand, implementing the principle that "two heads are better than one." As some ideas become clearer, they change "?" to "√."
9. Together, the readers list the questions they want to pose to the teacher or other students about ideas that remain unclear.
10. Readers proceed to the next section of the assignment.

Through this activity, students are learning in two ways: about the topic at hand and about strategies of study that other students find effective. Another advantage of paired study is that students realize they are not alone in their uncertainty. This cooperative learning develops a better understanding of how to learn more effectively and how to resolve problems encountered in reading.

■ Paired Questioning

We have taken the notion of paired reading one step further and devised a permutation of ReQuest (a technique we discussed in chapter 5) that students can use to engage in active decision making during reading. You may want to try this strategy with your students.

1. The class is divided into pairs of students.
2. Both students in each pair read the title or subtitle of a manageable section of text.
3. The students close their books. Each student in turn asks a question that comes to mind related to the title. The other student must give as reasonable an answer as possible.
4. The students read the section of text silently.
5. After completion of the reading, Reader A asks a question concerning the information and ideas in the text. Reader B answers, using the text if necessary.
6. Reader B then asks a question. Reader A answers, again using the text if necessary.
7. Reader A now tells what he or she believes to be the important ideas and the unimportant ideas in the section of text just read. In addition, the reader must explain why the ideas are important or unimportant and how he or she knew that.

8. Reader B must either agree or disagree with Reader A's choices and reasons and offer reasons for the agreement or disagreement.

9. (Optional) Each student writes a paraphrase or summary of the selection.

10. (Optional) Students read their paraphrases to each other and come up with a synopsis that they both agree accurately summarizes the passage.

11. (Optional) Students draw a picture that reflects the essence of their summary. (This is especially effective for lower grades.)

12. Students proceed to the next segment, switching roles for who goes first in each of the steps described above.

Here, students have an opportunity to share their decisions about many aspects of the ideas they discover in text. They also have a chance to practice their developing questioning skills, which can, in turn, help them frame good questions to guide their reading and thinking in anticipation of reading.

Imaging

The decision-making strategies we have presented thus far are foundational in that they offer students a way to approach text for the purpose of understanding. In effect, we want students to use strategies like INSERT, SMART, and paired readings to connect their own thoughts with the ideas presented in text. Sometimes imaging is also a help in making these connections. We discussed guided imaging activities as an anticipation activity; here we want to encourage readers to generate images themselves as they read. Imaging is picturing in the mind and it is particularly valuable when students are reading narrative text. By creating a visual image of characters and places, a reader makes a movie in his or her head and this mental "seeing" facilitates understanding and subsequent remembering. Some students may want to close their eyes when imaging to aid their concentration, but imaging should also be used when reading to create a movie in the mind using the text to cue the image making.

Imaging is also a useful strategy by which to picture relationships, somewhat in the same way that diagrams and other graphics are used in textbooks. If students are reading about the digestive system and the text provides no visual aids, students can try to generate an image of the various activities of digestion, fitting each phase of the digestion process into a "diagram" in their heads. By creating an image of events in a narrative text, students identify relationships and "concretize" ideas that might otherwise remain abstract and unclear. Think back to the selection on brown bears and polar bears in chapter 2. How might imaging have been useful when reading that selection? Students who sought to create images as they read would have envisioned forests and ice floes, and they could have related the two locales to the activities of the different types of bears. If students had then sought to relate the two locales, rather than perceive them as isolated elements (locale one and locale two), their images might have suggested the environmental differences between forests and ice floes. Any student who could have done this would have been closer to determining the "other means" of maintaining species distinctiveness. Students who seek to relate ideas to one another can sometimes accomplish this by creating a mental picture of how pieces of a puzzle fit together. If a text fails to provide a gestalt, then the reader must try to create one.

■ Imaging as Paraphrasing

Everyone agrees that the more active the reader, the better the comprehension. Dansereau (1978) found that when readers paraphrase their understandings as they read, comprehension and retention is greatly enhanced. What Dansereau means by paraphrasing is more than mere *re*phrasing *what* the author says. As much as possible, any paraphrase should express *how* the reader understands. The guiding question in such paraphrasing must be, "How might you explain this text to someone else?" In this sense, an excellent paraphrase of the brown bear/polar bear passage in the biology text would be "Distinctness in closely similar species, like brown bears and polar bears or mallard and pintail ducks is maintained by geographical separation and behavioral differences." Such a paraphrase represents what the paragraph was meant to express, although the author never quite accomplished that degree of clarity. The paraphrasing we want to encourage is a restatement and elaboration of "*" ideas that the reader has discovered. In effect, during reading the reader constructs an understanding of what the text is taken most importantly to mean.

   Now, let's reconsider imaging as akin to paraphrasing. While imaging can serve to help make connections and to create a framework for events in a story, it also is a form of paraphrasing. An image represents what the reader understands, the "poem" Rosenblatt refers to, and imaging creates a mental picture of that understanding. While imaging can facilitate the process of making connections, it can also serve as the product of the completed process. Once the connections are made, an image can help the reader clarify the connections and serve as a valuable aid to recall. In fact, Dansereau found that when imaging is used in tandem with paraphrasing, it can lead to as much as a 55-percent increase in retention.

Like any other strategies, imaging and paraphrasing will develop only with practice, practice that can be done in class—sometimes with you reading to the students, at other times with their reading silently to themselves. At times students may need to make their images concrete by drawing pictures or creating collages and to express their paraphrases orally to others. These specific techniques work for readers because they increase students' abilities to make connections and to recognize or form connections. Of course, they will not always work; therefore, students need opportunities to discuss their successes and difficulties in using these strategies.

THE TEACHER'S ROLE IN STRATEGY DEVELOPMENT

We've offered a few suggestions about strategies that readers can develop to increase their proficiency as learners. Now we'd like to make some suggestions about what can be done to teach those strategies. We have drawn on our own experiences and the metacognitive research projects of Anderson (1980), Brown (1980, 1981), and Dansereau (1978) to develop the following suggestions that we hope you will find helpful.

Place instruction of learning strategies in the context of meaningful learning experiences for students. Avoid isolating strategy instruction from content learning. Students will see more quickly the value of learning strategies you are teaching them if they can apply the strategies directly to their needs to understand what they are required to read. Recall one of our maxims offered previously: When learning to read and when learning to write, children should read about and write about things worth learning about.

Illustrate and demonstrate specific strategies by reading with *students*. Show them how you would use the strategies, explaining to them, for example, the basis for your INSERTs, how you arrived at certain images, and why you chose to paraphrase as you did. Much of what we are talking about here is learning about learning. Students need to know more about how learning occurs and how *they* can go about learning.

Let the strategies you share with students build on one another into a repertoire that can continue to expand. Distinguishing familiar from new ideas is a foundation for making distinctions between important ideas and examples. Deciding what is important in text provides a basis for creating a paraphrase or an image of the ideas in text. Learning to make decisions about ideas in text is a foundation for monitoring one's understanding. The strategies we are introducing to you are not isolated one from another; they are variations and permutations of one another.

Include feedback opportunities as part of students' practice with these strategies. Students can be given innumerable opportunities to share *what* they learned (as in paired activities) and *how* they learned. The importance of peer feedback sessions cannot be overstated. Daniel Fader (1976) builds his writing instruction program around feedback among groups of three students. He composes these groups heterogeneously, and no written exercise is submitted to the teacher until the group has approved it. Triads such as Fader describes work equally well for reflecting and reacting to reading assignments. The critical consideration is that students have an opportunity to compare the strategies they have used and the realizations they have made.

Make your evaluation of students' learning compatible with the kinds of learning you hope to encourage. Many students read to memorize details and definitions "because that's what teachers test." It may be true that teachers test details and definitions. At times, detailed recall may reflect broader conceptualization, but not if students seek only to memorize what is to be tested. For this reason, we ourselves have each, independently, stopped giving closed book, recall tests. The result has been fascinating for both us and our students. We have no reason to ask detailed, factual questions on tests because students can simply look up the answer in the book or in their notes. Our test questions, on the contrary, ask students to make connections between and among concepts that reflect breadth of understanding. This is, if you'll notice, more like "real world" kinds of questions, too. How often, in the real world (as contrasted to the world of school) does one have to remember details and definitions apart from application? Rarely! Since our test questions ask for clarification, elaboration, and application of ideas dealt with in class, our students have shifted their focus to understanding rather than remembering. As they understand broadly and as they come to real-ize connections among concepts, they also find that details and definitions make more sense and generalizations as well as details are easier to remember because they all fit into a sensible whole. Thus, our form of testing and evaluation has been revised to reflect the sort of learning we have sought to encourage in our students. We believe that if you want students to become thinkers, you must consider making your forms of evaluation more in keeping with the kind of thinking you hope to inspire and encourage.

REDUCTION OF FRUSTRATION POTENTIAL: TOWARD A LEARNING STRATEGIES CURRICULUM

■ ■ The immediate object of a learning strategies curriculum is to provide students with learning strategies that can help them learn more from their reading and study in school. The long-range object is to make reading a tool for learning throughout the student's life. There is nothing so important to learn as the process of learning, we have said. Now think about it this way: You've heard the old saying, "Give a man a fish and he'll eat for today; teach a man to fish and he'll eat for a lifetime." Consider this an analogy to learning how to learn: Teach students information you want them to learn and they'll pass the test on Friday; teach students how to learn and they'll pass the test for the rest of their lives.

Unfortunately, instruction in learning strategies is lacking in most schools; even good college students say no one ever taught them how to study or gave them any direction in alternative learning techniques. Many of the difficulties faced by students and teachers are, we believe, directly related to the absence of instruction in learning strategies. Students who do not know how to learn become distressed, frustrated, and even disruptive. Students who know how to learn are successful and enthusiastic about learning. It is for these reasons students need to learn how to learn at least as much as they need to learn the content in any subject field. Further, our first-hand experience tells us that the time for learning how to learn is when one is studying something worth learning.

The teacher's role in a learning strategies curriculum is to provide a conducive, supportive context for learning and to explain to students the strategies appropriate to learning the content they have been assigned. Further, the teacher must encourage students to use appropriate strategies and provide opportunities for students to practice those strategies: INSERT, SMART, paired readings, and so forth. Finally, teachers should help students monitor their progress with the strategies. This includes discussing how they used the strategy, encouraging students to describe their success or difficulty when using a strategy, and offering feedback that clarifies why a strategy may or may not have worked. Without this supportive context, students will not want to learn new things about their own learning nor will most of them make any conscious effort to become proficient learners. Helping students reach a high level of accomplishment such that they are in charge of their own learning will never be easy; however, if you fail to make a concerted effort to help them learn, learning for them will become more and more difficult as time goes by. Precious few of your students will learn how to learn on their own. They need structured, supportive, organized help from you.

7

Contemplations and Rememberings

SETTING THE STAGE

Contemplation is a natural activity for all of us. Think about how often you hear adults discussing with others what they have read or heard. The cosmic speculations of Carl Sagan, the current best seller by James Michener, the latest article on the pros and cons of nuclear energy—literature is a common topic among literate people. There seems to be in people an ever-present compulsion to share and discuss ideas with other people. When we share ideas with others, be they ideas from books or other sources, we are contemplating, saying, "This is how it seems to me; here is where I think it makes sense; how does it seem to you?" Such contemplations almost always lead to elaborated understandings and often to additional readings.

In settings outside of school we find people of all ages and all types engaged frequently in contemplative activities, often with one another. Parent and child, brother and sister, husband and wife, banker and client, Rotarian and Jaycee, all rely on others to sharpen their understandings and their perspectives. By comparing perspectives, recollections, and anticipations, two or more people usually gain a deeper understanding than any one of them could possibly achieve alone. Unfortunately in schools, we rarely find students engaged in reflection alone, much less in pairs or groups. Nor are students encouraged to contemplate, and therein lies the essence of our discontent. We maintain that a major part of teaching students to learn should include repeated and extensive opportunities to develop and exercise the habit of contemplation.

Contemplation is an essential feature of learning that is rarely engaged in today by the millions of young readers in our schools. Rather, many students seem to read from first word to last without serious concern for the ideas they are encountering. (One teacher friend of ours calls these readers "skip-along" readers, those who seem to skip through text but never get involved in what they're reading.) We are concerned that so few students seem to realize the importance of contemplations. One explanation for this may be that so many students read to remember detail, as we've said before. Our research indicates quite clearly that many adolescents read to memorize definitions and details. The irony is that remembering definitions and details is a particularly difficult task unless it also involves contemplated understandings. Think what they could retain if these same readers approached learning as an integrated, associative process!

The third phase of ARC, contemplation, is reasoned reflection that enables understandings to be synthesized. Reading, as an activity, begins with anticipation, proceeds through realization, and encompasses contemplation. (See Figure 4.2, p. 103.) As awarenesses and understandings emerge, the reader/learner must weigh ideas to discern their merit. As ideas are contemplated, understandings are refined and reinforced. Distinctions are made as uncertainties dissipate. Perceptions and feelings become crystallized. Cognitive synthesis occurs as readers give careful reconsideration to what they have learned.

Our concern stems from our observation that too few students give careful consideration to ideas they encounter during their study. Contemplation is our remedy to encourage students to reconsider their new learnings. Contemplation is simultaneously the essence of reconsideration and the foundation for remembering. Yet, before students can contemplate, they must learn how to contemplate. Here, then, are some activities and strategies that foster contemplation and, hence, better learning for all students.

CONTEMPLATION ACTIVITIES

■ ■ Our object throughout this book is to share strategies that help students think clearly and reasonably. Many of these strategies fall into a category we call contemplation activities. For your students to find these activities useful, you need only encourage them to go beyond their initial, once-over-lightly comprehension to discover, through contemplation, the extensiveness of their own thoughts and ideas. We are encouraged to find that as students discover how much they can elaborate their realizations, they then incorporate contemplation into their natural habits of study.

■ Read, Encode, Annotate, Ponder (REAP)

Developed by Marilyn Eanet and Anthony Manzo (1976), the REAP technique calls on readers to clarify and to synthesize their thinking after they have read a text selection. REAP is an acronym for

> *R*ead: student reads a selection,
> *E*ncode: writes a retelling of the selection,
> *A*nnotate: condenses the retelling into a summary, and
> *P*onder: then considers the importance of the ideas.

It is apparent that REAP can be used in the context of many other strategies such as PReP, categorical overviews, INSERT, SMART, and a content reading lesson. REAP is an activity to aid recall though a conscientious consideration of the ideas that emerged during reading. REAP is an activity used by an individual to clarify his or her own thinking. It begins with reading and proceeds through three subsequent stages. Let's examine each in its proper turn.

Immediately after reading a selection, students produce a written retelling. As you introduce the idea of written retellings, we suggest you encourage, even cajole, your students to elaborate their comprehension as much as possible. You want to jog their memories as much as you can. In a light-hearted way, you might also encourage them to write down more than anyone else in class, although quantity does not insure quality. At times you may find it helpful, especially with a new topic or a difficult selection, to encourage students to look back at the text from time to time to refresh their recall. (We mentioned look-backs in our discussion of realization strategies.) However, we advise that when a book is open during lookbacks, the student should not be writing. We mean to discourage copying! We'd also suggest limiting the number of look-backs for any given selection, again to discourage multiple reviews, memorization, and copying. What we do want to encourage is thinking, reasoning, and reflection. If multiple look-backs seem necessary for a student, that might imply a need for more time spent on understanding and realization.

As teachers we all know that remembering follows understanding, at least most of the time. If students have not adequately realized the meaning of what they read, they must devote further effort to understanding, and we as teachers must provide time for them to pursue their understandings. Once understanding has emerged, students should be able to produce an elaborated written retelling, at least in a first-draft form. In this instance, forgive them the indiscretion of inadequate spelling and grammar; they are writing for themselves in this activity, not for another reader.

In the third stage of REAP, students must now write summaries of their retellings. Although Eanet and Manzo emphasize the value of students' learning a variety of ways to annotate, we have found it as effective to allow students to follow their own instincts here. Our object is contemplation, not a lesson in varied forms of annotation, though we hope students do not digress too far from their original intent. Within this summarization activity is perhaps the key to the success of REAP. Presumably, as students condense their retelling into a summary, they find they must weigh the ideas they have found and then prioritize the ideas according to their importance and triviality. Important ideas are retained in the summary while trivial ones are omitted. The value here is that students practice making decisions about whether ideas are important or trivial, just as they did during the realization activity discussed in the preceding chapter. And students who can learn to make reasoned distinctions about the relative importance of ideas are well on their way to becoming accomplished readers, learners, and thinkers.

In the final stage of REAP, students ponder the significance of their newly discovered ideas. This stage serves as a final opportunity to reflect upon ideas and to reinforce recall. It also affords students a chance to *probe* their ideas (probe is, we think, an equally good name for this stage of REAP). Students would be likely to refer to the summary of their retelling for review, probing, and pondering, though some students will prefer to use their original retelling. Students may also realize the value of their retelling *and* their summary when time comes to review for a test or examination.

REAP provides students with specific guidelines for contemplation. Reading is followed by (1) an initial retelling that allows look-backs if necessary to cue recall, (2) a chance to prioritize concepts in the form of a summary, and (3) an opportunity to ponder and probe newly discovered ideas. This easy-to-use activity will facilitate students' practice with contemplation, and we have found REAP to be a helpful framework for reflection and reconsideration of ideas that is appropriate for students at all levels, even as early as second grade.

◼ Flip-a-Coin Quiz

This easy-to-implement activity is a favorite among students and teachers alike. Its simplicity is deceiving; its effect is often powerful.

The object of flip-a-coin quiz is to save class time for discussion of important ideas under study and to initiate that discussion as quickly after the tardy bell as you can. There are several variations on this activity, but they all involve previous study (for example, a homework assignment), provocative discussion, and an element of chance. This, then, is a story of motivation, exploration, deliberation, and intrigue.

As students enter the classroom, a pop-quiz is in full view on the chalkboard. From the time they enter the room until one full minute after the bell rings, students have an opportunity to examine the questions and to review their study from the night before. NO TALKING OR SHARING IS ALLOWED during this "centering" time. ("Centering" here refers to reordering students' focus of attention from their previous class to your class.) Centering helps save time often lost as students (and teachers) remain focused on their previous class. One minute after the bell has rung (plenty of time for attendance to be taken, and other necessary chores), you *flip a coin*.

If the coin comes up "heads," students take the quiz. We suggest that this quiz should be taken without reference to books or notes and that approximately five to seven minutes be allowed as time to take the quiz. As you can tell, this quiz format does not lend itself to simple, literal questions because the students can quickly look up those answers during the centering time. We encourage you to ask questions that cover ideas you deem to be most important for the day's lesson. One or two questions should suffice; in effect, you are asking for an elaborated retelling of some important idea. The object is not to be tricky or to find out what students do not know, but rather to stimulate students' thinking about a topic of central importance, something that is not a simple recitation from the text. If, for example, the assigned reading dealt with the early days of railroads in the United States, you might ask the question, "Why might both the farmers and the manufacturers have supported the expansion of railroads?"

If the coin is "tails," class begins with a discussion of the question(s) on the board. Several students might be asked to venture their responses to the question. Discussion would ensue as though no quiz had ever been considered. Likewise, after the quiz is taken, discussion would proceed on the question(s) as if no quiz had been taken. If the quiz is taken, however, you will likely see the benefits of students' having written a response, for it allows them to read aloud a point they want to make. This is also valuable for students who are often reticent and unwilling to contribute because they are unsure of their ability to think and talk at the same time. Which brings us to another benefit of written responses: students have usually thought before they talk!

If the coin comes up "heads" and students take the quiz, the papers should be graded *after* the discussion. Once all the grades are determined (for example, by students themselves or by swapping papers, monitored by the teacher), the teacher once more flips the coin. If it is "heads," the quiz counts! Students of all ages relish this one last chance for reprieve.

Of the numerous times we have observed this activity, it rarely fails to stimulate a lively discussion. When this activity seems not to work, the failure is usually due either to (1) difficulty students encountered when trying to understand the text or (2) rather bland question(s). As you try this with your students, keep in mind that the pop-quiz is more of a vehicle than anything else; flip-a-coin quiz is designed to elaborate understandings and to extend awareness while fostering recall. Oh, yes, there's one thing more. If students take the quiz and want their grade to count, we always let them count their grade, even if, on the second flip, the coin comes up "tails."

■ Save the Last Word for Me

This discussion-generating activity offers an extremely rich opportunity for student contemplation and interaction. Too, it is as student-centered an activity as we can imagine. Devised by Carolyn Burke and Jerry Harste, Save the Last Word for Me begins with students reading a selection. Either during or after reading, each student locates five statements from the selection that are of particular interest. They could easily be "X" "!" statements, but they must also be statements about which the student wants to make a comment. The student's intent is to say, "Here's a statement in the selection that I want to discuss. I'll share the statement and you tell me what it makes you think about. Then, when you have told me what you think, I'll get to tell you what I think."

Although this activity involves students finding five statements of interest in the selection, you may want to go with three statements; the number is chosen to provide ample "food for thought" for a classroom of students. On one side of an index card the student writes the statement of interest; on the reverse side the student writes what he or she wants to say about the statement. Discussion is triggered by the statements that students bring to class. First, the quote is read aloud. We have found it helpful for the student to locate the statement in the text for the class (for example, "This comes from the top of page 98"). This enables classmates to find the statement in its original context and helps keep discussion on the topic as intended by the author. Next, any student (or even the teacher) is allowed to comment on the statement. As you moderate the discussions, we suggest you limit the time for commentary on any one statement to a length reasonable for its importance and interest to the class. Don't allow a petty argument, even if you are deeply engaged yourself, to rumble on endlessly over an issue that has little benefit for anyone's better understanding of the main topic. Finally, the student who offered the quote gets to have the last word. Of course, after hearing others' ideas, the student who shared the quote may decide to change his or her comment altogether.

Several teachers with whom we have shared this activity have noted some reasonable concerns, two in particular. First, what if the student's final comment is resoundingly incorrect or even minimally misleading? Should a silly grin suffice to reflect the horrendous internal suffering within the teacher? Or should the teacher break the rules? A second concern is that the student who gets the last word has no response from peers or teachers. What kind of discussion is that?

While it seems that Save the Last Word for Me works well to initiate and extend discussions on topics where subjective responses are most appropriate, it could also be modified slightly to broaden its applicability. Several teachers have suggested the rules be altered slightly to allow a teacher to respond to the final comment only in instances where the student would leave others with incorrect information or misleading impressions. Further, the student who has the last word should be allowed, at his or her discretion, to invite comments from peers or the teacher. In such an instance, the student would call on those who want to respond for several minutes of extended discussion. (In press conferences, they call this follow-up time.) These modifications do not violate the spirit of the activity, and we encourage other alterations of this sort that make strategies more contextually appropriate. We caution, however, that the rules never be changed in the middle of the game. Rewrite the rules prior to any given discussion period.

■ Cinquains

We have a favorite among the contemplation activities. You may already know the cinquain (pronounced *sin-ꞌkān*) as a five-line poetry form with these features:

> The first line is a one word title, usually a noun.
> The second line is a two-word description of the topic, usually two adjectives.
> The third line is three words expressing action of the topic, usually three "-ing" words.

The fourth line is a four-word phrase describing the topic that usually shows feeling for the topic.

The fifth line is a one-word synonym that restates the essence of the topic.

Here's an example of a cinquain written by a fifth grader after she had read about geological disturbances:

> Volcanoes
> Red hot
> Erupting from within
> Nature's furnace of fire
> Inferno

Another example is the result of an eleventh grader's study of the concept of manifest destiny:

> Westward
> ruthless, destined
> expanding, civilizing, cultivating
> enhancing potential for all
> birthright

We first learned of cinquains as a poetry form, but we soon found them to offer particular potential for synthesis. You'll only need to try them to feel what we mean. Think of a topic, any topic. Start with an affective topic, like someone you love. Your parents. Your children. Your spouse. Do it here:

title (one word)   _____

describe (2 adjs.)   _____ _____

action (3 "-ings")   _____ _____ _____

feeling (phrase)   _____ _____ _____ _____

synonym (one word)   _____

There! You've got the hang of it. Next, do one on the subject you teach, or some concept within that subject, like one of the examples below:

> teaching
> complex, TOUGH
> challenging, invigorating, rewarding
> tying new to known
> educating

reading
fluid, active
participating, sharing, learning
glow in the dark
illuminating

Try them on your students. To write cinquains requires thought. Usually, the deeper the thought, the better the poem. The deeper the contemplation, the more permanent the image. Kids love them as much as we do. And because of the process involved, cinquains are as effective a tool as we know to foster contemplation.

SHARING AND SMALL GROUPS

■ ■ We find that shared learning in schools is as valuable as shared thinking outside of schools. Shared learning involves students working in pairs, triads, quads, or other small groups. While some of our recommendations include students working together in pairs, we also find that small group work is often a valuable setting for constructive interaction. We will discuss post-reading activities with the assumption that students will have an opportunity to discuss what they are studying. We will further assume that the setting of some of that discussion will be in small groups.

The primary value of the small group is that it allows differentiation of assignment by interest and ability. By teaching a class in three or four subgroups, flexibly arranged with different individuals comprising the groups at different times, you increase the likelihood of efficient, individualized learning. If discussion groups are to work well, it is recommended that the teacher maintain control over who is in which group and participate with each group whenever possible. Thus, the teacher is in direct control of each group, even when not present with the students as they meet as a group.

Under some conditions small groups may function well without teacher guidance. Such groups are those formed for solution of specific problems. These problems characteristically involve such activities as investigations in science, simulation exercises in social studies, problem solving in math and related subjects, and role playing or dramatization in literature. The problems best solved by self-directed groups are those with the following three characteristics: (1) the problem requires a multiple-step solution, where each member can offer something to the solution and no member is likely to have all the steps at his or her command; (2) every member of the group understands the problem and values the group in the sense of believing the solution will more likely be reached by the group than by an individual; and (3) the resources for solution of the problem are readily at hand.

Whether or not under direct supervision of the teacher, small group work is usually the best setting for contemplation, assuming that students have achieved a basic understanding of what they have studied. Small groups offer the opportunity for pooling ideas, providing a more extensive basis for new associations than one person might ever achieve alone. Let us now consider two specific contemplation activities that involve small groups.

Paired Summarizing

One example of a strategy that involves cooperative learning after reading is what we call paired summarizing, a variation of REAP. Immediately after reading, a student writes a retelling of the selection. If students have difficulty remembering, they should refer to the text to verify understandings and to re-cue thinking. During paired summarizing, however, we do not allow students to write any of their retelling while looking back at the text. We encourage students to approach look-backs in the same way that a race car driver sees a pit stop—something necessary but best done quickly. Of course, if minor or major repairs are necessary to the car (that is, understanding), the driver must take care of that before leaving the pit.

In paired summarizing, students might want to try to produce as extensive a written retelling as they can, to even out-do their partner. But in no case are students' retellings to be graded; they are rough drafts. The goal is elaboration, not fragmented thinking hassled by specters of spelling or ghosts of grammar and the pen that only writes red.

Once the respective retellings are completed, the partners swap papers. Then Partner A writes an abstract of Partner B's retelling and vice-versa. At this stage of the activity students are not allowed to converse with one another. If something is not clear to one of the partners, he or she must work to figure out what was intended. (If you use paired summarizing and decide you do want students discussing at this stage, you can always change the directions to fit your needs and preferences.)

When the abstracts are ready for comparison, the pair begins a discussion. The object of the discussion is (1) to specify what each reader understands, (2) to identify what they collectively cannot come to understand, and (3) to formulate questions for classmates and the teacher. Here is where the contemplation from the first three steps pays off. Students clearly realize what they understand, work together to resolve confusion, and agree to ask someone else for help if needed. This fosters understanding and increases self-confidence too.

Any activity involving pairs will not be particularly effective unless both parties complete their work to the best of their abilities. We find small group work is most beneficial when the individuals have each completed a task that is then brought to the group for discussion or reaction. Except in those kinds of instances we discussed earlier, when students try to complete a task together in groups, the most frequent result is confusion, chaos, and wasted time. Hence, we suggest that when you plan group work or paired activities, assign a task to be completed by individuals before the group work begins. In effect, the individual work is the student's "ticket for admission" to the group work where feedback and elaboration are available. For the student who fails to come prepared to a group activity, he or she is told to work on the prerequisite assignment during time set aside for group work. Presumably the lack of interchange will produce less learning for the unprepared individual, and the seclusion from interactive classwork may encourage completion of the tasks on other occasions.

Progressive Cinquains

Perhaps our bias toward cinquains is due to our success with an activity we call progressive cinquains. It begins with each student writing a cinquain on a specific topic. Notice we said topic, not title. We like to let students choose their own "title"—the word on the first line—based on a topic we give them. After two students have completed their individual cinquains, they are paired to produce another cinquain. "Combine the ones you have or write a new one," they are told. We suggest you have students raise a hand when they have finished their individual cinquain so you can assign partners. Once the assignments are made and the task is clear, students engage in active, lively discussion about how to create the best cinquain in the room (for this is a contest!). Occasionally, the pair chooses one of the original poems; at times students scrap the first efforts and take a completely new approach; usually, the pair integrates words and phrases as they revise and consent to one another's suggestions.

After a pair has completed its new cinquain, that pair is combined with another pair into a quad. The task of the four is to produce a cinquain better than either of the two developed by the pairs. Once again, parts are integrated into a new creation; sometimes a cinquain emerges that is completely different than either of those created by the pairs. The contemplation, the thinking, the realization, the interaction that occurs is dynamic.

Finally, one member of the group is chosen to write the group's effort on the board; a second member is asked by the group to read the cinquain aloud to win votes for their poem. When all cinquains are on the board, each is read aloud and the class votes for that cinquain it thinks best reflects the feelings, inclinations, and understandings of the topic being considered.

Our bias toward this activity is due to the enthusiasm and the energy expended during the construction of the paired and the quad cinquains. On occasion, ever so rare, verbal shouting matches have punctuated the discussions. Such is the worst that can occur. At best, students contemplate and share their perspectives. Elaborated thinking is observed as it emerges. Of greatest import to the students is the poem they create, for they want to achieve the "blue ribbon." For the teacher, who wanders among the groups observing students grapple with concepts for just the right word, the process of grappling excites and rewards. To instill in your students the spirit of shared contemplations, you may want to stipulate the following rules or guidelines as the need arises: (1) everyone deserves a chance to be understood, but no one should demand acquiescence; and (2) disagree with reason, not disputation.

Let us share some progressive cinquains that have been created by some of our students. The topic was "ARC."

Reading
Cued Thinking
Anticipating, Realizing, Contemplating
Combining Old With New
Comprehension

And one that included a bit of humor,

ARC
Adventuresome, Innovative
Braving New Ideas
Not belonging to Noah (nor Joan)
Odyssey

SPATIAL LEARNING STRATEGIES

■ ■ Recent research into students' rememberings (for example, Holley & Dansereau, 1984) suggests that learning is enhanced when students literally arrange concepts according to their relationships to one another. These activities require that students examine ideas in relation to previously realized concepts as well as to other ideas that emerge during study of a given topic. As students realize how concepts are related, they arrange the concepts on paper in a way that clearly depicts the relationships as the students see them. Thus, details are associated with main ideas and examples are linked to basic concepts. While the final graphic displays of such activities are often of value to students, the exercise of identifying relationships and spatially arranging concepts according to their logical associations is of even greater value to both realization and remembering. Two of the strategies we want to recommend you share with your students are graphic post-organizers and ConStruct.

Graphic Post-Organizers

The graphic post-organizer was first described by Richard Barron (1969; 1979) and Richard Earle (1976), though at that time it went under the name "structured overview." Few instructional activities require any historical background for understanding, but this is one that does. Dick Barron originally conceived of the structured overview as a solution to a problem. We'll let his words (Barron, 1979) explain the origins of this procedure:

> Several years ago I became interested in studying ways to help students read the text materials required in subjects such as science, mathematics, and social studies. To identify the problems students encounter with these materials, I became involved as a participant in a high school biology class. At first this proved to be somewhat damaging to my ego. Because I had little background in the subject, I found myself actually struggling to keep up with the kids!
>
> One day, early in the semester, the teacher introduced a new unit by listing and defining a long list of vocabulary terms. I became quite confused by this presentation and my initial reaction was, "My God, how will I ever keep all this terminology straight?"
>
> Later that evening, as I attempted to read the chapters associated with the unit, a simple fact began to dawn upon me. *All the vocabulary terms were related in some fashion!* I started to arrange the words in a diagram to depict relationships, occasionally adding terms from the two preceding units. Gradually, much of the content with which I had been struggling became clear.
>
> Out of this came a procedure which was subsequently labeled the "structured overview." It was defined as "a visual/verbal presentation of key vocabulary in a new learning task, in relation to broader, more inclusive terms (presumably) understood by students." The device was

incorporated into a larger set of instructional strategies under study at Syracuse University's Research and Demonstration Center in Secondary Reading and shared with a number of high school teachers. After they had used the structured overview for a period of time, most of these teachers reported positive feelings about its effects in helping their students to learn. (pp. 172–173)

What happened next is intriguing to say the least. After conducting several studies to demonstrate empirically the value of the structured overview, Barron (1979) found he could *not* find the support he expected. What had happened was that "we had been treating the structured overview as something teachers did *for* students." (1979, p. 173) To determine what had gone wrong, he talked with some students who had found the strategy helpful, and he discovered that ". . . these youngsters took an *active* role in the reading/learning task, they attempted consciously to relate the new, specific information to the teacher's introductory presentation." (p. 173) The key was that students had to take an active role in the development of this "visual/verbal" graphic display *after the reading*. Those students who passively observed teachers present their structured overview before the reading gained little if anything from the lesson. It was the active thinking by the students that made the difference, for when students ". . . constructed their own structured overview during or following a reading/learning task (they) would achieve higher test scores than those who received one made by the teacher or none at all."

Barron subsequently changed the name of this visual/verbal display to "graphic post-organizer." Notice here a critical shift in focus; he called it a POST-organizer, for he saw its direct application to facilitation of recall after reading. His suggestion is that students develop their own overview of what they have read by arranging and rearranging 3 × 5 index cards on which have been written terms related to the concepts underlying the reading selection. The purpose of such an activity is to devise an accurate, graphic account of how ideas understood from the reading are interrelated. An example based on the reading of a selection about our banking system is provided in Figure 7.1 to help you visualize this activity. If you are familiar with other spatial learning strategies (for example, mapping, semantic mapping, networking), you will surely recognize their similarity to graphic post-organizers.

We recommend that you help your students learn how to use graphic post-organizers. This strategy is not, however, learned quickly for practice is required to understand its intricacies and more practice

FIGURE 7.1   Graphic Post-Organizer for Selection on Banking System

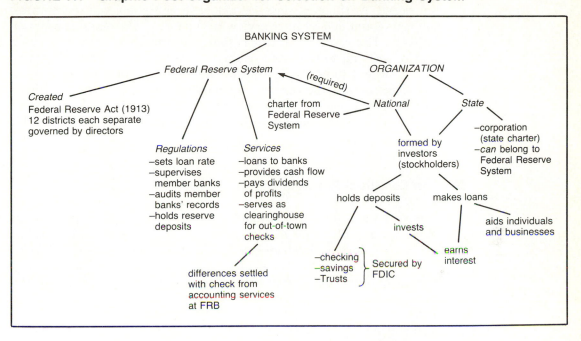

to master its potentials. Allow students to share with others their different versions of graphic post-organizers. Or, allow students to work in groups with 3 × 5 cards of ideas they think must be included in the array; students may choose ideas that they think are important (*), new (+), or particularly interesting (!). Having done this, students can then compare their display with that of other groups.

A creative use of graphic post-organizers was suggested to us by a group of high school teachers as they sought to integrate contemplation with anticipation. As an introduction to a unit of study, these teachers assign a general reading to all groups of students in their classes, a reading that surveys the major concepts in the unit. The reading might, for example, be a chapter in a textbook or the introduction to a chapter. Appropriate anticipation and realization activities would be used to help students understand as best they could. Following the reading students are placed into groups (assuming the reading did not occur in groups — another effective idea) where they discuss the selection in terms of what seems to them to be its major concepts. They then seek to display graphically (something they understand because their teachers have used structured overviews in their classes) the concepts as they are related to one another. Each group submits

its collective effort for review by the teacher, who makes comments as needed. At the next class session, each group is given ten minutes to display and defend its overview to the rest of the class. Discussion is lively. The result of all this is that students have a chance to read and reflect and to build out of their contemplations an anticipation of the content to be studied in the forthcoming unit. The concepts in the selection are the concepts for emphasis in the unit as a whole. What these teachers have done is to combine creatively the strengths of both contemplation and anticipation through the use of graphic post-organizers.

■ The ConStruct Procedure

It is very important that in whatever way reading is taught, students move toward independence in their abilities. Accomplished readers eventually develop strategies to deal with highly complex textbooks. ConStruct was created to help less accomplished readers learn to master highly complex text such as is often found in science, health, home economics, and social studies classes. ConStruct (Vaughan, 1982; 1984) is a technique students can learn and adapt for use in a variety of independent work settings.

The name for this procedure is derived from a blending of the ideas in the phrase *concept struct*uring. There are two features that serve to define it. First, it incorporates the common practice of reading the same text several times. One reading of any text is rarely sufficient for a complete understanding, regardless of the considerateness of the text. Different readings serve different purposes, each of which builds on the previous reading. The second feature is the evolutionary development of a graphic overview, a display similar to Barron's graphic post-organizer (which, by contrast, is developed in only one stage). These features will become clear with elaboration.

The *first* ConStruct reading is *a survey of the selection to formulate a skeletal graphic overview and to activate prior experiences relative to the selection*. Most first readings serve essentially the same function, but in this setting it is the first of three readings.

The *second* ConStruct reading is a careful, in-depth search for meaning often described as "study" reading. There is, however, a slight deviation from the usual sense of this term in that students are advised during this second reading (1) *to ignore anything they don't understand* and (2) *to pay attention to details but don't try to memorize them*. The purpose of this second reading is to facilitate as much understanding as possible while eliminating as much confusion as possible. (Let us remind you that this strategy is intended for use with very complex text; we certainly don't mean to recommend this strategy for all readers and all texts.) The second reading should be a highly positive experience; its purpose is clear realization, not strict recall. Students are encouraged at this point to include in the overview as much detail as seems appropriate to reflect the understandings they are developing. We also strongly discourage students from trying to memorize definitions and details they don't understand, as of course we would discourage them from merely memorizing anything.

The *third* reading in the ConStruct procedure is a combination of study, skim, and scan. First, *the reader returns to portions of the text not previously understood.* If the material remains unclear *and* the student has decided that an unclear idea is important to an overall understanding of the selection, help from another source (for example, another book, glossary, another student, teacher) must be sought. Readers can note these questions on their overview. It is in this third reading that questions can be more clearly formulated. Another part of this third reading is to *scan for details, trying to build ways to remember them in the context of their meaning.* (Mnemonics may be useful here.)

As we mentioned, ConStruct has two major features; the first is three readings. The critical second feature is the construction and elaboration of a graphic overview *during and immediately following each of the three readings.* This is important because it stimulates active involvement with the concepts and encourages continuous monitoring of comprehension. In addition, consider the potential it holds for allowing students to create a gradually evolving diagram of their independent realization of the text.

So, the ConStruct procedure integrates differentiated readings and graphic post-organizers, or graphic overviews as we call them. Research on the effectiveness of this procedure (Vaughan, 1984) leaves no doubt that it is easy to learn, though it does take care and time, and results in dramatically increased learning of both details and higher level concepts of a reading selection. Care must be taken, however, in the introductory period and the initial trial by students to help them understand its parts and its purposes. We have placed ConStruct here in the context of contemplation, incidentally, because it seems to combine so much of what is involved in reflection and the synthesis of ideas. The name seems perfectly fitting—it is a technique that facilitates the structuring of concepts in the mind of the reader.

In Figures 7.2, 7.3, and 7.4 you will see the three stages of graphic overviews designed by a tenth-grade student for a selection about the human digestive system. Note the initial framework in the first stage, the embellished form of the second stage, and the addition of minor details in the final stage.

FIGURE 7.2   ConStruct Overview, Stage One

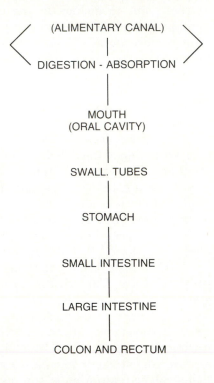

WHAT THE DIGESTIVE SYSTEM DOES

(ALIMENTARY CANAL)

DIGESTION - ABSORPTION

MOUTH
(ORAL CAVITY)

SWALL. TUBES

STOMACH

SMALL INTESTINE

LARGE INTESTINE

COLON AND RECTUM

Merely to see something that someone else has done is usually not sufficient to an understanding of it, so before you try to explain the ConStruct procedure to your students, try it out yourself on a text that you find complex to read—perhaps an encyclopedic entry on a topic that interests but eludes you. See for yourself how the successive readings and graphic construction of concepts from the reading can aid your own understanding.

In one demonstration of ConStruct for a group of students, we worked through an example with them, using one of the books they are assigned to read in their freshman biology class. You'll find this a good way to introduce ConStruct to your students; that is, start at the beginning of an assignment and walk through the steps with them. We'll explain by using the example from the biology class.

The chapter was twenty-three double-columned pages on the topic "Circulation." To use ConStruct, our first step was to SURVEY the chapter to see what it was about. Our survey indicated to us that the topic of the chapter was "Blood Circulation in Humans," so we

FIGURE 7.3 ConStruct Overview, Stage Two

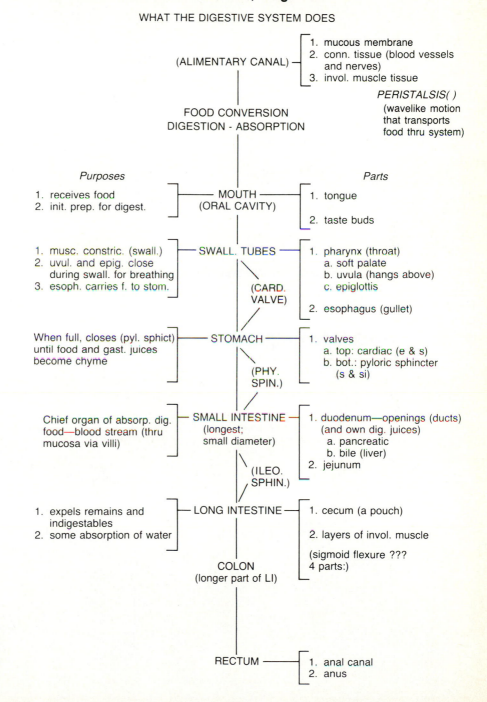

WHAT THE DIGESTIVE SYSTEM DOES

(ALIMENTARY CANAL)
1. mucous membrane
2. conn. tissue (blood vessels and nerves)
3. invol. muscle tissue

PERISTALSIS( )
(wavelike motion that transports food thru system)

FOOD CONVERSION
DIGESTION - ABSORPTION

Purposes

Parts

MOUTH
(ORAL CAVITY)
1. receives food
2. init. prep. for digest.
1. tongue
2. taste buds

SWALL. TUBES
1. musc. constric. (swall.)
2. uvul. and epig. close during swall. for breathing
3. esoph. carries f. to stom.
1. pharynx (throat)
   a. soft palate
   b. uvula (hangs above)
   c. epiglottis
2. esophagus (gullet)

(CARD. VALVE)

STOMACH
When full, closes (pyl. sphict) until food and gast. juices become chyme
1. valves
   a. top: cardiac (e & s)
   b. bot.: pyloric sphincter (s & si)

(PHY. SPIN.)

SMALL INTESTINE
(longest; small diameter)
Chief organ of absorp. dig. food—blood stream (thru mucosa via villi)
1. duodenum—openings (ducts) (and own dig. juices)
   a. pancreatic
   b. bile (liver)
2. jejunum

(ILEO. SPHIN.)

LONG INTESTINE
1. expels remains and indigestables
2. some absorption of water
1. cecum (a pouch)
2. layers of invol. muscle

(sigmoid flexure ??? 4 parts:)

COLON
(longer part of LI)

RECTUM
1. anal canal
2. anus

FIGURE 7.4   ConStruct Overview, Stage Three

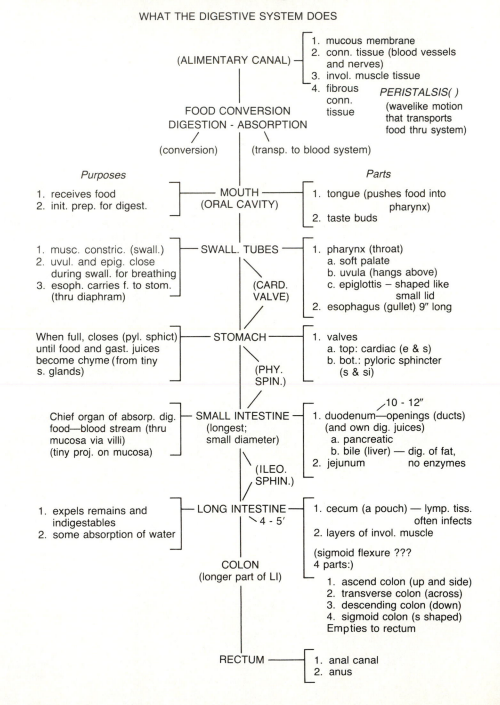

WHAT THE DIGESTIVE SYSTEM DOES

(ALIMENTARY CANAL)
1. mucous membrane
2. conn. tissue (blood vessels and nerves)
3. invol. muscle tissue
4. fibrous conn. tissue

PERISTALSIS( )
(wavelike motion that transports food thru system)

FOOD CONVERSION
DIGESTION - ABSORPTION
/ (conversion)   \ (transp. to blood system)

Purposes   *Parts*

MOUTH (ORAL CAVITY)
1. receives food
2. init. prep. for digest.
1. tongue (pushes food into pharynx)
2. taste buds

SWALL. TUBES
1. musc. constric. (swall.)
2. uvul. and epig. close during swall. for breathing
3. esoph. carries f. to stom. (thru diaphram)
(CARD. VALVE)
1. pharynx (throat)
   a. soft palate
   b. uvula (hangs above)
   c. epiglottis – shaped like small lid
2. esophagus (gullet) 9″ long

STOMACH
When full, closes (pyl. sphict) until food and gast. juices become chyme (from tiny s. glands)
(PHY. SPIN.)
1. valves
   a. top: cardiac (e & s)
   b. bot.: pyloric sphincter (s & si)

SMALL INTESTINE (longest; small diameter)
Chief organ of absorp. dig. food—blood stream (thru mucosa via villi) (tiny proj. on mucosa)
(ILEO. SPHIN.)
10 - 12″
1. duodenum—openings (ducts) (and own dig. juices)
   a. pancreatic
   b. bile (liver) — dig. of fat, no enzymes
2. jejunum

LONG INTESTINE 4 - 5′
1. expels remains and indigestables
2. some absorption of water
1. cecum (a pouch) — lymp. tiss. often infects
2. layers of invol. muscle

(sigmoid flexure ???
4 parts:)

COLON (longer part of LI)
   1. ascend colon (up and side)
   2. transverse colon (across)
   3. descending colon (down)
   4. sigmoid colon (s shaped)
Empties to rectum

RECTUM
1. anal canal
2. anus

gave our overview this title. The chapter was subdivided conveniently into sections. The sections did not seem to us at the survey reading to be of equal importance, but we decided to arrange our skeleton overview around them all anyway. Later, we could do some rearranging. Here's what we started with:

Blood Circulation

circulation   heart   vessels   pressure   hemostasis

Our next step was to READ the chapter as carefully as we could, without trying to memorize or even to remember anything particularly. We were just trying to get enough of the details *as we understood them* (which wasn't any too well) to support the major ideas in our basic overview. We read the chapter one section at a time, sometimes once more and sometimes twice more, as the text and our understanding seemed to require. For example, after a second reading of the first section, entitled "Systemic and Pulmonary Circulation," we had the following additions to the graphic overviews:

circulation

systemic (to body)   pulmonary (to lungs)

from (right side) heart   from (left side) heart

into arteries   to lungs

into arterioles   through veins

into capillaries (beds)   back to heart

into venules

into veins

back to heart

In pencil form, this was a bit messier but didn't take up as much room. It was squeezed beneath the heading "circulation" with alot of lines and arrows. Actually, in reading the next section of text ("The Human Heart"), we realized that systemic circulation originates on the right side of the heart and pulmonary circulation on the left side, so we went back to do a third reading of the first section and added the right side/left side distinction. In that next section, we learned about systole and diastole atrial and ventral alternation and many other things *that came clear to us only as we were able to put it into a graphic picture.* Yes, ConStruct often leaves us with questions, and it can't make comprehensible what is incomprehensible, even after three readings. But our personal experiences and the experiences of the students we've worked with assure us that ConStruct can be a lifesaver for students who have to read complex text.

As a final comment about ConStruct, we realize it can seem rather elusive, especially as we have explained it. We suspect that because it is a rather intricate process, it is more difficult to explain than to use. Perhaps it can only be learned, not taught. Yet, we have helped students learn how to use it in grades as low as seventh, and a colleague, Vicky Proctor, has taught it successfully to fifth graders in Winnetka, Illinois. If you sense uncertainty about ConStruct, all we can suggest at this point is to try it yourself on a passage of some difficulty for you. After you use it a couple of times, the subtleties of our explanation may become clearer, and then you'll be ready to help your students learn how to use it.

CONTEMPLATIONS, ANTICIPATIONS, AND REMEMBERINGS

Worthwhile rememberings are founded on clear understandings. Accomplished readers know that, but many have yet to learn it. We also suspect that many students know little of the relationship between understanding and remembering. That is why we strongly encourage you to help your students realize that remembering, especially information as opposed to stories, requires an intent to remember and the use of certain activities that aid recall. We find it hard to believe that students do know what is required to facilitate remembering but instead opt for the short-term shortcut of memorization. If students can accomplish the difficult task of memorizing definitions and details, they can most certainly master the process of remembering what they understand.

Of course, we know that there's more to comprehension than linking understanding with remembering and that rememberings serve as the prior experiences on which new learning can then be built. In that sense, memory works both ways. But let's let Alice (of Wonderland) tell it in her words,

> "I don't understand you," said Alice. "It's dreadfully confusing."
> "That's the effect of living backwards," the Queen said kindly: "It always makes one a little giddy at first . . ."
> "Living backwards!" Alice repeated in great astonishment. "I never heard of such a thing!"
> ". . . but there's one great advantage in it, that one's memory works both ways."
> "I'm sure *mine* only works one way," Alice remarked. "I can't remember things before they happen."

"It's a poor sort of memory that only works backwards," the Queen remarked.

"What sort of things do *you* remember best?" Alice ventured to ask.

"Oh, things that happened the week after next," the Queen replied in a careless tone.

The week after next? you might ask. How can the Queen remember things that happen in the future? Of course, the whole idea is self-contradictory, but so are a lot of other things that happen "through the looking glass." If we suspend logic for a moment, however, we can quickly realize that the Queen is able to remember forward because of what she can make happen. Perhaps such a connection will seem less dreadfully confusing if we consider the activity called reading from the view of Wolfgang Iser (1974). "The activity of reading can be characterized as a sort of kaleidoscope of perspectives, preintentions, recollections. Every sentence contains a preview of the next and forms a sort of viewfinder for what is to come; and this in turn changes the "preview" and so becomes a "viewfinder" for what has been read." (p. 130) Iser, like the Queen, is pointing us to the inextricable relationship between contemplation and anticipation. Anticipations are based on well-established prior experiences. Contemplation is the stuff through which prior experiences become well established. Anticipations form the basis for contemplations while contemplations provide the substance for further anticipations. (See, it really isn't so illogical after all!)

A VIEWFINDER ON CONTEMPLATION

■ ■   The point we want to emphasize is that understandings depend on the relationship between what is known and what is to be learned, that is, the known and the new. When you seek to learn something, your potential for success can be predicted, to a large extent, on the basis of how much you already know about it. While we have explored this issue at length, given its critical importance to ARC and the cycle of reading, we want to emphasize that the understandings that serve as our prior experience in any new learning endeavor are formulated and framed by the degree to which we have seriously contemplated those experiences. Those understandings that have been only casually developed provide little advantage in new learning situations. During reading activities, understandings that we evoke neither commence nor cease with the reading itself. Anticipation brings our associations to the reading activity; contemplation is an equally important element, as we have explored throughout this chapter. Anticipations, realizations, contemplations . . . ! They are as inseparable as honey and bees.

Learning begins with an established network of awarenesses. To understand is to build new awarenesses into that established network. To remember is to be able to identify and locate the links and connections in the network that hold ideas together; recall is the ability to produce consciously those experiences that are of use at a given moment. Likewise, when we anticipate, we call to consciousness those awarenesses that are most appropriately linked to what we will be learning. When we contemplate, we seek to establish clear and well-defined links and ties among our awarenesses. It is these links, associations among concepts, that increase our chances of recalling our awarenesses at will. The clearer our contemplations, the more effective will be our anticipation, for our anticipations are founded on our prior contemplations. Irrespective of how we relate awarenesses to one another, our reflections and our memories, somewhat like the Queen's, extend in both directions, backwards in our contemplations and forward in our anticipations.

As we have said, learning will be difficult for students who insist on trying to memorize tidbits that teachers test. Rememberings are built on contemplations of understandings. If students learn and apply that principle, they will reduce their frustration potential found in efforts to remember without understanding. When students become impatient to remember and resort to memorization at the expense of understanding, they will surely ignore contemplation. Students must learn the advantages of contemplation, and that means times set aside and opportunities for them to learn.

8

Thinking and Questioning

SETTING THE STAGE

A major idea undergirding this book is that the ability to think and to reason can and should be taught in the context of all instruction. For example, a major consideration in the design and plan of content reading lessons is, what kinds of questions should be used with students, that is, what kind of thinking should be stimulated? It's easy to say, "Good questions and high-level thinking," and perhaps anyone would agree. And though it's not quite so easy to do as to say, there are ways to accomplish good questions and high-level thinking with virtually all students.

The first step is to decide that thinking is an important and valued educational objective. In itself this is not always easy for a teacher to do, as Peter Schrag (1965) pointed out twenty years ago.

> Too many schools, too many teachers, too many communities are fearful of the one thing that education is supposed to achieve: the capacity to think. Thinking students ask nasty questions. Thinkers get too big for their britches. They want to change things. If you challenge students too much they may turn around and challenge you. Ask them real questions and they start discussing things that the teacher or the community doesn't like to discuss: why Negroes are treated badly, why adults aren't a little more honest about sex and morals, why the local politicians are corrupt. In the Bible belt the idea that God created the universe in six days is not a discussable issue, and all the ideas and prejudices rooted in rural South fundamentalism and racial segregation remain almost as untouchable now as they ever have been. J. Evetts Haley, one of the right-wing Texans for America, issued a manifesto a

few years ago proclaiming that "the stressing of both sides of a controversy only confuses the young and encourages them to make snap judgments based on insufficient evidence. Until they are old enough to understand both sides of a question, they should be taught only the American side." (pp. 276–277)

To which you might like to reply, "But things have changed in the last twenty years." No one would argue with you, certainly, though the change you mention may not be as great as you would hope. In Texas, for example, there is a mandate in textbook adoption specifications (issued March 12, 1983) that "positive aspects of the USA's history must be stressed in world history texts used in public schools." We aren't suggesting that the negative aspects be emphasized. We do suggest that there is a great deal to be learned in trying to understand both sides of any issue or question. Our plea is for good questions and high-level thinking, and our object in this chapter is to explore what those terms mean.

A long string of research beginning approximately with the work of Frank Guzak (1967) suggests two things about questioning in the classrooms:

First, the quality of answers students give to questions asked by teachers and the quality of questions *asked by students* is directly related to the quality of questions asked by teachers. When factual recall questions are typically asked, the level of students' answers is, not surprisingly, at a factual, literal level. But when questions are asked that require more sophisticated reasoning, students become more sophisticated thinkers accustomed to such thinking and reasoning. The 1981 study of reading, thinking, and writing conducted as part of the National Assessment of Educational Progress (NAEP) has reported that "students (notably secondary school students) seem not to have learned problem-solving strategies and critical thinking skills. . . . These findings seem to be a direct reflection of current practices in testing and instruction." (Petrosky, 1982) In addition, Appleby (1981) reports in an extensive study of writing in secondary schools that less than 4 percent of writing activities engaged in by high school students is more than a paragraph in length. Those findings were true for both in class and outside of class activities. We cannot categorically say that there is a relationship between Appleby's findings and NAEP's data, but we strongly suspect a direct correlation. Questioning, writing, and reasoning are integrally and inextricably linked, at least according to such noted authorities as Jerome Bruner, Lev Vygotsky, and Jean Piaget.

Second, a consistent conclusion about questioning in the classroom is that teachers don't ask for much. According to Guzak, fewer than 15 percent of teacher questions require any appreciable depth of thought by students. The NAEP data and Appleby's findings confirm that Guzak's conclusion in 1967 is at least as applicable today as it was then. Presumably, teachers are trying to ask questions students can answer; teachers also seem to assume that questions of detail requiring memory are easier to answer than questions that call for sophisticated reasoning skills. This is probably not true for questions following reading and almost certainly not true for questions preceding reading.

Keep in mind the purpose and role of questioning in the classroom. Questions should invariably stimulate rather than evaluate. If you find your students responding more on a factual, literal, "phase one" level, consider how often you ask questions in search of a "correct" answer rather than a reasoned answer. Questions should guide students to (1) analyze prior understandings, (2) synthesize different bits of information by determining their relationships to one another, and (3) evaluate critically their understandings about ideas and their relationships. The three stages of PReP are intended to lead students to these kinds of inquisitiveness, as are other activities we have shared. We might add that memorization type questions induce a relative passivity in readers and tend to encourage them to strive for memorization without understanding. Yet, when encouraged to understand bits of information in relation to one another and in relation to larger, broader concepts, students not only understand more, they also remember more, including the details teachers so often test.

The framework and context for good questions and high-level thinking is, we'd propose, ARC, which provides multiple opportunities for a repetitive cycle of questioning to spur thinking, reading to test predictions, and contemplations to refine thinking. Too, as you might guess, many of the activities for anticipation, realization, and contemplation discussed previously can be integrated into the context of the content reading lesson, but whether we speak of the content reading lesson or activities used within the framework of ARC, the defining feature is the kind of questions the teacher can ask and the kind of thinking the students engage in. Questions that best stimulate students' thinking are generally of the kind, "What do you think?" "Why do you think so?" "Can you prove it from what you've read?" Keeping that in mind, along with the idea that the objective is to stretch students' thinking to the highest levels possible, we'd like to offer a few ideas for framing different kinds of questions to stimulate different levels of thinking.

KINDS OF QUESTIONS

■ ■ Norris Sanders (1966) defines seven different kinds of questioning for teaching modeled on Bloom's earlier treatise (1956). The difference between the two perspectives is that where Bloom was concerned with questions to evaluate learning, Sanders is concerned with questions to facilitate learning. Each of the seven kinds of questions Sanders discusses is designed to elicit a different level of thought. Without meaning to negate any of the value of Sanders' work, we would point out that questions themselves have levels only in a manner of speaking. The same question might require different levels of thought from different people depending on how they arrive at their answer.

It is Sanders's implicit assumption, and one with which we agree, that the "better" question will require more sophisticated thought on the part of the learner. As a general rule, we suggest you always try to ask the question that will stimulate the most creative thought in the learner. The seven levels of thinking Sanders's questions are designed to foster are presented by him in roughly ascending order of sophistication: **memory, translation, interpretation, application, logical analysis, synthesis,** and **evaluation.** (Those familiar with Bloom's taxonomy will notice that Sanders's list is the same except that the categories **memory** and **translation** are substituted for the single category that Bloom called **comprehension.**)

Memory questions ask the learner to recognize or recall information. There is research evidence to suggest, unfortunately, that 85 percent of teacher questions are of this kind (Guzak, 1967). Surely memory is important to learning, but when students are asked only for what they remember, two things happen. One, they come to believe that the memorization of facts is a desirable and sufficient goal for their study. Two, they are given no opportunity to develop the skills to help them understand and remember what they are studying.

Translation questions ask the learner to change information into a different form. This different form might be a paraphrase or a drawing or any product that requires the learner to express an idea in a form different from the way it was presented in text. No great creativity is required of the reader to answer such a question, but as we have implied before, translation is a good strategy for learning and certainly worth cultivating.

Interpretation questions lead the learner to discover relationships among ideas, facts, definitions, and values. Questions of this kind require the learner to compare ideas, to draw inferences about relationships among ideas, to infer cause and effect between ideas, and other similar cognitive activities. Such comparisons and inferences require a minimum of creativity, actually, since they ask the reader merely to manipulate or rearrange ideas.

Application questions lead the learner into attempts to solve real-life problems. At this level of thinking, for example, the reader combines ideas from what has been read with ideas from prior knowledge to derive new ideas. Or, as Harold Herber (1970) states it, ideas at this level of thinking are "used" in the sense that "they are applied to previous knowledge and experience to determine if there is corroboration or contradiction. If the former, the specific ideas are strengthened; if the latter, specific ideas are modified." (p. 13)

Logical analysis questions ask the learner to analyze and judge the quality of the logic inherent in a statement or an argument. For example, such a question might lead the reader to see fallacies in a syllogism or detect a propaganda device or identify an advertising ploy. Or, a question of this type might guide the learner to several alternative conclusions from the same information and ask for a choice of which conclusion is most likely or logically appealing, which is least likely or logically appealing. This kind of question emphasizes the quality of argument and reason behind a statement (a statement, for example, like "All men are created equal," or "A well regulated militia being necessary to the security of a free State, the right of the people to keep and bear arms shall not be infringed") or an event (an event, for example, like the dropping of an atom bomb on Hiroshima to usher in a new form of warfare, or the controversy surrounding the refutation of the geocentric concept of the universe). The issue or event is not at stake, but the logic that underlies it is the interesting point to be discussed; in the process students will learn to analyze the reasoning that lies behind statements and events.

Synthesis questions require the learner to solve a problem with original, creative thinking. This sort of question will vary greatly in complexity. Consider the following questions as examples: "What would be a better title for this story, and why?" "If you were publicity manager for OPEC, what would you emphasize in an attempt to gain wider acceptance of OPEC policies?" "What conclusions can you draw from the fact that 9 percent of the gross national product of this country is spent on the health care industry?"

Evaluation questions are meant to inspire judgments of good or bad, right or wrong, according to specific standards. Answers to such questions need to be justified with reference to explicit criteria of judgment. *Consumer Reports* is a good source of examples of evaluative answers justified against criteria. Sanders points out two steps in evaluation: "The first is to set up appropriate standards or values and the second is to determine how closely the idea or object meets these standards or values." (p. 141) However, the evaluation question gives rise to the problem of distinguishing facts and values, especially in cases where students (or teachers) may treat some values of their own as facts that "any people would disagree with."

Each of these seven kinds of questions has a place in some phase of ARC and within every content reading lesson where they can stimulate anticipations, guide realizations, and structure contemplations. That is *not* to say anyone should somehow try to ask each type of question in designing every lesson. We want to point out again, though, that most questions asked in the classroom are not as good as they could be because they require so little sophistication in thought and stimulate such minimal discussion among students. An awareness of alternatives has helped many teachers to move away from questions that solicit literal facts to questions with much greater potential to stimulate readers' thinking. The result has been an improvement in their students' memory and thinking. We think this has occurred because the awareness we speak of helps teachers in the following three ways:

1. To distinguish different levels and kinds of thinking and to identify how they are related to one another,
2. To define a broad range of objectives of instruction, and
3. To provide a way of structuring class activities to foster a variety of intellectual abilities and habits with whatever subject or content is being taught.

Before moving on to the issue of kinds of thinking, we'll first illustrate and summarize what we've already said about kinds of questioning, using as our example a passage of text and accompanying the questions we first used in a journal article (Estes, 1979). With tongue only half in cheek, we ask you to read the familiar poem:

"Jack and Jill"

by M. Goose

Jack and Jill
Went up the hill,
    To fetch a pail of water;
Jack fell down
And broke his crown,
    And Jill came tumbling after.

When you're sure you understand the poem, contemplate your own understanding with these questions, each meant to stimulate a different kind of thought about the same poem.

1. *What did Jack and Jill do?*
   This is a question of memory, asking for mere recall of information. It probably stimulates very little if any interest in you about the poem, though it is unfortunately too typical a kind of question. Little thought is required to answer it, and so it is not a very good question to ask.

2. *Draw a picture (at least in your mind) of the scene depicted in the first three lines. Then, on another sheet of paper, draw a picture of the scene depicted in the last three lines.*
   This "question" is one of translation, asking you to change the information from the first question into a different form. It does require at least a minimum of thought and forces a comparison and sequencing of events. It might lead to an appreciation of cause and effect. What, after all, caused Jack to fall down and Jill to tumble after?

3. *Why do you think Jack and Jill went after water? Why did they take only one pail?*
   Now we begin to get to some interesting thought in a question of interpretation. The question requires you to see relationships in the information given. Incidentally, it is Sanders's opinion that all higher level questions are refinements of the intellectual processes required in interpretation. It is our opinion that comprehension *is* interpretation, as we keep saying.

4. *Is it reasonable to go up a hill after water?*
   This is a quesion of application, the answer to which requires the reader to combine his or her prior knowledge with information in the poem. The judgment asked of the reader requires some knowledge of where water is likely to be found and where wells are likely to be dug. Those who justify their answer on the basis of an illustration they recall from a children's book have a chance to do some genuine critical reading and thinking.

5. *Would it be reasonable to suggest Jack and Jill had other motives in going up the hill?*
   This is a question of logical analysis since it asks the reader to judge the validity of an inference being drawn from the poem, namely that one or both of these children's motives is less than honorable.

6. *What are some things this couple might do to avoid suspicion in their behavior?*

Take along a pail, of course! This is a question whose answer requires creativity and originality. (These questions have probably by now led you to thoughts about this nursery rhyme you never before had.) A simple problem is posed by the question, the solution of which lies in a synthesis of the content of the text with the common sense of the reader.

7. *Do you think Jack and Jill should have gone up the hill? Does the outcome of their misadventure, revealed in the second part of the verse, provide a moral?*

Here the reader is asked to make an evaluation on the basis of specifiable standards of behavior and poetic justice.

To restate the obvious, the point of these different kinds of questions is not to direct comprehension by constraining thinking but to facilitate comprehension by stimulating divergence and creativity. The idea of using questions to stimulate thinking would probably appeal to many teachers, at least in principle. But in practice, teachers are far from unanimous on this point. By and large they view questions as evaluative, judging answers on the sole criterion of agreement with information in the text. Albert Kingston, in leading a discussion of cognition and reading at a reading conference, once suggested a variety of interpretations of the Jack and Jill story, such as:

Jack and Jill were a king and a queen.
Jack broke the top of his tooth.
Jill fell down because she was trying to help Jack.

Would you accept these interpretations from children as evidence of good understanding? If such comments arose in a discussion, how would you handle them? According to Smith (1980) who reported the discussion in a journal article, Kingston's audience was about evenly divided between "those who would accept these interpretations as demonstrating comprehension and those who insisted that the children had included ideas . . . not allowable in this context." (p. 101)

In discussing the issues that divided the audience, Smith points out that there are two related questions at stake: (1) Does comprehension encompass only what the text says? (2) Or does it by necessity include relevant prior knowledge? To our way of thinking, these questions pose no serious practical or theoretical problem. Why not? Because we believe all comprehension requires some interpretation. Who were Jack and Jill? A boy and a girl about six to ten years old, you say, and certainly that's an allowable interpretation. But it is important to realize that it *is* an interpretation. Some history-minded reader might say, in answer to the same question of Jack and Jill's identity, that they are Cardinal Wolsey and his coadjutor, Bishop Tarbes, who are on their way to France to arrange the marriage of Mary Tudor. If you've never heard that interpretation, or think it too outlandish, have a look at *The Annotated Mother Goose* (Baring-Gould & Baring-Gould, 1967). And there are other interpretations of this simple poem. For example, some say the water at the top of the hill is symbolic of the holiest of holy water, in reference to Cardinal Wolsey's papal ambitions.

What shall we allow or disallow as comprehension, especially beyond the level of memory? This question is itself a question of evaluation, asking you to make a judgment on the basis of specifiable standards. Perhaps the answer has to be found in the mind of each individual teacher. For us, at least, these are the specifiable standards we would appeal to in our own judgments:

1. Interpretations should not contradict the text,
2. Interpretations should be justified with evidence from the text,
3. Interpretations should be logically connected with ideas in the prior knowledge of the reader.

If you agree with us, in principle at least, about the need to pose stimulating questions more frequently than evaluative questions, you may also be asking, "But how do I do it?" Having been there ourselves, we appreciate the sense of frustration that can come from recognizing a goal but being uncertain as to the means to fulfill that goal. We will address the "how-to," but first let's examine the corollary to kinds of questions, namely, kinds of thinking. We prefer to discuss application of questions and thinking at the same time; remember, they are inextricably linked.

KINDS OF THINKING

Our idea of kinds of thinking as the complement to kinds of questions is drawn directly from a seminal book on semantics by Albert Upton (1961). One of Upton's students, Richard Samson, has translated this work into a critical-thinking skills program published by Innovative Sciences, Inc., in Stamford, Connecticut. This thinking skills program, packaged as a series of exercise workbooks, is structured around six basic ways in which human beings make sense of the world. Our proposal to you is that the questions and exercises you provide students in their study of any content can prompt various kinds of thinking in the context of ARC.

We will take three approaches in our discussion of kinds of thinking, *à la* Samson. First, we will list the six kinds of thinking with a brief definition. Second, we will describe the six kinds of thinking with reference to a selection of text you have already read, examining the kinds of thinking possible in contemplation. Third, we will look afresh at some reading passages to consider the kinds of thinking and kinds of questions one could anticipate applying to the passages.

■ **Kinds of Thinking Defined**

Here, with thanks to Richard Samson, are the six kinds of thinking we will be dealing with:

1. *Thing-making* — People make things and use words as labels for what they make. They shape their reality with their language.
2. *Qualification* — Having made something, people describe it by specifying the qualities that distinguish it.
3. *Classification* — On the basis of their qualifications, people put like things together and separate different things.
4. *Structure Analysis* — People divide wholes into parts and put parts together to form wholes.
5. *Operational Analysis* — People describe things, ideas, and events across time.
6. *Analogy* — People see similarities in relationships among otherwise different things, ideas, and events.

■ **Six Ways to Think About Crocodiles**

Sometime back, you will recall, you read a selection about power, sex, predation, and violence — a newspaper selection about crocodiles. We used the selection as an exercise in INSERT, or Interactive Notetaking System for Effective Reading and Thinking. Now we'd like you to think about those crocodiles in the six ways Richard Samson has suggested.

As you reconsider the crocodile article, which you'll find in chapter 6 on pp. 138–140, in what ways does the text help the reader *let words mean things?* One good example is the author's use of metaphor in reference to the breeding of crocodiles as an assignation, an appointment between lovers. The author allowed the mating of crocodiles to become more than mere breeding. Such is the power of words to imply, and hence, to mean things. Consider, too, the distinction we make between crocodiles and alligators simply by giving them distinct names. In fact, by attaching words to concepts we give discrete recognition and meaning to the concepts themselves. Extending this idea, how much thought is given to things for which we have no words? For example, because we, unlike the Eskimo, have no words for all the kinds of snow an Eskimo can distinguish, we give no thought to the possible different kinds. Even if there is a distinction we can make, without words to do so, we won't make it—for example, the distinction between "hot" tasting food and "hot" weather, which the Romance language speaker can make with words but we cannot. Thus, when the author describes some of the differences between crocodiles and alligators, she helps the reader "make" two different animals. Because words mean things, it is important that students come to appreciate the power of language to shape and express understanding.

Having made something and given it a label (or name), between the animals we call alligators and the ones we call crocodiles, the next human inclination is to *qualify* the animals by specifying the differences between them. This is more abstract than it seems, especially for the young person whose thinking remains at a pre-formal stage, in Piaget's terms. To talk about the qualities of crocodiles as separate from crocodiles is to abstract the qualities. In the present example, this seems all too easy, but were the idea of crocodile somewhat less familiar, as is so much of what students are required to learn in school, the task wouldn't seem nearly so easy. And just to show how abstract the task actually is, try now to name a few of the differences between crocodiles and alligators and specify what quality belongs to which animal.

With their qualities specified, crocodiles can next be *classified,* meaning grouped with other things that have similar qualities and separated from things with unlike qualities. Thus, crocodiles are classifiable among things that lay eggs, things that are large, things that are fearful, and so forth. Albert Upton (1961) points out that questions of qualification are typically of the forms, "What is this a sort of?" or "What are the sorts of these?"

The author of the crocodile passage does not deal with her topic in terms of *structure* to any great extent, though she does mention the importance of some parts of the animal—skin and teeth particularly. It is possible and appropriate, however, to consider the article itself in terms of *structure,* the parts of which may vary depending on one's approach. In one sense, the parts are power, sex, predation, and violence in Africa. Or, in reflecting on the content of the article, readers might want to think in terms of the geography, characteristics, and habits of crocodiles. In either case, the reader is making decisions about how to structure the ideas in the article. Questions of structure typically take the forms of "What are the parts of this?" or "What is this a part of?" (Upton, 1961)

With the addition of a fourth dimension, time, it becomes possible to *operationally analyze* a selection or the ideas it contains. When we speak of reading as anticipations, realizations, and contemplations, we are analyzing the process of reading as an operation. When the crocodile article speaks of the life stages of the animal, this is operational analysis. Here we're talking about something akin to what Harold Herber (1978) calls "time order," with the difference that the primary focus now is on the stages of events rather than the time separating them. First the assignation, then the egg laying, then the hatching, then the struggle against predators, and always our focus is on stages. The typical forms for questions of operation are "What are the stages of this?" and "What is this a stage of?" (Upton, 1961)

Analogies may well be the most complicated kind of thinking in Samson's list of kinds of thinking, but in some ways they are easiest to understand and to teach. Perhaps it is human inclination to see one thing in terms of another, in part because understanding depends on making connections. All connections are based on some relationship. The author of the crocodile article says they lose their teeth like mittens, implying an analogy between the disregard children have for handwear and crocodiles have for teeth. When the author describes how a crocodile's grin is like an evil, insincere smile ("a toothy simper"), she builds an understanding of one way in which the croc is particularly human, or at least lives up to a human stereotype.

These are but a few examples from the crocodile article of the kinds of thinking possible. The examples are meant to imply instructional objectives.

THE CONTENT READING LESSON REVISITED

■ ■ We'd now like to show you a plan for directing the reading of a selection in any content area. The following questions and exercises will help you think about and understand the ideas presented by the authors and is an approach we suggest you use with your students. The questions we ask and exercises we have designed are of one of the kinds suggested by Sanders, and each is designed to tap one or more of the kinds of thinking suggested by Upton. For our purposes, the plan has been designed around a particular section, in a biology textbook, entitled "The Community." The actual content of the selection is unimportant except in providing us with an example in which to explain our questions and exercises.

To *anticipate* what you are going to read in this selection, think about what a community is. You probably live in one. But the concept of community in the context of biology (the study of life) is at once different from and similar to the more common concept of community. How do you think the biological concept differs from the ordinary concept of community?

This is a question of interpretation since it asks for a comparison, and the kind of thinking it calls for is thing-making. It requires you, the reader, to apply a label to the same idea in two different domains to further define the concept by comparing its application in those two domains (the community you live in and biological communities).

The discussion of community is organized in the selection around four subtopics: (1) Living Things, (2) Food, (3) Energy, and (4) Food Production and Transfer. How many things can you think of to describe the idea of a community? You might try to organize your own thoughts into these four categories.

This is a question of application since you are asked to apply prior knowledge to understand information in the text. The kind of thinking the question requires is qualification: you are asked to specify qualities that define the idea of community.

It is sometimes helpful to turn subsection headings into questions that help you anticipate the ideas to be encountered. Thus you can ask yourself: What are the living things of my community?

This is a question of memory asking for structure analysis.

Where do the living things of my community get food?

This is a question of interpretation since it asks you to examine relationships among ideas (such as the fact that certain foods are available only in certain seasons). It asks for operation analysis since one would have to consider production and transportation procedures in some time frame (first the food is planted, then the crops are harvested, and so forth).

Where do the living things of my community get energy?

This question is one of interpretation and classification—interpretation because it asks you to infer relationships among facts (perhaps concluding that all energy comes from the same source) and classification because it asks for the sorts of energy in your community.

How is food produced and transferred in my community, considering all food needed and all the ways in which living things get it?

This is another question of application, applying prior knowledge in an attempt to understand new information, and it requires operational analysis since production and transfer can only be considered in relation to time.

To *realize* the meaning of what you read, we'd suggest you try INSERT, the system we introduced in the context of the crocodile passage. This would help you compare what you know about your community to what you know about biological communities, because *INSERT is an activity requiring interpretation, application, analysis, synthesis, and evaluation and all possible kinds of thinking. Primarily, though, it requires interpretation (the discovery of relationships among ideas, facts, definitions, and values).*

Assume now that you have read the selection on communities in the biology textbook. The number of questions and activities for *contemplation* is practically limitless. Here are a few examples.

How does what you read compare with your previous thoughts about communities? Does a knowledge of biological community help you to understand human communities? Is the reverse true as well?

These are questions of evaluation requiring qualification since you are asked to judge the worth of what you read in terms of your previous understanding and to specify the qualities of new and old information that led to your judgment.

Regarding the section, "Living Things":

1. How would you define "community" after reading this section?
   This question asks for translation and requires thing-making thinking.
2. Is your definition now more specific?
   This question asks for interpretation and qualification.
3. Is your definition more specific than the one the author states (a community is a naturally occurring group of plants and animals living in a certain area)?
   This question asks for evaluation and qualification.
4. The selection ends with two questions for discussion: How did early humans affect their community? How do humans affect their community today? A famous conservationist, Aldo Leopold, said, "Conservation is a state of harmony between man and land. . . . Harmony with land is like harmony with a friend." (*A Sand County Almanac*, 1949, p. 189.) Draw an analogy between the ideas of community, conservation, harmony, and friendship.
   Different people will draw different analogies and justify them in different ways. Here, as often is the case in open-ended

questions, there is not so much a right or wrong answer as there will be good and better reasoning in the process. The exercise requires synthesis and analogy.

Regarding the section, "Food":

1. Members of a community are either producers or consumers of food. You are a consumer because your body can't produce any of its own food. What producers have you consumed today?
   This is a question of application and classification, asking you to classify the food you have eaten into one of two categories.
2. If you have a garden or if you raise animals to eat, you may think you produce some of your own food. In a sense you are correct, but in biological terms why are you incorrect in your thought?
   This is a question of application and thing-making. It asks you to think of two senses of the same word and how different ideas can have the same label, one loosely applied, another a technical term.

Regarding the section, "Energy":

1. Consider the analogy the author sets up in this section: the automobile engine is to gasoline as a human being is to food. The relating factor is energy source. In what ways is this analogy *false?*
   This is a question of evaluation that uses analogy.

Regarding the section, "Food Production and Transfer":

1. Why might one say "The sun is the source of all energy on earth"?
   This is a question of evaluation that calls for operational analysis.
2. To "Transfer" is to move from one place to another. How does this definition apply in an explanation of the food chain?
   This is a question of translation, the restating of a principle, and it requires operational analysis.
3. Oxygen, carbon dioxide, water, and carbon are recycled but energy is not. Why doesn't a community run out of energy?
   This is a question of logical analysis since it asks you to deal with logically different phenomena (elements in the atmosphere and the abstract concept, energy); to decide they are different

> *one has to inquire as to the nature of each, and in this way*
> *the question requires classification.*

All these questions are meant to illustrate one point: that various kinds of questions can be asked and various kinds of thought can be simulated for the same reading passage. Again, you needn't worry about trying to fit your plans to include all of these kinds of questions. But when you make plans to guide reading in the manner of the content reading lesson, we do suggest you be conscious of the variety of questions that are possible. With just that much attention, you will be amazed at the kinds of thought your students are capable of. And all because someone cared to ask the right kinds of questions.

"KIDS HAVE THE ANSWERS: DO YOU HAVE THE QUESTIONS?"

This was the title of a feature article that appeared in *Instructor* magazine, in November, 1980. In this feature, Hilarie Bryce Davis described eight ways she's found of converting less challenging questions into questions that really stimulate thought. In summary form, here are her excellent suggestions for quickly improving anyone's questioning. All of these suggestions are applicable to the improvement of questioning in the content reading lesson.

1. "Yes, but why?" Ask students *why* an answer is correct. "Why is the product of two negative numbers a positive number?" "Why do we begin each sentence with a capital letter and end with a period?" "Why did Japan ally itself with Germany in World War II?"
2. "What's the use?" To convert from recall to use of information, ask questions that get students to apply what they remember. As Davis suggests, "to the question 'Why do you need to know the effect of light on plant growth?' students might answer, 'To do landscaping, know where to plant a garden, or decide which houseplants to buy for the light exposure available.' "
3. "What's different now?" This conversion strategy is to change something about basic information that causes students to consider implications and meaning of that information. There are a number of tactics for this change (Osborn, 1963):
   a. Adapt—borrow an idea from somewhere else. "How would our lives be different if we hibernated all winter long as some animals do?"

b. Modify — make a small change for the better. "What would be the effect if the relationship between inches and feet and between ounces and pounds were the same (for example, if both were 10 to 1 instead of inches to feet being 12 to 1 and ounces to pounds being 16 to 1)?

c. Substitute — use something or someone else. "How would the poetic effect of Hamlet's 'to be or not to be' soliloquy be changed if it were translated into French?"

d. Magnify — add, multiply, or extend. "If earth had three moons and two suns, what would be the effect on our lives?"

e. Minify — make it smaller, omit something, divide it. "What if there were no paragraph breaks in written language?"

f. Rearrange — revise the order of things. "What if every country were an island equidistant from all other countries?"

g. Reverse — turn things completely around. "What if we were to adopt the habit of counting to the left on a number line instead of to the right, that is, in descending rather than ascending order?"

h. Combine — add two or more things together. "How would the world be different if each continent were only one country?"

4. "Can you prove it?" This conversion strategy asks for support of an answer. The question, referring to the main character in Somerset Maugham's *Of Human Bondage*, of "What event in Phillip's young life affects his later personality?" becomes "What aspects of Phillip's relationship with Miriam would show that his personality was warped by his birth defect?"

5. "Right, wrong, or neither?" This is the question that can have no right or wrong answer, much like most of the interesting questions in real life — the question is open-ended. "Why do people name places and things instead of using another identification system such as numbers, do you think?" (This would surely be an interesting sort of question to pose in discussion of Orwell's *1984*.)

6. "All of the above?" This question has many answers. For example, "If a noun is a person, place, thing, or idea, how many of the words on the board are nouns?" (Show the students, on the chalkboard, a list of many words including examples of all the parts of speech.) "How many nouns can you add to the list?"

7. "Alike or different?" This type of question is of the comparison-contrast form. "How are Thomas Jefferson and Abraham Lincoln and Martin Luther King, Jr. alike? How are they different?" "How is a short story of Edgar Allen Poe similar to a story

by Arthur Conan Doyle (creator of Sherlock Holmes)? How are the two different?"

8. "Square peg and round hole?" This kind of question asks of the reader thinking that James Adams (1980) calls "conceptual blockbusting," breaking out of old ways of thinking to see new relationships. "If the parts of speech were members of a family, what parts of speech would have which family roles? Why do you think so?"

We hope that all of these adaptations suggested by Hilarie Bryce Davis will help you see how the simplest question can be transformed into a thought-provoking exercise. Any teacher has a role to play as thought provoker, and good questioning is the best way to play that role. A good content reading lesson depends on it.

■ What's Your Questioning IQ?

The following quiz appeared as an insert to the *Instructor* feature on questioning. The quiz was designed by Robert Schirrmacher and Michael Kahn.

What's Your Questioning IQ?

Below are questions you might ask children after reading "Goldilocks and the Three Bears." Write L after the questions that call on only lower-level thinking skills. Write H after those questions that involve higher-level thinking skills.

_____ (1) How many bears are there in the story?

_____ (2) What is porridge?

_____ (3) How would you have felt if you were Baby Bear?

_____ (4) Should Goldilocks be punished for breaking the chair?

_____ (5) Who went into the house where the three bears lived?

_____ (6) What happened first in the story?

_____ (7) What happened after Baby Bear's chair broke?

_____ (8) Do you think the three bears will lock their door the next time they leave their house?

_____ (9) Is this story like another bear story we've read? How?

_____ (10) Are all little girls like Goldilocks?

(Davis, 1980, p. 66)

We will leave you to share this exercise with others and to discuss with colleagues various questions that could be asked about this story. All that we mean to suggest about questioning and thinking comes to naught unless you are able to actualize the key principle: Questions should be designed to stimulate rather than just to evaluate. Good thinking comes from practice and the practice comes with provocative questions.

9

Vocabulary Instruction

SETTING THE STAGE

Throughout our discussion of ARC and its importance for comprehension, we have emphasized the importance of students' conceptual awareness of the topics they study. Understanding the vocabulary of a reading selection is equally essential to its comprehension. We are referring here not only to the technical vocabulary defined in context or in a glossary, but also to the general vocabulary authors assume is familiar to their readers. If students lack familiarity with any vocabulary in a reading selection, their efforts to understand will be impeded to some degree.

Because vocabulary knowledge is such a vital factor in comprehension, it is common practice in schools to pre-teach new vocabulary before students read a selection of text, and to assume subsequently that students know the words. So why don't we just take up the cadence and go directly to a discusssion of ways to pre-teach and reinforce vocabulary? We don't because the research evidence suggests that in most classrooms the pre-teaching of vocabulary has little effect on learning (e.g., Petty, Herold, & Stoll, 1968) and that vocabulary instruction rarely affects comprehension (Anderson & Freebody, 1981). Also, we don't pick up the cadence because we don't quite hear it— our experience has led us to hear a different drummer, and we want you to listen with us a moment to see if you might hear it too.

WORDS AND CONCEPTS

■ ■ Effective vocabulary instruction is based more on an understanding of the nature of vocabulary than familiarity with a repertoire of strat-

197

egies and activities for instruction. Teachers who use vocabulary instructional strategies effectively are those who understand what vocabulary is and how it is learned. The cadence of the drummer they and we hear has vocabulary instruction embedded in the teaching of subject matter, and in the teaching of meanings and uses for words.

Vocabulary, as defined by Webster's *New Collegiate Dictionary* (1976), is "a list or collection of words or of words and phrases . . . ; a sum or stock of words employed by a language, group or individual in a field of knowledge." (p. 1310) The essence of vocabulary clearly lies in the nature of words. The Russian psychologist Lev Vygotsky (1962) provides us with a viable point of departure in our thinking: "A word without meaning is an empty sound; meaning, therefore, is a criterion of 'word,' its indispensable component." (p. 120) At the risk of oversimplifying Vygotsky, we might say a word without meaning is only a label, "an empty sound."

But, you might well ask, *when* is a word only a label? Doesn't a word inherently have meaning (excluding, of course, nonsense words)? Let's think about that. As a start, let us ask you to consider the following sentence: Betsy looked out the window and exclaimed, "Look, there's that padnag in the yard again!"

What was it that Betsy saw? Anyone who can read knows the answer, surely. Betsy saw a padnag. But what is a padnag? To answer, you must have a meaning for the word "padnag" or you're merely uttering empty sounds. Now maybe you think we're pulling your leg a little, that padnag is not a word at all. We assure you it is, though it's not a very common word. It occurs in a poem entitled "Old Man's Wish," by Pope:

> With a spacious plain, without hedge or stile,
> And an easy padnag to ride out a mile.

But we've still got the word quite separated from its meaning. We're hoping you get the idea that a WORD is comprised of a label *and* a meaning, that meaning is truly an "indispensable component" of a word. Take away meaning and you have no word. If you have no meaning for it, "padnag" for you is not a word, we would maintain. It will become a word for you only when you are able to associate a meaning with it. In this case it happens that you do have the concept for the word, but the label is probably unfamiliar to you. A padnag is a slow-moving, old, run-down horse. If you can conceptualize that, padnag is now for you a word.

The nature of word meaning goes even deeper than this. Try once more to answer the question, "What is a padnag?" but use your own words, not ours. Your answer will be what padnag means to you. Is that meaning the same as for your friends? Your colleagues? Others who have read this book? Precisely the same? We think not. Close your eyes and picture a padnag. Is what you see what we see? Probably not! Similar, yes, but not precisely the same. In that sense, at least, what a word means to any two people must be different. If word meanings were the same, exactly the same, for any two people, their experiences and their conceptualizations associated with the word (the label) would have to be exactly the same, and that is by the nature of things impossible. Reducing all this to a technical level, then, words are an individual's verbal representations of concepts, and word meanings are direct extensions of individual experiences. Words don't have meanings, really; people have meanings for words. The essence of one's vocabulary lies within the experiences one brings to words. Without the appropriate experiences and conceptualizations that cause words to be full of meaning, and hence meaningful and useful, a person has no use for them as labels. It is here we find the nature of words and how they should be taught.

Do you hear that drummer yet?

LEARNING NEW VOCABULARY

When words are perceived as verbal representations of concepts, the learning of new words can be understood to progress in a manner similar to the learning of new concepts. The logical way to pursue the learning of new words is to begin with the learning of new concepts. This need not always be true, however, for there are times when one fully understands a concept and needs only to know the word that represents that concept. That is probably what happened for you with padnag. But what often happens for students in school is they understand neither the concept nor its verbal representation. Thus, we maintain, particularly in school settings, the teaching of new words must begin with the teaching of new concepts. This is the reverse of the traditional notion that the first step in teaching concepts is to teach vocabulary. (We're getting close to the essence of *our* drummer's cadence.)

As we emphasized in our discussion of anticipation, the learning of new concepts, or the elaboration of known concepts, begins when one relates existing awarenesses, experiences, and understandings to an exploration of new ideas. As new ideas come into focus and become understood, one is compelled to find an economical way to express those ideas and to relate those newly learned ideas to other ideas. Until one understands a concept, there is neither need nor desire to communicate the idea or to explore it further.

In a related sense, the learning of new words is also a matter of entitlement; that is, one is not entitled to a new word until he or she has a need or a use for it. James Michener provides an apt example of this when he describes something that happened to Potato Brumbaugh in *Centennial:*

> He was only a peasant, but like all men with seminal ideas, he found the words to express himself. He had heard a professor use the words "imprison" and "replenishment" and he understood immediately what the man had meant, for he, Brumbaugh, had discovered the concept before he heard the word, but when he did hear it, the word was automatically his, for he had already absorbed the idea which entitled him to the symbol. (p. 678)

There are two important points to be made here. First, there are times when people have a good concept for a word, and when the word is met in speech or print it is as surely theirs as if they had invented it themselves. But, and this is our second point, there are also times when people encounter words for which they have no concepts, and in this case, no amount of teaching of those words *per se* is *ever* going to make the words theirs. The learning of new words begins with the learning of new concepts.

■ Evolution of Word Meanings

We have yet to mention one important dimension of words and word meanings: word meanings are fluid and dynamic, not static. As Margaret Donaldson (1978) puts it, "It is a common but naive assumption that the understanding of a word is an all-or-none affair! You either understand it or you don't. But this is not so. Knowledge of word meaning grows, it undergoes development and change." (p. 75) Just as a teacher's meaning for a word is not a student's meaning, so too a student's meaning does not remain constant, especially if the student is learning more and more about concepts that words represent. Meanings develop and change as the understandings of concepts evolve.

This brings us to the basic premise that supports all our suggestions about teaching vocabulary, the essence of our drummer's cadence: *effective vocabulary instruction is responsive to the evolutionary development of students' understandings of concepts.* We ask you to keep this in mind as you examine with us an approach to pre-teaching vocabulary based on this premise, which has been validated to be highly effective (Vaughan, Castle, Gilbert, & Love, 1982).

PRE-TEACHING VOCABULARY

■ ■ The purpose of pre-teaching vocabulary should not focus on the development of readers' vocabularies; instead, the focus should be on facilitating readers' comprehension. Our observations suggest that words introduced prior to students' interaction with concepts are usually little more than labels, empty sounds. At best, students have only a superficial understanding of the meanings of terms typically pre-taught; in effect, students are not yet "entitled" to the symbols. Let us clarify this important notion.

Assume that we want you to read an article about the relationship between a theoretical perspective on reading and ways to teach based on that perspective. Included in that article are several important technical terms: *ideational, subsuming, schemata, and macrostructure.* How might we pre-teach that vocabulary for you? We know several traditional ways; how do you react to them?

Approach Number One:

We want you to read a selection in which the following words appear:

> ideational
> subsuming
> schemata
> macrostructure

Before you read, however, look up these words in a dictionary. Write out the definitions and keep them close at hand when you read.

Approach Number Two:

Look up the following words in a dictionary and, using the definitions, correctly use each in a separate sentence:

> ideational
> subsuming
> schemata
> macrostructure

Share your sentences with another student and compare your uses of the terms. We will discuss your sentences before you read.

Approach Number Three:

Before you read this selection, look over the definitions of the following terms that we have provided you on this sheet:

ideational:	related in some way to ideas or concepts, especially as they are in the formative stages
subsuming:	integrated with; a part of, especially when something is a small portion of a larger element
schemata:	(*pl.* of schema) the dynamic and changeable

representation of ideas, especially as they are related to other ideas

macrostructure: hierarchically, the top-level ideas; the most important ideas presented in a selection

Do you have any questions about these definitions? Keep this list handy as you read.

Approach Number Four:
Use the definitions of the words given to you in Approach Number Three. For each word, write a sentence in which you use it correctly.

Approach Number Five:
After doing any one of the exercises above, write a paragraph using all four of these words appropriately.

What is your reaction to these exercises? Each of these approaches we have shared in this exercise was taken verbatim from classroom observations; only the vocabulary words have been changed to present you with words you are not likely to know. Although the intent of each of these approaches may be to familiarize you with words and their meanings, the focus is clearly on the labels. This would have become even more apparent to you if you had actually tried to accomplish the tasks in any of these approaches. Had you looked for these words in a dictionary, even a good dictionary, you would not have found macrostructure, and the primary definitions for the other terms do not resemble the usage in a selection on reading theory. In those approaches where we gave you appropriate definitions, we used the sort of terminology found in teachers' manuals or in glossaries because that is what students most often rely on. We suspect that even when we gave you definitions, they may have been insufficient for you to consider these terms "your words" in light of your conceptual development relative to these terms.

Perhaps this brief encounter with new words, important though they may be, will remind you of what students encounter daily with these kinds of vocabulary activities. Perhaps too it has led you to understand more clearly why we contend that labels should be avoided until it is clear students understand the concepts those labels represent. Even if you use the technical terms in your introduction of concepts, as textbooks often do, students will hear "empty sounds" and that leaves gaps that confuse rather than facilitate. We doubt that students generally have enough conceptual awareness of those types of words that are typically pre-taught (for example, technical terms) to justify pre-teaching these terms as labels. The only situation in which the pre-teaching of labels might be appropriate occurs when the students *clearly* understand the concepts and the only thing new is the labels. As we discussed earlier in this chapter, however, we must determine the level of conceptual awareness through discussion and exploration, never assuming what we should be teaching (Herber, 1978).

It may seem that we are boxing ourselves into saying that vocabulary should not be pre-taught. That is not quite true. We fully recognize that much of what students are expected to read, especially in content area textbooks, is laden with precise, technical language. We also realize the difficulties students will encounter learning the concepts unless they know the terms, because the textbooks rely so heavily on the terms to explain the concepts. Sounds a lot like catch-22, doesn't it? It is, and the only way around the catch is for teachers to intervene in the reader-text connection.

■ Preparation for Pre-teaching Vocabulary

The purpose of pre-teaching vocabulary is to facilitate reader comprehension. There are three fundamental steps in the preparation for pre-teaching vocabulary:

1. Identify the concepts you want to emphasize during the lesson;
2. Determine the key vocabulary words that are essential to understanding the concepts specified in step one;
3. Identify words that (a) reflect approximately the same concepts as the key vocabulary words chosen in step two *and* (b) are words the students would be familiar with.

To apply these steps appropriately, you probably need to know why we suggest these steps in particular. The primary purpose of identifying concepts for emphasis is to help to focus instructional objectives. Identification of concepts tends to shift the emphasis from details to broader perspectives. When teachers establish and maintain their instructional focus on general concepts, concepts that students are more likely to remember than empty labels, a context is created, a gestalt that gives greater meaning to the ideas being considered. This context or gestalt provides a framework that students can use to learn subconcepts and details, because students can perceive the subconcepts and details in relation to the broader framework and to one another.

As we mentioned earlier, many expository textbooks found in classrooms rely on technical vocabulary to convey and explain essential concepts. If you doubt this, examine some of the textbooks for your classroom. Because this is true more often than not, our second step in preparing to pre-teach vocabulary is intended to help in identifying those terms that are *essential* to students' understanding of the concepts to be emphasized. You must notice here that the vocabulary chosen for pre-teaching should be limited to those *few* words that students must know if they are to understand the key concepts. For reasons that we don't really understand, there is a tendency to pre-teach too many words, and this creates a problem for teachers and students alike. Teachers often find little gained by the time spent in pre-teaching, and the activities tend to leave students confused. This is particularly true in subjects like science, health, and social studies.

Consider all that we have discussed about the relationship between prior knowledge and comprehension and the nature of learning new words. Examine the way textbooks in your classroom tend to introduce and use new, technical terms. Until you realize the degree to which vocabulary and the learning of new concepts are interrelated, you will not appreciate the difficulties that some of your students might have.

The object of pre-teaching anything, concepts or terms, is to facilitate new learning. Evaluating the situation in your classroom will determine your instructional objectives. If you pre-teach too many new concepts or new words you may inadvertently stress words and concepts that are not essential to students' understanding of the most important ideas; you may also inadvertently overload students with excessive words and concepts that confound understanding rather than facilitate learning. We suggest that as you decide what should be pre-taught to facilitate students' learning, you make your choices judiciously. You will minimize potential difficulties when you perceive the pre-teaching of vocabulary as an opportunity to familiarize students with important concepts rather than new terms. When you maintain this perspective, you will naturally limit the number of new words and concepts to those that will facilitate comprehension of important ideas.

We should emphasize in passing that those key terms you choose to pre-teach may or may not be new to the students. The pre-teaching of vocabulary need not be, nor should it be, restricted to *new* words. Often textbook authors use terms to explain new concepts that the authors assume students will know, when in fact, the students may have either no experience with the terms (they may know the concepts but not the labels) or their experience with those terms is too limited to help them learn the new concepts. For us, vocabulary instruction is inseparable from the learning of concepts; therefore, the pre-teaching of vocabulary must proceed within the context of pre-teaching concepts.

At times the pre-teaching of concepts may be most appropriately facilitated with a combination of familiar and new vocabulary.

For students to be prepared for new labels, they need first to understand the concepts the labels represent, preferably in terms the students understand. If you share this view with us, the third step in the preparation for pre-teaching vocabulary may be self-explanatory. Since the pre-teaching of anything should evolve from a discussion of concepts and terms familiar to the students, as your point of departure you must first identify those terms and concepts that likely will be familiar to most of the students you are teaching.

To facilitate your understanding of how to apply the three steps in preparing to pre-teach vocabulary, let us share with you our plans for a textbook selection, "How Did People Live During the Middle Ages?" If you feel comfortable with our discussion to this point, you might prefer to work through each of the steps yourself before examining what we did. If you do so, keep in mind that this selection is intended for use with sixth graders.

How Did People Live During the Middle Ages?

After the fall of Rome a way of life called feudalism developed in Europe. Under the feudal system, the land in a kingdom belonged to the king or to the high nobles, who were usually dukes or counts. A high noble would grant the use of parts of his land to lesser nobles. These lesser nobles then became his vassals. Each vassal took an oath of loyalty to his lord. He promised to support his lord in any quarrel, and to supply him with arms and men when they were needed.

The nobles lived in huge stone castles. Most castles had high walls and were surrounded by a water-filled ditch called a moat. One entered the castle by crossing a drawbridge, which could be raised and lowered. With the drawbridge raised, the moat made it almost impossible for enemies to enter the castle. In times of danger, the people took shelter behind the castle walls.

Outside the castle walls were the farm fields and the small, crude homes of the serfs. Serfs were farmers who lived on the estate of a noble. In return for the protection of the noble, serfs gave the noble part of their crops. Serfs were also expected to take care of the noble's roads, fences, and fields.

Most of the common people in the Middle Ages were serfs. There were a few free farmers, but it was difficult for them to live without the protection of a noble. The serf could not leave the land without permission from his lord, but the serf was not a slave. He could not be sold like a slave. However, he had few rights and his life was not very happy. Serfs worked hard and barely made a living.

The Middle Ages was a time of thousands of small wars. Much of the fighting was done by knights, who were warriors on horseback. Only the son of a noble could become a knight. Knights had special equipment and special training and even a special code of behavior, called the code of chivalry. Chivalry comes from a French word meaning "man on a horse." Knights were expected to be loyal to their nobles, to protect the weak, and to be courteous to women.

A young noble started training to be a knight by first becoming a page. As a page he was expected to learn proper manners and to serve as a sort of messenger boy in the castle. When he was about fifteen years old, the young page became a squire. As a squire he was taught to ride a horse and to use a sword, lance, and battle-ax. The squire became a full-fledged knight when he was about twenty-one. He then entered the service of a noble to whom he took an oath of loyalty. Every knight hoped that someday he would receive his own lands and become a lord in his own right. Many knights never did become lords and lived out their lives fighting endless wars.

In the Middle Ages most people believed that a man was born into a certain station in life. They felt nothing could change that station. Most people believed that kings and nobles were born to rule, and that common people were born to work and to obey. They thought that was how things had always been and always would be.

The key concepts we identified for the study of this selection were the following:

1. During the Middle Ages, people believed that a few people were born to be rulers, but that most people were born to work for their rulers.
2. The rulers were kings and nobles who owned land and protected the other people.
3. Most people were farmers, called serfs, who farmed the land owned by the king and nobles.
4. Some people were soldiers, called knights, who protected the king and nobles and their lands.

These concepts may seem to be too general to you. For us, they reflect the essence of the selection, its broad context, and when considered together, these concepts represent a general idea we might reasonably expect students to remember several years after their study. Too, we have expressed these concepts in terms students will understand after they complete their study. Notice that each concept is expressed in a complete sentence; we have found that complete sentences, unlike phrases, clarify and specify the concepts as we hope students will understand them. Had we simply listed "serfs," "kings," "nobles," and "soldiers" as new words, we would not have specified the concepts we wanted students to learn.

The key words that we deemed essential to facilitate students' understanding of the major concepts are listed in the order in which we would introduce them: rulers, kings, nobles, serfs, knights.

Words familiar to students that could be used to begin a discussion of these concepts are:

rulers: people in charge
kings: rulers of a country
nobles: rulers of parts of the country
serfs: farmers, laborers, servants
knights: warriors, soldiers, officers

Before we discuss how to pre-teach the vocabulary for this selection, we must point out that our choice of how to pre-teach is only *a* choice, not the *only* choice. There may be other ways to accomplish the same objectives and there may well be other concepts, even different concepts, that you or another teacher might want to emphasize. In fact, if you followed our suggestion and prepared to pre-teach this selection before you looked at our plan, you may well have designed a very different sort of lesson plan. But certainly if you have a different plan and followed the framework of what we proposed your plan may well be every bit as effective as ours.

The actual presentation of the lesson should follow steps similar to those for preparing to pre-teach except that the order of the steps is changed a bit:

Steps for Pre-teaching Vocabulary

1. Discuss with students the familiar words or phrases that reflect the concepts to be emphasized. Initially, this discussion should be kept within a context familiar to the students.
2. As the discussion evolves, introduce the meaning of the terms as they will be treated in the selection to be read.
3. After discussion of the concept as it is treated in the selection, then introduce students to the new label.

NOTE: Each of the key terms should be introduced in turn using each of these steps. It is also helpful to continue to use key terms (labels) that have already been introduced during earlier portions of such discussions. (Notice as you work your way through our plan that we discuss the concept of each word before introducing its corresponding label, and that as the lesson proceeds we reinforce words introduced earlier in the discussion.)

Lesson Plan to Pre-teach Vocabulary
for
"How Did People Live During the Middle Ages?"
(*The script is intended for demonstration purposes only.*)

Before we get to the chapter we will be discussing today, there are some ideas I want to discuss with you that will help you understand this chapter better.

To begin with, who can tell me who's in charge of this school? What do we call this person? What does he or she do?

Now, then, who helps the principal and what do they do? (Construct a list on the board and discuss responses.) Can we make a chart of these people and what they do? (Notice the similarity of what we're suggesting here and the categorical overview activity we discussed earlier.)

Now who can tell me who's in charge of our country? What do we call someone who's in charge of a country? (Discuss various titles.)

While we have lots of different names for people who are in charge of countries, there's one term that can be used to mean all of these different titles, and the term I'm thinking of is "ruler." (Write the word *ruler* on the board.)

That's right, Wanda, it's the same word as the ruler you have on your desk, but it means something different. You see, a word can mean different things. OK, a ruler is a person in charge of a country. Why do you think that such a person is called a ruler? (Discuss responses, making the connection between rulers and someone who makes rules.)

In this chapter you'll find out about two kinds of rulers. One is called a king. (Write "king" on the board.) What do you know about kings? (Discuss their responses.)

Now remember, I said we'd learn about two kinds of rulers. A long time ago, in the Middle Ages, when kings ruled countries, each country was divided into parts. While the king was in charge of the whole country, some other people were in charge of each part of the country. And these other people were called nobles. (Write "nobles" on the board.)

Now, who can tell us why the king needed some nobles to be in charge of parts of the country? (Discuss their responses; use the comparison of governors of states if necessary to stimulate further discussion.) (If they don't mention it, include a comment about the difficulty of getting from place to place in those times. Build the concept of the conditions of the time.)

The king is in charge of the country and the rulers of the parts of the country were nobles. Also in each part of the country, there were lots of other people. What do you think those people did? (List responses on the board. Then arrange the list in a categorical overview.)

Ok, we have a pretty good list. In this selection you will find out about kings and nobles and some other people who did certain things during the time we call the Middle Ages. Let's talk about a couple more terms you'll see in this selection.

Theresa, you said that some of the people were probably farmers. You are right, but they were different from farmers we know today. These farmers grew crops and gave part of their crops to the nobles and to the king. These farmers were called serfs. (Write "serfs" on the board.) And what do you think the nobles and the king gave the serfs in return for the crops? (Discuss their responses.) OK, those were all good answers, but there's one thing you didn't mention. The king and the nobles keep each part of the country safe from robbers and other people who wanted to take away the land. Remember earlier when John said that some of the people were probably soldiers? Well, he was right and the soldiers helped protect the people and the king and the nobles. They were there to be sure other people didn't try to take over the land and hurt the serfs. Some of these soldiers were officers, just like we have officers in our army and our police force. In medieval times, these officers were the sons of the nobles. Only the sons of the nobles could be officers, and they were called knights. (Write "knights" on the board.) So what we'll be studying today is how people lived in a time long ago when there were kings, nobles, knights, and serfs. This was during a time called the medieval period (write "medieval" on the board above the other words) or what we often call the Middle Ages. (Write "Middle Ages" in parentheses next to "medieval.") After you read this chapter, we'll talk about why this period is called medieval, or the Middle Ages.

And so the vocabulary introduction lesson is complete and the students are, we hope, ready to read. What we have attempted to do in this lesson is to introduce students to the concepts they will explore as they study this chapter. Because the concepts within the chapter are presented with many new terms, students need some familiarity with the key terms they will meet.

Notice, however, by re-examining the selection itself, that we did not introduce any other of the many new terms that might often be pre-taught. We did not include, for example, *feudalism, counts, vassal, moat, chivalry,* or *station.* The students will come to understand these concepts through their reading and through further discussion after the reading. There are two other things we might mention about the terms we included in the list of words not pre-taught. First, if you reread the selection, you'll notice how incompletely the text deals with these terms. They are tossed in with little regard for the superficiality of the discussion that was intended to explain these concepts. That suggests our second point about these terms: if you want the students to know and understand these terms you will have to plan for considerable discussion after the reading.

Before we leave this passage and our experience with a sixth grade class who read it, we must share with you something that we could not have predicted. One student in particular was very concerned about the serfs and the protection they were to receive in times of war. His concern stemmed, we finally discovered, from this particular part of the selection:

> The nobles lived in huge stone castles. Most castles had high walls and were surrounded by a water-filled ditch called a moat. One entered the castle by crossing a drawbridge, which could be raised and lowered. With the drawbridge raised, the moat made it almost impossible for enemies to enter the castle. In times of danger, the people took shelter behind the castle walls.

Can you guess what in this segment caused Donald to be concerned? It was the phrase "the people took shelter behind the castle walls." He perceived that in times of danger, the drawbridge was pulled up to protect the soldiers and the nobles or the king. The people were left outside and they took shelter behind (in back of) the walls. If the enemy were attacking in the front of the castle, the serfs were protected. If the enemy came around to the back, they would be in real trouble. Donald was much relieved to learn that "behind the castle walls" meant inside the walls of the castle, within the castle walls. However, explaining this concept wasn't easy because Donald moved from having the serfs outside the castle to inside the walls. He didn't quite understand how they got put inside the walls. Were the insides of the walls big enough for all the serfs and their families? Give us an infinite number of chances to predict the difficulties children will have with text, and we'll never predict them all.

In conclusion, let us say that the pre-teaching of vocabulary, as we have discussed it here, applies to any instructional situation. It is not limited to a particular reading selection, or for that matter to reading. The key vocabulary for an entire unit or course can be pre-taught effectively in this manner, likewise for a film, slide-show, recording, or lecture. One need only remember that the learning of vocabulary begins with the learning of concepts. With that idea established, we can now move to further consideration of how to develop the vocabulary of readers.

PREMISES FOR LEARNING VOCABULARY

The following two premises will summarize the discussion to this point: (1) the learning of vocabulary begins with the learning of concepts, and (2) one's learning of vocabulary is evolutionary.

Consider how many students have heard the terms *sine, cosine, tangent, cotangent, secant, cosecant,* and yet have never understood the concept of trigometric functions? How many have learned to spell and copied definitions for terms like *tragedy, climax,* and *denouement;* or *sonnet, epic, meter, verse, cadence,* and *metaphor*? It would have been possible for these same students to have understood the concepts related to these words *before* encountering the words. Lacking the concepts, the words remain hollow shells in the recesses of most people's memories.

To base vocabulary instruction on our first premise alone, however, is not sufficient to insure effective vocabulary learning. Recall Donaldson's comment that vocabulary is not an all-or-none affair. Students' understandings of words *evolve;* understandings do not suddenly emerge full-grown and then remain fixed.

One's learning of anything begins with awareness, extends through understanding, and subsequently progresses to remembering and application. So it is with learning vocabulary. Awareness of words emerges during anticipation when certain key concepts are introduced and explored. Understanding evolves as realization occurs, during reading, for example. Remembering and application appear as the learner synthesizes understanding and prepares to demonstrate that he or she is entitled to the word(s). The pre-teaching of vocabulary, as we have discussed, sets the stage for understanding to occur during personalized study. Let us now consider activities you can use to help students increase their usable vocabulary, activities that appropriately fit it into the contemplation stage of ARC.

VOCABULARY DEVELOPMENT IN THE CLASSROOM

■ ■ Plans for any unit of study should include specification of concepts to be emphasized, description of experiences that will lead to understanding those concepts, and identification of precise, new vocabulary that will be important as students progress toward those understandings. The question this raises, then, is: What vocabulary should you specify for emphasis in a unit?

In some instances the question of what vocabulary to highlight seems easily answered. In math and science, for example, technical terminology is often highlighted by textbook authors. But should a teacher rely on textbook authors to identify vocabulary for emphasis? Actually, we think not. Our own rule of thumb is this: Vocabulary important enough to teach is vocabulary essential to an understanding of the concepts being taught. Since a single textbook provides only one avenue for learning major concepts, highlighted vocabulary in a text provides only a general clue to the words that should be emphasized.

The best way to determine the vocabulary for emphasis in a unit of study is to form a list of all the possible terms you consider relevant to each of the concepts to be studied. In doing so, you can include terminology at various levels of sophistication. In effect, we are suggesting you make a concerted inspection of the vocabulary for each topic of study. From that inspection, choose the vocabulary that should be emphasized.

For example, when planning a lesson on forms of government, a social studies teacher might list this and similar concepts for emphasis: "Democracy is government 'of the people, by the people, for the people.'" What are the important words that come to mind when we recite this idea? Equality, representative government, constitution, self-government, home rule, vote, Congress, law, populace, people, public, majority rule, common man, silent majority, plebeian, proletariat, democrat, republican, and so forth. Dozens of words can be listed. In effect, a thesaurus can be built for the unit as terms relevant to each concept are listed. From this list the teacher can select those words that, at various levels of sophistication, represent the kernel or basic ideas underlying each concept. Certainly not all the vocabulary relevant to a concept will come to have meaning for all students. However, from such a broadly inclusive list, a teacher can select words of varied sophistication and incorporate them into a variety of exercises designed to enhance vocabulary development for students of varying ability.

INTRODUCING THE LABELS

Throughout previous discussions, we have emphasized that prior knowledge is a major contributor to new learning and it stands to reason that this is basic to our notion of teaching vocabulary. Recall also our assertion that the purpose for pre-teaching vocabulary is to facilitate reader comprehension rather than to build students' vocabularies. The proper time for students to increase their stock of labels is *after* they have conceptualized the essence of word meanings that the labels represent. In this case, "conceptualized" means, for us, that students have come to know *of* the concept; one need not fully understand a concept before being entitled to its label. In fact, given the vocabulary/concept paradox, a full understanding of a concept may be impossible without knowledge of the label. Thus, the most appropriate context for the acquisition of labels is in the setting of contemplation. When vocabulary development is integrated with contemplation, the new labels can be introduced in the context of synthesizing ideas that have recently become familiar. The exact timing of the introduction of new labels is impossible to specify because it should come when students' evolution of the concept can make the label useful. The timing is very important and it will become easier for you to determine the right timing if you hold steadfast to this guideline: *teach vocabulary and concepts as part and parcel of the same thing and keep both in close proximity to ideas and terms with which students are already familiar.*

VOCABULARY ACTIVITIES

Like Potato Brumbaugh, students will naturally "pick up" some of the vocabulary of any subject as they come to understand it better, much as young children acquire words to express relationships they have come to understand. Through their experience with activities related to concepts, the words used to express the concepts will become more meaningful. Experience with words in specific vocabulary activities is essential, however. Vocabulary cannot be left to chance without considerable risk: risk either that words may have little or incomplete meaning for learners or that learners may lack the proper terminology in which to express their understandings. Vocabulary activities must be designed to allow systematic exploration of words in relation to concepts, phenomena, and other words. What follows is a series of suggested activities that allows for such exploration.

Vocabulary Reinforcement Activities

Through the pre-teaching of vocabulary and by reading the assignments, students will develop an awareness and understanding of the words, but the time arrives when they are entitled to make the words their own. This occurs during the contemplation phase. On the following pages, we illustrate various types of vocabulary exercises that can be used as reinforcement activities. We encourage you to develop these activities for students, but more strongly we urge you to have your students engage in creating vocabulary exercises.

■ Designed by Students

Learning vocabulary, like learning concepts, requires active involvement. While we can wish for students to increase their vocabularies, our desire can become reality only when we provide time and opportunity for students' involvement. We fully realize that considerable time and effort is required to construct good vocabulary exercises and that teachers often do not have the necessary time. Therefore, we strongly encourage you to teach your students various formats for vocabulary activities and have them construct activities for other students to complete. While you may want to identify certain terms they should include, you can also encourage them to use words they think are important as well.

We have found that when teachers follow this suggestion, their students "get turned on to words," and their vocabulary development surpasses imagination. Of perhaps greater benefit, students begin to develop a sense of words that carries over to future learning of vocabulary. While the students often find such involvement to be great fun (if you don't believe us, try it), the teacher accomplishes a major goal at no great expense in time or effort. When finished, you will have upwards of thirty vocabulary exercises per class as compared to one or two you might be able to accomplish in an evening. Completion of other students' vocabulary activities can be required or students might receive extra credit; they also serve as magnificent "time fillers" at the end of classes.

Frank Molina, a vocational agriculture teacher, devised a system whereby students could earn extra credit on the unit test based on vocabulary activities. He gave two points extra credit for each vocabulary exercise that included at least fifteen "unit words" up to a maximum of six points. He also awarded one point extra credit for every two puzzles correctly completed up to a maximum of four points. Thus, students could earn up to ten points extra credit, but more importantly, they learned the vocabulary. Student involvement—à la Molina & Wigginton—is a dimension too often forgotten or ignored.

Now consider the following examples of vocabulary activities and then hustle down to a nearby drugstore for word puzzle books that will suggest other varieties of activities to develop and reinforce students' vocabulary.

□ *Matching Exercises*
This type of exercise seems very simple, and in fact it is little more than a recognition exercise. It does, however, concern meaning. Vocabulary items are listed in two columns on a sheet, in random order.

They may be synonyms, antonyms, roots and derivatives, terms and definitions, etc. The task for the learner is to match the items in one column with those in the other. The form is familiar:

```
_____ 1. ........  a. ........
_____ 2. ........  b. ........
_____ 3. ........  c. ........
_____ 4. ........  d. ........
```

Students are asked to place the lowercase letters in the blanks before the arabic numerals to indicate a match between the items. Consider this exercise:

_____	1. diamonds	a. lowest suit
_____	2. spades	b. one suit higher than clubs
_____	3. clubs	c. one suit higher than diamonds
_____	4. hearts	d. highest suit

The novice bridge player who works this exercise may become more familiar with the relationship among suits. Notice that the exercise tends to be self-correcting. If a mistake is made, it is apparent in the failure of a subsequent match. In other words, a person can reason his or her way to the correct answer even if he or she has only partial understanding of the terms. This is a desirable feature of such exercises since it allows relatively more teaching and less testing. All exercises should have this feature built in whenever possible.

Here is another exercise of the same type, again set up so that errors are somewhat self-correcting. Match the symbols on the right (lettered a, b, c, etc.) with the definitions on the left (numbered 1, 2, 3, etc.) by placing letters in the blanks before the numbers. If you come to a definition that you cannot at first match with a symbol, skip it and go on. From those matches of which you are sure, you may be able to figure out the ones of which you are unsure.

	Definitions	*Symbols*
_____	1. identical with	a. $>$
_____	2. not identical with	b. $=$
_____	3. not greater than	c. $\equiv$
_____	4. equal to	d. $<$
_____	5. is to; ratio	e. $\neq$
_____	6. greater than	f. $\geq$ or $\gtreqless$

_____ 7. greater than or equal to   g. $\approx$

_____ 8. not equal to   h. $\not>$

_____ 9. less than   i. :

_____ 10. congruent to   j. $\neq$

Some of the symbols in this exercise may be unfamiliar to students, but almost all will know at least the equals sign. By deduction and elimination the others may be reasoned out if the student has even the vaguest idea of how the definitions and symbols fit. For example, if = means "equals," the best guess for "not equal" might be $\neq$, which is correct. By deduction, | must mean "not." If the student couldn't remember > and <, he could deduce it from $\not>$, "not greater than." Notice that $\not<$, "not less than," is not included since to have done so would have been to require complete knowledge of the symbols being taught.

Many exercises of the matching type are, unfortunately, better tests than teaching tools. It is admittedly more difficult to build the self-correcting (for example, teaching) feature in, but it is that feature more than any other that makes such exercises worthwhile.

☐ _Categorization Exercises_

One of the best and most flexible of meaning exercises, the categorization exercise may frequently serve as a good follow-up to matching and other types of exercises. The basic form of the exercise is the categorical column head based on concepts to which terms are related. For example, an exercise related to a unit on nutrition might look like this:

DIRECTIONS   The basic food groups are carbohydrates, proteins, and fats. Certain foods are known for their particularly high content of these substances. List these foods under the group with which each is associated: cheese, butter, cereal, fruits, corn oil, fish, shortening, flour, bacon, drippings, eggs, sugars, milk, vegetables, olive oil. Then add other foods you think might be closely related to one or another basic group.

Carbohydrates	_Proteins_	_Fats_
_____	_____	_____
_____	_____	_____
_____	_____	_____
_____	_____	_____
_____	_____	_____
_____	_____	_____

Students should be allowed to discuss their categorizations in small groups following completion of this sorting exercise. The categorization exercise will be most effective when:

1. Students have completed reading something that discusses the concepts used as column heads.
2. Either before or after the reading, but preceding the categorization exercise, students have completed a recognition or word study exercise (to be explained presently) that used vocabulary similar to that in the categorization exercise.
3. As they complete their categorizations, students can refer to the reading selections in which the vocabulary and ideas used in the exercise appear.
4. Students are allowed to compare their responses to the exercise in small groups. The task of the group is to resolve any differences and to present the group's completed categorizations to the rest of the class or to submit it as a group effort.

In the atmosphere described by these conditions, the pressure for the "right" answer may be relieved. In fact, there may often be no right answer, only various defendable choices. Being able to make and defend choices in the face of good and better reasoning is the most important lesson anyone can learn about vocabulary. The categorization exercise can demonstrate this and that is its strongest asset as a vocabulary development tool.

☐ *Crossword Puzzles*
Long a favorite of word hounds of all ages, the crossword puzzle can be found on almost any topic through educational supply houses. Many people enjoy working them, and there can be little doubt that they foster curiosity about words.

For classroom use, especially where the objective is to build students' familiarity with particular words, the teacher-made crossword may serve best. It allows the teacher opportunity to use words most closely related to concepts under study and to associate the words with most appropriate definitions. Despite their complicated look, they are also rather easy to construct. Using either graph paper or a Scrabble board and tiles and working from a list of conceptually related terms, a crossword puzzle can usually be worked out in less than an hour. What it may lack in professional appearance will improve with practice and is more than made up for by the effectiveness of the activity and the enthusiasm it generates among the students. Let's look at some examples.

For a fifth grade unit on oceans, one instructor developed a crossword puzzle that does more than provide her students a chance for vocabulary reinforcement. Notice that this one includes several multiple meaning words that also extend students' word knowledge, for example, the clues for one across and eleven down.

ACROSS

1. a shellfish; to *shut* up
2. periwinkle; s-l-o-w
3. very well "armed"
4. flat, tasty fish; struggle
5. has a "pearly" shell
11. Jaws; a tricky person

DOWN

1. an 8-legged shellfish; a grouch
2. the giant is deadly
7. is caught in a pot
8. a very "bright" fish; You may see it in the sky!
9. has many stingers; Great with peanut butter.
10. underwater mammal; huge
11. small, curved shellfish; a puny person

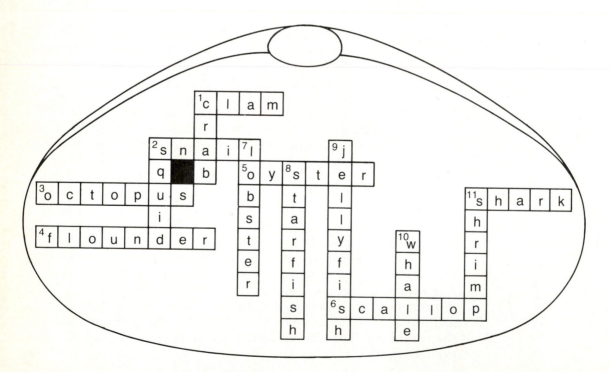

Here's an example from an eleventh grade unit on grammatical elements related to composition skills. We'll let you try your hand at this one.

CROSSWORD PUZZLE

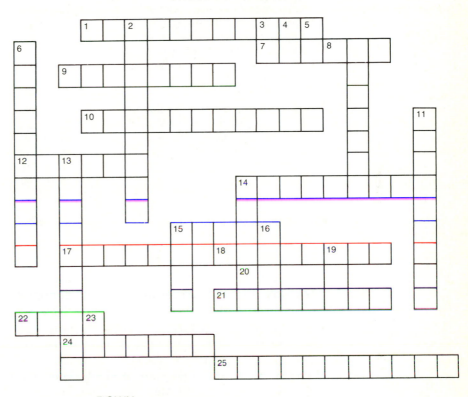

DOWN

2. _____ Clause: A clause that depends on another clause in the sentence.
3. Tap dancer Eleanor Powell's initials.
4. Abbreviation for New Hampshire.
5. Theodore Roosevelt's initials.
6. A verb form that modifies nouns and pronouns.
8. The person or thing about which a verb asks a question or makes a statement.
11. _____ verb: A verb that does not use *ed* or *d* in the past participle.

13. A noun or pronoun placed beside another noun or pronoun to explain it more fully.
14. _____ Clause: A clause used to modify verbs, adjectives, and adverbs.
15. A word or group of words used to express action or being.
16. A period is used when a sentence _____.
19. _____ Clause: A clause used in any way that a noun may be used.
23. A direction.

CROSSWORD PUZZLE, *continued*

ACROSS

1. _____ Clause: A clause that can stand alone.
7. A group of words without a subject and verb, used as a single word in a sentence.
9. Two or more simple sentences joined by a coordinating conjunction.
10. A word that connects sentences, clauses, phrases, or words.
12. Part of a sentence, with a subject and verb.
14. _____ Clause: A clause used to modify verbs, adjectives, and adverbs.
15. Enthusiasm; energy; vigor

17. _____ Sentence: A sentence with only one subject and one verb.
18. A group of words that expresses a complete thought.
20. Abbreviation for *road*.
21. _____ Phrase: Phrases that have no grammatical connection with any part of a sentence but are related in meaning.
22. _____ Clause: A clause that can stand alone as a sentence.
24. Verb forms that are used as nouns, adjectives, or adverbs.
25. _____ Conjunction: connects a subordinate clause with a main clause.

Individuals or groups of students often enjoy making their own crossword puzzles. The reading and discussion involved in group construction is often most rewarding as it requires close examination of the concepts under study and the terminology in which those concepts are expressed. In addition, if other students have a chance to work the puzzles constructed by their peers, chances are the level of difficulty of the puzzles and the words used in the exercises will be appropriate. In fact, we have found that student-made puzzles are often more effective learning activities than those made by teachers. Making puzzles may be more instructional than working them.

A word of caution, however, on student-made puzzles: it is vital that you take the time to instruct students in exactly how to make them. The time you spend modeling this activity will pay off in the long run with less confusion on the part of your students. We have found the following simple instructions useful when launching students on this project:

1. Start with the concepts to be reinforced.
2. List the words that reflect those concepts. They become the answers in your puzzle.
3. Arrange the words into a crossword puzzle configuration. Use either graph paper or a Scrabble board to simplify this task.

4. Create clues or descriptions to go with each word.
5. Set the clues up into "down" and "across" categories to correspond to the puzzle design. Number the clues and boxes in the design to coincide.
6. Transfer the outline of the squares for the crossword puzzle onto a ditto or paper for duplication.

Once you have collected your student-made puzzles you can either duplicate the best ones for class use or merely have students exchange and work each other's puzzles. We have found that students benefit greatly from the time they have spent wrestling with concepts and meanings in their creation of a crossword puzzle and their final products often outshine ours!

☐ *Magic Squares*
The magic square is another popular puzzle format with an unusual twist. This puzzle has a self-correcting aspect because students are not only matching words and meanings, but are also looking for a "magic number" as well. If the correct meanings are matched with the terms, the numbers in each straight row (not diagonal row) will add up to the same total.

As with most matching puzzle formats, this one can be made more difficult by adding foils, or extra clues that will not be used.

Here's an example taken from an earth science lesson:

5 geologist	3 fold	7 strata
9 crustal movement	4 sediments	2 pressure
1 decompose	8 fault	6 salt domes

DIRECTIONS: Put the number of the clue below in the square with the appropriate term. Check your answers by adding the numbers to see if the sums of all rows both down and across add up to the same "magic number." The magic number is 15.

Clues:

1. to decay or break down the original parts.
2. A bearing-down or squeezing.
3. A wave-like tendency seen in rock formations due to pressure and heat.
4. The fragments and solutions of decayed and crumbled rock.
5. One who studies the history of the earth as recorded in its rocks.
6. Formations caused by masses of salt in the earth reacting to heat and pressure.
7. Layers.
8. A break in the continuity of a rock formation.
9. The shifting and settling of the earth's strata.

Given below are some additional numerical combinations that add up to a magic number. Those that do not include all consecutive numbers 1–9, or 1–16 include foils in the definitions.

7	2	9
8	6	4
3	10	5

5	7	9
12	8	1
4	6	11

10	8	6
2	9	13
12	7	5

3	2	16	13
10	11	5	8
6	7	9	12
15	14	4	1

12	18	7	2
15	11	5	8
3	6	17	13
9	4	10	16

☐ *Central Word Puzzles*
A variation and simplification of the crossword is the central word puzzle. These are very easy to construct and simple to work, but they are appropriate for students who might be unable to work the more complicated, traditional crossword.

As an example, you might work the following puzzle. The central word expresses the major concept under consideration.

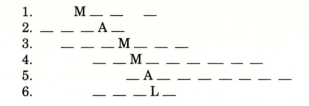

1.   M __ __   __
2. __ __ __ A __
3.   __ __ __ M __ __ __
4.   __ __ M __ __ __ __ __ __
5.   __ A __ __ __ __ __ __
6.   __ __ __ L __

1. small powerful burrowers (pl.)
2. rabbit-like, small, and almost tailless; also called conies (pl.)
3. the order that includes monkeys, apples, and humans
4. probably the oddest mammal, it carries a plate of armor.
5. meat-eating
6. the largest animal ever to inhabit the earth.

Quite a variety of these puzzles is possible, all related to one general subject. For example, *carnivore* could serve as a central word, around which would be arranged different members of this zoological order (raccoon, bear, otter, hyena, lion, civet, badger, and seal, for example).

Here's another central word puzzle for a geometry class.

CONGRUENT TRIANGLES

Directions: Use the clue provided to complete each word below.

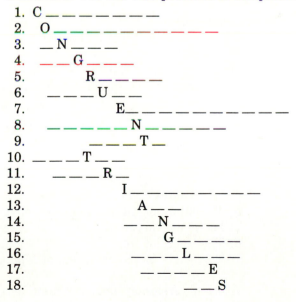

1. C __ __ __ __ __ __ __
2. O __ __ __ __ __ __ __ __ __ __
3. __ N __ __ __
4. __ __ G __ __ __
5.   R __ __ __ __
6. __ __ __ U __ __
7.   E __ __ __ __ __ __ __ __ __ __
8. __ __ __ __ __ N __ __ __ __ __
9.   __ __ __ T __
10. __ __ __ T __ __
11. __ __ __ R __
12.   I __ __ __ __ __ __ __ __
13.   A __ __
14.   __ __ N __ __ __
15.   G __ __ __ __
16.   __ __ __ L __ __ __
17.   __ __ __ __ E
18.   __ __ S

Clues:
1. When one figure (triangle) is physically placed on top of another like figure (triangle).
2. When two triangles lie partially in the interior of each other.
3. A part of a triangle used in proving triangles congruent.
4. A triangle is a geometric _____ .
5. A type of triangle that contains an angle by the same name.
6. Same clue (different answer) as #5.
7. A triangle with all three sides equal.
8. A triangle with all three angles equal.
9. A type of triangle containing all three angles of the same kind.
10. A special point in an angle.
11. Equal angles and segments come in _____ .
12. A type of triangle with only two angles and two sides equal.
13. The method of proving triangles congruent that involves two angles and the included side.
14. Segments have _____ .
15. The first step in a "proof."
16. A type of triangle with all three sides of different lengths.
17. The last step in a "proof."
18. The method of proving triangles congruent that involves three sides.

☐ *Beginnings and Endings*
In this last meaning exercise, a beginning or ending element is listed that is common to many words or to words that are conceptually related. Definitions for the words are listed in one column, the words in another, with blank spaces for all but the common element. Try this for an example:

LOGY QUIZ

1. The scientific study of man.   _ _ _ _ _ _ _ _ logy
2. The study of fossils   _ _ _ _ _ _ _ _ logy
3. The ethnology of early man   _ _ _ _ _ _ _ _ _ logy
4. The study of ancient animals   _ _ _ _ _ _ _ _ logy
5. The study of the influence of heavenly
   bodies on human events   _ _ _ _ _ logy
6. The study of weather   _ _ _ _ _ _ logy
7. The study of the evolution of language _ _ _ _ _ logy

Another version of the same game lists common beginnings and asks for endings. You may find this easier:

ANTHRO QUIZ

1. The scientific study of man   anthro _ _ _ _ _ _
2. Attributing human
   characteristics   anthro _ _ _ _ _ _ _ _ _
3. Resembling man   anthro _ _ _ _ _
4. Of or pertaining to man   anthro _ _ _
5. Study of the origin of man   anthro _ _ _ _ _ _ _ _

Or, try this one:

Par one, two, three, . . .

1. To peel   par _
2. A hooded fur jacket   par _ _
3. Equality in amount   par _ _ _
4. A model of excellence   par _ _ _ _
5. Being equal distance apart at
   every point   par _ _ _ _ _
6. A distinct division of written
   work   par _ _ _ _ _ _
7. Oval protozoans   par _ _ _ _ _ _ _

■ Recognition Exercises, Games, and Puzzles

When followed by the use of the word in meaningful context, simple word games may be useful. Basal reader manuals have traditionally called for recognition exercise in the recommendation that the teacher write "new" or "unfamiliar" words on the board and pronounce them with children. Seemingly, a bond between the sight (look) and sound (say) would be established by this look-say technique. The problem is that the technique teaches something else, that reading is saying words.

An alternative to the show-and-tell method of building word recognition is the variety of word games and puzzles that students like to play. Newsstands are full of examples that can be copied, and students who enjoy working them are usually happy to try their hand at building games and puzzles. When they are centered on vocabulary related to a unit of study or area of concern to the course, such word exercises may have real value, particularly to the student who makes them up! They cause and reinforce genuine curiosity about language, just as traditional crosswords have done for so many years.

Two common and popular examples of word games that can easily be adapted for class use are the cryptogram and word hunts.

☐ *Cryptograms*

These are coded lists of words that may be related to the same topic. The code is such that letters stand for something other than themselves. In the same puzzle, however, letters are substituted for one another consistently. An example from the puzzle is given as a clue to the other words. Our sample cryptogram will strain your memory of history:

CIVIL WAR GENERALS

example: Grant

M D L E V R Q

— — — — — — —

P H D X H

— — — — —

J U D Q W

— — — — —

O H H

— — —

V K H U P D Q

— — — — — — —

M R K Q V W R Q

— — — — — — —

Z R U U H V W

— — — — — — —

☐ *Word Hunts*

This is one of the most popular puzzles of the day, known by a variety of names—ring around the world, seek-a-word, search and find. Newsstands carry multiple sources for word hunts, and they are almost as easy to make as to find.

FAMOUS ARTISTS

```
A   R   T   I   R   E   M   I   N   G   T   O   N   A
R   E   M   B   R   A   N   D   T   I   I   S   U   W
E   B   P   S   D   E   G   A   S   N   J   U   D   Y
Y   M   I   C   H   E   L   A   N   G   E   L   O   E
N   U   C   V   E   S   A   L   V   R   P   L   B   T
O   S   A   L   E   B   U   V   W   E   E   Y   O   H
L   E   S   R   O   B   T   I   S   S   A   N   B   C
D   I   S   M   O   N   D   R   I   A   N   V   L   N
S   S   O   D   F   G   C   E   Z   A   N   N   E   W
V   T   H   D   E   L   A   C   R   O   I   X   Y   Z
```

If you want to convert word hunts from a recognition task to a meaning exercise, consider the following example:

READING AND REASONING

Directions: Find and circle the words that appropriately correspond with each of the following:

1. author of a readability formula
2. should be used as stimulators rather than evaluators
3. a purpose of pre-reading
4. with label, it comprises "a word"
5. knowledge isn't static, it _____
6. contemplation focuses on this
7. reading is really a search for this
8. Wigginton is almost synonymous with this
9. the essence of reading in the content areas is "_____ in every classroom"
10. the first principle of interpersonal relations is the ability to be this

Reminder: the words can be backwards, diagonal, or upside down as well as horizontal or vertical

```
I   L   F   O   X   F   I   R   E   Q
E   I   A   P   O   R   M   N   U   M
V   T   L   K   D   Y   R   E   A   L
O   E   A   V   L   R   S   E   I   J
L   R   A   P   A   T   Z   H   P   S
V   A   T   U   I   Y   G   B   M   X
E   C   C   O   N   C   E   P   T   Y
S   Y   N   L   C   U   I   D   T   F
E   S   T   D   A   R   C   T   D   W
Q   G   R   M   E   A   N   I   N   G
S   I   S   E   H   T   N   Y   S   A
```

And here's one designed for an ecology unit in a biology course.

```
D E R T F G I O L O G B J E R E T T I K O E
N O R Y E T O P C W H I C H N T Q U I C K R
M I O H P R T I F R O A D I T O P W E C E E
O P C T O T E R R E S T R I A L O O N C S H
S V E Y E M C I E L U A N O I T A L U P O P
B O O G O C O N S U M E R S O I T D X C Y S
T I E O I P S M H Q M P L A N T O E Q R S O
R O W L N E Y E W O E F I S H R E C O E N C
I I I O T R S A A T R U E D P O B O I E X E
N V N C E O T W T W A T E R H O N M W E N T
I N T E R D E P E N D E N C Y R O P S N O W
T I E C V I M C R E M N E X S O E O R G E Z
C C R P E N M A E N O V C N I O T S E P S O
W H V N N I T I R I C I N H C D W E Y B C D
B E E O T O W N M C W R O C A K L R T Y I T
J O N B I O L O G Y E O M O L B T R E E T S
P O T E O W Q K N C F N E N V I I T O Y O X
K L I V N Y T I N U M M O C O E M T O U I S
I R O J A C K L E R P E S T O L T Y A D B V
R E N Y G O L O G Y E N R F C B G Y N T I M
N M P E R S I S T E N T C H E M I C A L S U
W H Y D O Y O U T H I N K I A S K E D Y O U
```

The words defined below are hidden in the puzzle. Can you find them and place them in the line before the definition?

_____ relying upon each other for existence and support of the sea.

_____ that niche that is largely composed of plants

_____ the total role of an organism in the ecosystem

_____ those chemicals that do not readily decompose

_____ ecosystem that includes ponds and streams

_____ natural surroundings

_____ all ecosystems on earth

_____ study of the relationships between living things and their environment

_____ group of organisms of one kind in a given area

_____ that niche that is composed of bacteria

_____ ecosystem that includes forest and deserts

_____ group of populations in given area

_____ interference

_____ where an organism lives
_____ study of life
_____ composed of physical environment and living organisms
_____ they eat producers
_____ substance that combats disease
_____ one that destroys

SUMMARY

The learning of vocabulary beyond the primary grades usually involves more than becoming aware of new words or labels. More often than not, learning of vocabulary includes the learning of new concepts. And the learning of new concepts is evolutionary, beginning with initial awareness, followed by gradual understanding, and eventually remembering. As a new concept is understood, a reader/learner finds needs for the word that represents this newly acquired understanding and along with the needs comes an entitlement to the word itself. This entitlement occurs only when the concept is understood.

Vocabulary instruction must be based on a realization that vocabulary knowledge grows as conceptual awareness grows, for words do not have meanings; people have meanings for words. To assume that an exposure to a definition of a word ensures that learners know, understand, and can remember the word is faulty logic at best. Vocabulary instruction begins with initial awareness of concept and label during the anticipation phase of the lesson. Realization of meaning emerges and evolves during reading as the reader encounters the word and its corresponding concept. Once the concept has been understood during reading, reinforcement during the contemplation phase facilitates remembering. Hence, the understanding of a word is rarely an all-or-none affair; knowledge of word meaning grows, develops, evolves, and changes. Vocabulary instruction must account for the evolutionary nature of vocabulary learning.

The teaching of vocabulary beyond the primary grades should begin by facilitating the reading comprehension of students in real learning situations. The words to be pre-taught are not necessarily those that are new but those essential to an understanding of the selection to be read. After students read for understanding, vocabulary instruction proceeds to help students remember the new words and their concepts. Teacher-directed, concept-based discussions prior to reading foster the awareness phase, and student-developed vocabulary exercises facilitate the contemplation phase of vocabulary learning.

10

Attitudes and Interests

SETTING THE STAGE

In *Remembering,* his classic treatise on experimental and social psychology, Sir Frederick Bartlett (1932) makes a remarkable observation on which we will build the thesis for this chapter:

> When a person is being asked to remember [something read or anything else], very often the first thing that emerges is something of the nature of attitude. The recall [that follows] is then a construction, made largely on the basis of this attitude, and its general effect is that of a justification of the attitude. (p. 207)

To us this seems a rather precise description of how a reader remembers something he or she reads. One remembers first an attitude and all that follows is a justification of that attitude. This is a remarkable idea. Think for a moment about it and why it is so remarkable.

Virtually every study that has examined the relationship between general interests and specific comprehension has shown a positive result (Asher, 1980; Belloni & Jongsma, 1978; Bernstein, 1955; Estes & Vaughan, 1973; Pauk, 1974; Shnayer, 1968). Given two things to read of equal difficulty but one on a topic of high interest to the reader, the other on a topic of low interest to that same reader, the selection on the topic of higher interest will be comprehended better. Bartlett helps us to understand that one's attitude and one's comprehension are inseparable. Students who have a good attitude toward a subject will be likely to achieve best in that subject, and few teachers would argue with the idea that attitudes are critical determiners of learning, be they positive or negative. In fact, it is easier for students to learn those things in which they are most interested. (What a pleasure it is to teach students who have good attitudes!)

Throughout this chapter, we will consider three facets of the role of attitudes and interests in classroom instruction. First, we will explore affect in relation to what a learner brings to learning, what a reader brings to reading, and how learning and reading might influence students' attitudes. Then, we will share some ideas about how attitudes can be changed—what makes them change and what can be done to make them change. Finally, we will suggest ways to measure attitudes, a neglected dimension in most school testing programs.

EXTENDING OUR PERSPECTIVE

■ What a Learner Brings to Learning

Here we'd like to use an example of learning requiring little if any reading. We'll consider the learning involved in realizing geometric principles from a construction and a demonstration included in a plane geometry unit on circles. First, look at Figure 10.1.

The directions would tell you to place the circle at the top of Figure 10.1 over the arrow-like lines so that (1) when points A and C are on the circle, the center of the circle is somewhere on the line segment BD, and (2) if you trace segment BD twice, each time with A and C set at different points on the circle, the point at which the BD lines cross will mark the center of the circle.

Perhaps you'd like to try this exercise yourself. Either trace the lower portion of Figure 10.1 (the "arrow points") and manipulate it over the circle to draw your extra BD segments. Or, you can draw your own circle with a compass on a piece of paper. Then draw your arrow point so that line segments AB and BC are congruent. You can do this with your compass and a ruler by drawing a line through A and through BD and perpendicular to it. Point C will be on this line at the same distance from BD as A is.

You may be wondering what this is all about. We want you to examine what it takes to learn from such an exercise. Consider your own learning here. Perhaps you can't explore your own learning because you haven't stopped to try the exercise for yourself. Maybe you're still playing around with the problem. (What happens to the exercise if segment AC is perpendicular to BD and runs through B?) Your present state of mind depends on your attitude about geometry, about the

FIGURE 10.1 Geometry Construction Activity

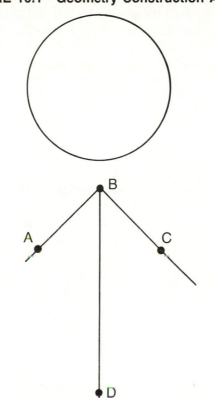

language of mathematics, about doing anything like this exercise in the context of a textbook you're reading about reading. In general, learning depends on attitude toward the topic under study and toward the particular context of its occurrence. In this specific instance, if your feelings about mathematics and geometry are positive, if you are inclined to follow such geometric puzzles through to some conclusion, and if your understanding of such things is characterized by curiosity (that is, if you're interested in such things) you will have learned something from the activity. But if the opposite is true about your attitude specific to this instance (for example, you feel quite unfriendly toward anything vaguely mathematical, you are inclined to avoid anything at all numerical or purely logical, and your understanding of math is that it is something dull and to be memorized) then you certainly won't have learned anything from trying to manipulate a circle over three line segments of any description.

Hence, the result of any attempt to learn is a direct function of the attitude the learner brings to the learning task. And the learner's attitude is in turn affected by the result of the learning. You are just a little more or a little less inclined right now, for example, toward geometry and mathematics, you feel just a little differently about the context created by this text, and perhaps too you may be feeling a bit more strongly, one way or another, about us because we asked you to engage in this activity. Regardless of how you feel, though, about any of these factors, our point is that you *do* feel and your feeling affects your learning.

What a Reader Brings to Reading

Because reading and learning are such similar processes (can we say that reading is a way of learning?), by now you have every idea of what we're going to say about reading and the reader's attitude, but for purposes of clarity, let's say it anyway. What a reader experiences and realizes during reading is due largely to the attitudes the reader has toward the topic, toward the kind of reading being done, and toward the context of the reading. Where the reader's feelings, inclinations, and understandings are positive, the reading is likely to be successful; where the feelings, inclinations, and understandings are negative, so too will be the reading experience. When helping someone toward a positive experience in reading (and that's what teaching reading should be), it is the role of the teacher to foster and build upon attitudes that can make the reading successful. To elaborate this in an affective way, let us suggest you take a moment now and return to the section To the Reader so that you can read again Belita Gordon's poem, "If Wishes Were Horses, Emperors Would Wear Clothes". Do you feel the distinction in what she suggests? Of course you can understand her view, but until you can blend the learning with the feeling, you're still missing something essential about the role feelings and attitudes play in successful learning.

A content reading lesson often illustrates for a teacher the importance of directing students' reading in ways that help them feel good about what they're doing. Many students have real difficulty in reading anything very technical, such as geometry. Often when students approach a reading of anything technical, they come with a bad attitude about the topic, about the language, and about the context in which the reading is being done. (Some people are simply afraid of math courses; how do you feel about your tests and measurements course, or are you still avoiding it?) But notice that a content reading lesson enables you to guide your students' learning in a way that will practically ensure their success, edging them slowly closer to the idea with each step. And success breeds success; can positive attitudes be far behind? Rarely do we find students to be successful and yet have a negative attitude. Hence, there are two sides to this coin: affect influences learning and learning affects attitude.

What, then, do we know about readers' attitudes and their understandings? We know that it takes a certain frame of mind or attitude to realize the meaning of "Theorem 10-6: In the same circle or in congruent circles, congruent chords have congruent arcs." A teacher who seeks to help students have positive experiences with reading will also help those students develop positive attitudes toward the topic, the subject, the language of the subject, and even toward their teacher(s) and themselves.

The Teaching of Text

It was Dolores Durkin's (1978–79) conclusion that most of what goes on in classrooms in the name of teaching comprehension is in reality *testing* comprehension. Exercises designed to teach comprehension are frequently, almost always, in the form of "read this selection and answer the questions at the end." Not that there's anything wrong with questions *per se*—they're a time-honored and powerful teaching tool. But questions must derive from the potential and realized meaning of text rather than, as is usually the case, from what someone assumes to be the literal meaning of a selection of text. Most attempts to question readers have a negative effect on attitudes because the questions usually asked are disrespectful of the reader *and* the text. To our way of thinking, detailed questions over trivia and "literal" meaning are an affront to good text, one whose meaning potential is rich. Mostly, the kinds of questions we're deploring are put after reading selections by textbook writers, editors, or anthologizers. To the teacher we'd like to say *caveat emptor* ("let the buyer beware") when it comes to these questions. And we say so because to ask trivial questions is to reduce text to trivia for readers, with an inevitably negative effect on their attitudes.

In an anthology of literature for high school English classes, we found one of the most beautiful stories in print, Truman Capote's *A Christmas Memory*. If you haven't read it and can lay your hands on a copy, drop everything, search it out, and read it. What a wonderful selection to share with adolescents! To teach reading with stories like this is to take full advantage of the effect a story can have on the attitudes of readers—the story deeply touches most of its readers. The story centers on Capote's memory of a few weeks around Christmas time many years ago when he was a child of seven living with relatives. He and one relative particularly were the closest of friends, and most of his memories, beautifully and poignantly detailed, concern his relationship with his friend. It is a story of love and friendship and Christmas. But too often we find questions like these following on the heels of the story:

1. What are the various uses for the dilapidated baby carriage?
2. What evidence is there in the story that the rural setting is located in the southern area of the country?
3. How do the two friends earn money for fruitcake ingredients?

These questions have nothing to do with who the story is about or with how the story affects its readers. In the face of that effect, these, and other questions like them, are an insult to anyone who does understand the story, and no help at all to anyone who doesn't.

As if it weren't enough that texts include these kinds of questions at the ends of stories or chapters, companies publish worksheets of questions for popular selections in ready-to-ditto form. Although we explored questioning at length in chapter 8, we want you to consider the effect bad questions might have on the attitudes of readers. Look at these questions intended as follow-up to the venerable *Silas Marner*:

1. Silas's first meal for Eppie is a bowl of porridge sweetened with (1) brown sugar, (2) maple syrup, (3) honey, (4) cinnamon.
2. The table and chair given Silas for his living room are made of (1) oak, (2) mahogany, (3) maple, (4) pine.
3. The only relatives of Silas mentioned in the novel are (1) his mother and sister, (2) his mother and father, (3) his mother and brother, (4) his mother and grandmother.

These questions, and all questions like them, ridicule the very thing they intend to develop: understanding.

Why are these kinds of questions so prevalent? We think because of a widespread conception of learning from text that goes something like this: Readers read first for details from which they then derive interpretations. As you know by now, we disagree and suggest instead: Readers realize meaning in the form of interpretations that are continuously modified or confirmed and that assign differing status to bits of detail. That is, detail is important, not trivial, to the degree it can be used to justify interpretations a reader wants to make.

One of America's best contemporary writers, Flannery O'Connor, once put these matters in slightly different terms, talking to a group of college students about the relation between analysis and enjoyment of a story:

> Last fall I received a letter from a student who said she would be graciously appreciative if I would tell her "just what enlightenment" I expected her to get from each of my stories. I suspect she had a paper to write. I wrote her back to forget about the enlightenment and just try to enjoy them. I knew that was the most unsatisfactory answer I could have given because, of course, she didn't want to enjoy them, she just wanted to figure them out.
>
> In most English classes the short story has become a kind of literary specimen to be dissected. Every time a story of mine appears in a Freshman anthology, I have a vision of it, with its little organs laid open, like a frog in a bottle. . . .
>
> A story really isn't any good unless it successfully resists paraphrase, unless it hangs on and expands in the mind. Properly, you analyze to enjoy, but it's equally true that *to analyze with any discrimination, you have to have enjoyed already.* . . . (pp. 107–108, italics ours)

Think how readers interpret what they read. We can define interpretation as an understanding, a feeling, and an inclination, all of which are tied up with enjoyment and appreciation, in short, "a construction, made largely on the basis of . . . attitude." (Bartlett, 1932, p. 207) This means that reading should be followed by the kind of questions that call forth a personal interpretation: "What do you think about what you just read?" or "What impressed you in this selection?" and then, "Why? What parts of the text had the strongest effect on you?"

When discussing a selection with students, we should first focus on what they understood and felt about the selection, from a broad perspective. As teachers concerned about reader comprehension, we'd do well to remember Bartlett's notion that ". . . the first thing that emerges is something of the nature of attitude . . . [and what follows is] a justification of the attitude." (p. 207) We have found that observant teachers notice that students often provide an affective response to comprehension questions; unfortunately, those of us who tend to use questions to evaluate rather than to stimulate sweep past students' feelings in search of their understandings. This happens all too frequently when we press for students' responses to detail questions.

What, though, if we initiated discussions with broader, more thought-provoking questions, as we have suggested frequently in earlier chapters? Then, if in readers' responses, the details that Silas sweetened Eppie's porridge with brown sugar or that the living room furniture was made of oak or that the only mention of Silas's relatives is a reference to his mother and sister happen to come out, then wonderful. It is in just this kind of context, a context of thoughtful response, that recall of such detail can be important. Outside of this context, though, these details and isolated bits of information will be of little value to the reader.

One objection you might raise if you're a science teacher or a social studies teacher or a math teacher is the importance of facts in text. They are important to us, too, but we will say that for content textbooks as well as short stories or novels, details become meaningful as they clarify readers' understandings and interpretations. One problem, admittedly, is expository textbooks don't have as great a potential to affect readers, at least not in a positive way. On the contrary, we are tempted to add parenthetically, content area textbooks generally tend to affect readers in a negative way. And this may be particularly so in elementary grades due to the inexperience young students have with expository texts. Aware of this, many teachers have put these books on the shelves. Thus, reading expository material in their classes is no longer a part of the learning that is going on. This is a grievously bad choice to make. Students need to learn how to learn even from textbooks that are not excellent.

SUSPICIONS REGARDING ATTITUDE CHANGE IN SCHOOLS

■ ■ There simply isn't a great deal known for sure about why students' attitudes toward school and school subjects form or change as they do. We have, however, some firm suspicions about attitudes borne out of experience and common sense, which we'd like to share.

Attitude and achievement are not the same thing, which means that learning and feeling good about school are not quite the hand-and-glove fit people sometimes take them to be. Many of you were probably very good students, yet it would come as no surprise to us if numbers of you have strong negative feelings about school. Knowing you were a good student simply wouldn't say much about your attitude toward school. (You see, even being a good teacher doesn't mean you like school. Why, some of our best friends abhor school but love kids, and they're excellent teachers!) So anyone who wants to change students' attitudes for the better will have to take that as a specific goal and do things to make it happen, rather than hoping for attitudes to slide along on achievement's coattails.

Teachers allow students' attitudes to influence grades. We noticed this when we were studying attitudes and achievement test scores and found their relationship to be weaker than the relationship between attitudes and grades. On the surface, that may seem reasonable; any humane teacher would tend to give better grades to cooperative class participants than to hellish troublemakers, even if the achievement of both were the same. It's a way of rewarding good behavior, which counts in school. But it is also a way of punishing bad attitudes.

Classroom climate is a very important factor in determining student attitudes. Have you read the introduction to *Foxfire 2* yet? Remember Carlton and what Eliot Wigginton had to say about him? If not, refer back to pp. 5–6 in chapter 1. The contrast makes our point.

Student's attitudes toward school get worse the longer they're in school. For many pupils, the longer they're in school the less fun learning becomes, until they finally drop out one way or another. For one thing, what they are required to read may appeal less and less as their tastes in reading enter the adolescent phase of development. As Robert Carlsen (1980) put it, "this is the crucial period when many potential readers stop reading. Paradoxically this is also the period when the young person may devote more time to reading than at any other period of his life, provided his interest is not killed." (p. 23) We think the quote would be equally justifiable if you changed the word "read" to "learn" in all three places. In the interest of "quality," schools have in the last few decades moved more and harder subject matter into earlier grades. The result is not only that pupils may understand set theory but not know how to do long division, but also that schools can become nonsense to them. Why the furor to teach everyone everything in twelve years? After the loss we suffered in Sputnik, we won the race to the moon, but some people are wondering, "What prize were we after, and what price did we pay?" The effect on schools was not altogether healthy, especially where we forgot that "To everything there is a season, and a time to every purpose under heaven." Are you familiar with *The Hurried Child* by David Elkind? He argues convicingly for our concern.

The classroom teacher has a greater affect on students' attitudes than does anything else in the school. College students especially find the following activity interesting. First, write on the left-hand side of a sheet of paper your favorite subject (or subjects) when you were in school. Then, on the other side, list the teachers who were your favorites. (Do they match?) Next, list all of the things you think made those subjects and teachers your favorites. (If possible, compare your list of reasons with someone else who has done the same activity.) We think the results will tell you a lot about the effect of teachers on attitudes in school.

Here's another one. Think about the two best experiences in your life and describe them briefly. Now, by "best" we mean experiences that affected your life, your personal development, in a positive way. Then think about and describe the two worst experiences in your life, ones that retarded your personal development, experiences you had to overcome later.

If what you put down in this activity is anything like that found in a study by Banan (1972), the overwhelming number of experiences (86 percent according to Banan) involved other people. And of that 86 percent, the largest group of other people were teachers. Banan asked only for negative experiences, but our replications of the study suggest that results hold for positive experiences as well. Teachers have a lot to do with the attitudes of students. In the eyes of the student, it is the teacher who is democratic or authoritarian, interesting or boring, fair or unfair, student-centered or subject-centered.

A close friend and student, Susan Drigant, once shared an experience that seems apt in the present context:

> After a lengthy unit on poetry which encompassed examining many specific genres, interpreting images for deeper meaning, and defining numerous terms, the teacher assigned the students to write poems for homework. They were allowed to choose any topic they wished, but they were required to demonstrate several poetic devices in their writing. A 17 year old girl, a high school senior, handed in the following poem.

> This poem does not come from the heart!
> Nor does it reveal the smoldering depths of my soul.
> (It does not even hint at a lost love.)
> This poem contains no symbolism.
> (Not one mention of man's eternal quest.)
> This poem has no similes or metaphors.
> "Let Shakespeare compare Thee to a summer's day.
> (I would rather not compare Thee at all.)"
> This poem makes no attempt to rhyme.
> And if it does accidentally, it's no fault of mine.
> (I mean myself.)
> There is no aliteration. (None, Nothing, Never!)
> Nor sensory images to cause sinus congestion.
> It has no definate rhythm.
>   All of
> the lines are of varying lengths and the only
>   definate meter is the one
> that demands a dime when you park your car.

This poem is not for analization,
interpretation, or discussion.
This poem is for publication,
for it is no reflection of me.

The poem was returned several days later, the errors circled in red; misspellings, usage, punctuation, and so on. There was also a comment written on top. "You try too hard to be clever. Avoid cliche and hackneyed phrases."

The student had indeed tried to be clever, and had been found guilty. The next day, the girl handed in another poem. She simultaneously and silently vowed never again to attempt writing poetry. Her second poem read as follows:

Each line of my poem you dissected.
Each error you promptly corrected.
But I realize, that
You must criticize.
You're a teacher; it's to be expected.

Incidentally, Susan still writes poetry, but she's very selective about whom to share it with.

IMPLICATIONS FOR CLASSROOM PRACTICE

What is known or supposed about affect is useful only if it can be translated into practical implications and suggestions. "Practical" means "capable of being put into practice," and we will limit our discussion to suggestions that have practical possibilities. (For example, if parents have bad attitudes toward school, so will their children, more than likely. But changing the parents' attitudes is all but impossible, and it might serve little purpose to discuss the problem and its unlikely solutions by teachers or schools.) Factors under control of the teacher that have bearing on student feelings may be divided into four categories: (1) curriculum factors, (2) classroom setting, (3) student characteristics, and (4) teacher characteristics.

Curriculum Factors

Generally speaking, if what is taught is taught in a way that is appealing to students through materials that are appropriate for them, the chances of their liking it are increased. That is, if learning is pleasant and successful, then students' attitudes toward what they learn are likely to be positive. Conversely, if learning is unpleasant, students will reject what they are taught. They simply won't buy.

There are always determinations to be made regarding curriculum, particularly what to teach. Whatever the choice, one result will be that students' attitudes will be touched. Therefore, choices of what to teach should relate to consideration of interest, appeal, and usefulness to students. In other words, what is taught in a course should relate in some way to students' present or future needs and be taught in a way appropriate to those needs. Since it is impossible, in any course, to teach everything, what is taught could (and should) be chosen to emphasize what is potentially interesting and useful. To do so improves the chances that students will continue to learn more of what they will be taught. Then, too, we are assuming that you have some control over what is taught. If you feel you don't determine what is taught in your classroom, might it not be worth the effort to alter the learning atmosphere?

Not only what is taught, but how it is taught must be considered in relation to affective change. For example, attitudes are likely to be more positive where students are allowed to express their thoughts freely. A classroom characterized by an open and honest atmosphere that stimulates creative and critical thinking is conducive to positive attitudes. Students, like all people, feel good when their ideas are considered worthy. They tend to feel bad when the learning atmosphere is autocratic and threatening. The outcome is practically axiomatic: if students associate good feelings with what they learn, they will likely continue to learn more of it; if they associate negative feelings, they will likely avoid learning it. Classroom atmosphere plays a big role in this outcome.

The manner in which assignments are made to students is another example. For assignments to be completed successfully and for students to feel good about their work, directions and purpose for the task must be made very clear. Where they see little reason for what they must do, students' attitudes suffer. However, where assignments are made very clearly, with the purpose explained and suggestions given for completing the task efficiently, students are more likely to enjoy their accomplishments, and their attitudes toward what is accomplished will be better.

Curriculum materials also bear on students' attitudes. Textbooks selected for a course should be carefully chosen for a pleasing, readable style. Moreover, a variety of texts and other materials should be used in a course. Surely an economist must have invented the single-text approach; teachers know that no textbook can serve all pupils equally well. We might also add that big books with hard backs tend to be intimidating rather than inviting to many students, even college students. Teaching materials are learning tools and if the tools suit the needs of learners, their attitudes toward what they experience will be more positive.

■ Classroom Setting

The effect of physical surroundings was the object of study in the classic "Hawthorne Experiments," from whence derives the term "Hawthorne effect." Actually, these were industrial experiments conducted by the Western Electric Corporation. One of the significant findings of those studies was that variety and change in surroundings had a positive effect on workers' production. All people seem to react badly to boredom and sameness in their surroundings.

Some characteristics of the physical surrounding may be out of the teacher's control. The thermostat for the room may be in an office down the hall, lights may need replacing but budget won't allow proper upkeep, desks may be old and dilapidated. Nevertheless, there are always so many factors about the teaching setting that *can* be controlled or changed that those that can't are made bearable. While there are many striking exceptions, the brightness, activity, and receptiveness of so many classrooms of grades one through three are often a contrast to typical classrooms of grades ten through twelve. (By the way, those striking exceptions of high-school classrooms invariably contain students whose attitudes are also exceptional.)

Wall space and bulletin boards can be used creatively for instructional and aesthetic purposes at any grade level, and somewhat ingeniously by students when given the chance. Where possible and appropriate, facilities and settings other than the classroom can be used for instruction. Within the classroom, desks and other furniture can be arranged and rearranged in a manner to serve a variety of instructional needs. (Straight rows of desks are good for two things: listening to lectures and sweeping between. These suggestions are meant to exemplify the kinds of features of the learning environment that affect moods and attitudes toward learning. Learners invariably associate attitude toward what they learn with attitude toward how and in what surroundings they are asked to learn.

The classroom setting is defined not only by physical surroundings but also by that intangible element called "atmosphere." For example, where quiet is maintained at high expense, the atmosphere can be oppressive. Where the classroom is active and buzzing with purposeful activity, the atmosphere is stimulating. (A teacher friend recently made this suggestion: "I tell my students when they're working in groups that if I can hear *what* they're saying, it's too loud.) To hold interruptions to classroom activity to a minimum is to respect the importance of what kids are doing. Conversely, if, and this by recent actual count, the interclass P.A. system interrupts thinking and learning fifteen times a day, students may believe there are many things more important than their study and learning. The effect on students' attitudes is painfully predictable.

■ Student Characteristics

If schools were designed to teach young people what they *can* learn instead of what they *should* learn, they would learn more and feel better about it. Students might, for example, be allowed to group themselves on the basis of interest in topics relevant to the course curriculum and then to pursue those topics under the aegis of the course. For example, a group of social studies students could put together an interpretation of the early 1900s through music, focusing on Scott Joplin. Their research on the time period could bring them to an expert understanding. Contrast their resulting attitudes with those of students who read a small portion of their dry text with a drier title like "America Turns the Century."

Individuals in a class can and should be given freedom to choose a maximum depth to which they will study. So many texts and so many courses are superficial surveys from which students learn little. But school can be a place to study in depth under teacher guidance, even inspiration. Where this is so, student attitudes flourish.

The most important student characteristic to consider, however, is the "self" each student brings to the learning setting. What education comes right down to is kids, young people. If they are given a voice in the decision affecting them, if the "system" seems to care for them, if they are helped to see their needs within the context of the needs of the larger group, then they will often return the respect in the form of cooperation. The course curriculum, and the way it is taught, can be cooperatively chosen by students and their teacher. The result will assuredly be more positive attitudes on the part of students.

Eliot Wigginton (1975) offers the following insight on the importance of a positive self-image:

> I work with a great many students who have been damaged. In many cases, because of the treatment they have received from peers

("Boy, are you stupid!") and/or adults ("Can't you do anything right?") they have come to believe there is little they are good at. Consequently, there is little they attempt. It's not much fun to try something and get laughed at by peers or failed by adults as a consequence. Once burned, one approaches matches with caution.

I believe that before a student can act *effectively,* he has to know he can *act.* I believe before he can become truly sensitive to, and concerned about, other poeple's egos and needs, he has to have his own ego and needs satisfied. I believe that he can't often move beyond himself until he is comfortable *with* himself and his capabilities—convinced of his worth. These things seem obvious to me. (p. 17)

■ Teacher Characteristics

As we discussed before, a person asked to name his or her favorite subject and favorite teacher in school will likely give answers that correspond. The overwhelming influence of the teacher on student attitudes can hardly be overstated. There is no more potent force in the classroom; the teacher above all other factors affects student attitudes and achievement. This is true, we believe, because of the influence the teacher has on various dimensions of the school experience.

For example, a teacher's effectiveness in influencing attitudes toward a course is undoubtedly related to that teacher's own interest in the course and his or her conviction of its value in the curriculum. If the teacher approaches a course with enthusiasm and excitement, the students will often catch the feeling and begin to share it. Pity the teacher (and students of) who is assigned a course because no one else would take the assignment. The price of such expediency is staggering. Whatever the course, whoever the teacher, the image and practice of the teacher is an important determiner of student attitudes. Students need a resource in teachers, not a taskmaster. They appreciate fair grading and discipline, realistic expectations, adequate attention to detail. It is all of these characteristics that cause students to judge a teacher as good, and the corollary to that judgment is a better attitude toward the course, and in turn, better learning.

THE MEASURE OF ATTITUDES

■ ■ Direct measures of attitude are distinguished by the fact that it is clearly evident what the scale is measuring. Such measures have the advantage of relatively high reliability, though critics will point out that answers to direct measures can be easily faked, that students may try to lie for fear of admitting dislike for a socially or academically desirable behavior. Research done on attitude measurement suggests this is not the case, however (for example, see Kennedy & Halinski, 1975). The Estes Attitude Scales (Estes, et al., 1981) are direct measures of students' attitudes toward English, math, science, social studies, and reading. The scale is available in two forms, secondary and elementary. We include on pp. 246–247 the reading subscales of the Estes Attitude Scales as examples. For validity and other statistical data on these scales, answer sheets, directions for scoring, contact the distributor, Pro-Ed, Inc., of Austin, Texas.

ESTES ATTITUDE SCALES

(Secondary Form)

© 1981, PRO-ED

DIRECTIONS: These scales measure how you feel about courses taught in school. On the front and back of this sheet are statements about school subjects. Read each statement and decide how you feel about it. Rate each statement on a scale of 1 to 5, as follows:

5 will mean "I strongly agree"

4 will mean "I agree"

3 will mean "I cannot decide"

2 will mean "I disagree"

1 will mean "I strongly disagree"

Use the separate answer sheet to indicate your feeling toward each statement. Show your answers by putting an X in the proper box. Please be as honest as possible in rating each statement. Your ratings will not affect your grade in any course.

Reading

31. Reading is for learning but not for enjoyment.
32. Spending allowance on books is a waste of good money.
33. Reading is a good way to spend spare time.
34. Books are a bore.
35. Watching TV is better than reading
36. Reading is rewarding to me.
37. Books aren't usually good enough to finish.
38. Reading becomes boring after about an hour.
39. Most books are too long and dull.
40. There are many books which I hope to read.
41. Books should only be read when they are assigned.
42. Reading is something I can do without.
43. Some part of summer vacation should be set aside for reading.
44. Books make good presents.
45. Reading is dull.

ESTES ATTITUDE SCALES

(Elementary Form)

© 1981 PRO-ED

DIRECTIONS:

These Scales measure how you feel about subjects taught in school. On the following pages you will find some sentences about school subjects. You will be asked to rate each sentence on this scale:

| A | will mean "I Agree" |

| ? | will mean "I Don't Know" |

| D | will mean "I Disagree" |

Please be as honest as possible in rating each sentence. Your ratings will not affect your grade.

Example:

Playing ball is fun for me. | A | | ? | | D |

Reading Attitude Scale

	Agree (A)	Don't Know (?)	Disagree (D)
15. Reading is fun for me.	A	?	D
16. Books are boring.	A	?	D
17. Reading is a good way to spend spare time.	A	?	D
18. Reading turns me on.	A	?	D
19. Books do not make good presents.	A	?	D
20. Reading is rewarding to me.	A	?	D
21. Reading becomes boring after about a half hour.	A	?	D
22. Free reading teaches me something.	A	?	D
23. There should be time for free reading during the school day.	A	?	D
24. There are many books I hope to read.	A	?	D
25. Reading is something I can do without.	A	?	D
26. A certain amount of time during summer should be set aside for reading.	A	?	D
27. Books usually are good enough to finish.	A	?	D
28. Reading is not exciting.	A	?	D

CONSTRUCTION OF DIRECT MEASURES

■ ■ Direct measures of attitudes are those that (1) are rather obvious in intent and (2) require little if any inference in interpretation. Raw scores on such measures are directly interpretable; the higher the score, the better the attitude.

One of the best and most popular procedures for constructing measures of attitudes was formulated by R. S. Likert (1932). Likert-type scales present the student with a series of statements related to a "psychological domain" (for example, school, English class, curriculum design, or anything about which people might hold varying opinions). The task is to indicate agreement or disagreement with each statement. For example, in a scale to measure attitudes toward school, the following might appear:

> 5 will mean "I strongly agree"
> 4 will mean "I agree"
> 3 will mean "I cannot decide"
> 2 will mean "I disagree"
> 1 will mean "I strongly disagree"

1. School is worthwhile.

2. Most courses in school are useless.

There are two points to be made concerning these items. First, notice that item 1 is positive, item 2 is negative. This means that the scored values of responses to the items are opposite in magnitude. That is, strongly agree to item 1 would be scored 5, whereas strongly agree to item 2 would be scored 1. (The numbers in the response boxes merely refer to response choices.) The general rule is this: from strongly agree to strongly disagree, score positive items 5, 4, 3, 2, 1; score negative items 1, 2, 3, 4, 5.

The second point about scoring is that an individual's score on a scale is the sum of response values across all items. For every item, an individual's response is scored 5, 4, 3, 2, or 1. These values are then summed across all items on the scale. The total represents a quantification of the person's attitude. For example, if a scale had 15 items, the possible scores for any individual would range from 15 to 75, or 15×1 to 15×5. Do you see why?

The writing of items for any attitude scale is the most critical step. (For a model for scale construction, consult the Estes Attitude Scales [1981] and the technical manual that accompanies them.) In addition, refer to criteria for items that have been published by Edwards (1957). The following suggestions for writing items are adapted from Edwards's list. Examples are provided to illustrate the criteria.

1. Avoid statements referring to the past rather than the present.
   Poor: Science was an exciting subject in elementary school.
   Better: Science is an exciting subject.

2. Avoid factual statements.
   Poor: Science is a required subject in the eleventh grade.
   Better: Science should be a required subject in the eleventh grade.

3. Avoid statements capable of multiple interpretation.
   Poor: The job of the science teacher is to transmit information. (Is to transmit information, good or bad?)
   Better: The study of science offers the opportunity for search and discovery.

4. Avoid statements irrelevant to the subject.
   Poor: School is worthwhile.
   Better: The study of science is worthwhile.

5. Avoid statements likely to be endorsed by almost anyone or by no one.
   Poor: All of man's progress has stemmed from his scientific endeavor.
   Better: The most important aspects of man's progress stem from scientific endeavor.

6. Use simple, clear, direct language in the form of concise statements.
   Poor: The study of science, while beneficial to the welfare of mankind, is nevertheless a double-edged sword, since it has the potential for accruing to man either his guaranteed immortality or his inevitable destruction.
   Better: Scientific endeavor provides a better way of life.

7. Each statement should have only one complete thought. (See example for 6.)

8. Avoid terms such as all, always, none, never, only, just, and merely.

9. Avoid use of words perhaps incomprehensible to students.
   Poor: Indefatigability is high during the study of science.
   Better: Studying science is less tiring than studying other subjects.

10. Avoid use of double negatives.

Poor: It is not true that not enough science is offered in high school.
Better: More science should be offered in high school.

The use of these criteria is essential in achieving the content validity of any attitude scale. To the degree that items conform to the criteria, the scale is likely to provide a true measure of attitudes.

Because item construction is so crucial in the development of attitude scales, we suggest you try your hand at it. Follow these steps:

1. Write ten statements (five positive and five negative) that could be used in a Likert scale for your subject area.
2. Ask someone (for example, your students) to read the items for clarity.
3. Ask students to respond to your items and indicate whether they think the items are positive or negative. (This is another check on clarity.)

Check to see if any problems with the items are like those cautioned in Edwards's list. These criteria should also be useful to you in choosing from among prepared scales listed in standard reference sources (for example, Buros [1978]). In recent years a variety of scales for measuring attitudes toward school subjects has become available. One day, perhaps, attitude measurement will assume its rightful place in all school testing programs. It will do so when we who teach recognize the critical importance of attitudes in any learning situation.

SUMMARY

Several years ago we heard someone say that prior knowledge is the single greatest determiner of new learning. We were inclined to agree. Now, however, since we have come to understand the power of affect and volition, we'd have to include the disclaimer, "if by prior knowledge you mean understandings *and* affect *and* inclinations."

We attach great importance to the affective role in learning. Naturally, then, we wrestled with where to place this chapter in the context of this book. Perhaps, for you, we have erred in our decision and should have emphasized the influence much earlier. That is a judgment call, but in no sense does our placement imply that we have relegated interests and attitudes "to a spot at the back of the book."

Indeed, we'd now encourage, even challenge you to return to

each topic where we emphasized the cognitive dimensions of learning and integrate all that we have suggested about attitudes and interests. We have tried to suggest that a content reading lesson, for example, breeds success and success affects attitudes. We have also stressed the subtle influences on learning that can be altered with positive effects, such as classroom setting and even attitude toward students or subject matter.

In closing, we are reminded of a scene from *The Little Prince*. The little prince has stumbled upon the king of asteroid 325 and the prince has just plucked up enough courage to ask a favor of the king:

> "I should like to see a sunset. . . . Do me that kindness. . . . Order the sun to set. . . ."
>
> "If I ordered a general to fly from one flower to another like a butterfly, or to write a tragic drama, or to change himself into a sea bird, and if the general did not carry out the order that he had received, which one of us would be in the wrong?" the king demanded. "The general, or myself?"
>
> "You," said the little prince firmly.
>
> "Exactly. One must require from each one the duty which each one can perform," the king went on. "Accepted authority rests first of all on reason. If you ordered your people to go and throw themselves into the sea, they would rise up in revolution. I have the right to require obedience because my orders are reasonable."
>
> "Then my sunset?" the little prince reminded him; for he never forgot a question once he had asked it.
>
> "You shall have your sunset. I shall command it. But, according to my science of government, I shall wait until conditions are favorable." (p. 38)

Might not we, in our teaching, seek more often for conditions that are favorable? And for opportunities to create favorable conditions?

11

The Art of Study

SETTING THE STAGE

The ability to study efficiently is a characteristic of most good students. Conversely, many poor students are unproductive because they lack good study skills. And yet when asked how and when they learned to study, most college students report that no one ever taught them; they just developed their study habits more or less on their own, with little help from teachers or books. And we're talking here about college students; how much more helpless must less able students feel when it comes to studying? Studying is too important a skill to be left to chance.

We are in hopes that much of what we have suggested about ARC and more specifically about anticipation, realization of meaning, and contemplation will find application in your teaching and in your students' study. In the contexts of those chapters we mentioned a wide variety of study skills and learning strategies. Recall INSERT, the Interactive Notation System for Effective Reading and Thinking we introduced in our discussion of how readers realize meaning. (Remember? We asked you to practice INSERT while you read the article about crocodiles in Zimbabwe.) Recall, too, paired readings. And SMART. And cinquains and ConStruct and paired summarizing. As we consider the art of study, we'd like to suggest a number of categories for different study skills, as well as some additional learning strategies that can help students become more accomplished in their study.

We assume by this point you are prepared to agree with the idea that when learning to read and write, students should read and write about things worth learning about. Let us extend our proposition to suggest that study skills can and should be taught in the context of meaningful literacy instruction, but to do so may necessitate a broad view of study skills, such as that proposed by Adams, Carnine, and Gersten (1982): "Beginning in intermediate grades and continuing through high school and college, a large part of a student's school time is spent in reading textbooks to acquire information. . . . The process by which students learn information from textbooks is commonly referred to as study skills." (p. 29) Unfortunately, there is much research to suggest that little if any instruction in study skills goes on in schools today (Durkin, 1978–79; Wertsch, 1978; Schallert & Kleiman, 1979). Yet where it exists, many positive effects result—students learn more of what they study and often transfer their learning skills to other classes. (Gillis & Olson, 1982).

STUDYING, IT'S NOT "JUST READING"

■   ■   When students are asked to say what the difference is between studying and "just reading," they generally reply that studying is reading to remember. At first that answer struck us as humorous, since it implies that some reading is not to be remembered. On reflection, however, we think we have a better sense of what these students are saying: that is, studying is purposeful and deliberate in a way that normal reading is not. Paraphrasing Paul Wilson, a researcher at the Center for the Study of Reading, the activity of reading is so automatic in the mature reader that he or she is hardly conscious of it. But the act of studying is never automatic; it is always a conscious, industrious activity. In this sense, it is different from ordinary reading; it is reading to remember. And those students who remember what they study are those who do things to enhance their memory as they read.

So what, exactly, are the activities that constitute industrious study? Several seem to stand apart from the rest, and they all reflect the use of a system of study, like ARC. Within any system of study, successful students frequently apply strategies like previewing, note-taking, using resource and textbook material effectively, and reviewing for and taking tests. Let's examine these as key elements of the art of study.

■   Previewing

Mortimer Adler and Charles Van Doren (1972), in their now classic book, *How to Read a Book,* devote much of their attention to a discussion of what they call inspectional reading, which is similar to previewing. To read inspectionally is to search for the form and structure of a reading selection. Much of what we suggest students do in anticipation of what they are about to read is related to the concept of inspectional reading, reading to find out what they're going to find out about. Almost all of what we suggest are activities that can be accomplished individually.

Effective study is something more than "skip-along reading," as one child coined it for us, where the reader starts to read at page one and reads straight through to the last page of an assignment with hardly a pause or a look-back. Effective study is strategic in that it is planned and then implemented. The planning part requires selectivity, and if a reader is to read selectively, as must be the case during previewing, what shall he or she select? Davis & Clark (1981) suggest keys to textbook previewing, ten focal points for attention during the preview stage. They are (1) the title, (2) the introduction, (3) the summary, (4) pictures and maps, (5) chapter questions, (6) subtopic titles, (7) first paragraphs following the subtopics, (8) first sentences of paragraphs, (9) words in special print (for example, italics), and (10) bold print (such as occurs for technical vocabulary).

Previewing, however, is more than knowing *what* to preview; effective previewing requires knowing *how* to preview. Let's elaborate on this facet of previewing in a way that will make sense to your students. (Thanks to Don Dansereau for his willingness to share many ideas that have stimulated our thoughts on these matters.)

1. Think about the title of this selection, asking yourself what you already know about this concept. Look in the table of contents to see how this assignment fits with other topics you have studied in the course. It is very important to be clear about what you already understand that can serve as a basis for learning new things.

2. Read any questions or summaries that may appear at the end of sections or chapters. This will give you some idea of what is important in the chapter (although after a thorough reading, you may disagree with the summary on what the important points are). It will also help establish in your mind what the reading is going to require and help you highlight major points so you'll know what to try to remember.

3. Notice how the chapter is divided into sections; the divisions will usually be marked in italics or boldface. It may help you to think of the chapter as a series of pieces that you will take one by one. Ask yourself which of these subtopics

you already know about, which you think will require more study to understand.

4. Take a good look at all the pictures and graphs in the chapter so they will be easy to refer to when they are mentioned in the text. This will also help you anticipate what the chapter is going to be about, what sorts of things you are going to have to try to understand.

5. Make a few preliminary notes about what you expect to learn from the reading. If possible, compare your notes with those of classmates. Maybe others will be anticipating things for this chapter that hadn't occurred to you, and vice-versa. By sharing, you can help each other to understand.

6. Think about the reading you are about to do in relation to the goals it will serve. Are you reading for a homework assignment or in preparation for a test or to write a report or just what? If you can be clear about why you are reading this selection, you will find it easier to approach the reading in a proper frame of mind to understand the new information.

7. Place this reading in a specific schedule of work, established on the basis of the relative importance of all you have to do. This will lend you some perspective on the reading assignment and help you establish the amount of time and effort needed to devote to it.

8. Put yourself in a proper mood for study—in effect, try to talk yourself into spending a certain amount of time on the task you face. Be assured that everyone tries to avoid work, but for those who are successful at getting work done it is usually "mind over matter." Try to approach each reading task in the belief that the experience will be a successful one. If you find you cannot do this, talk to your teacher about the problem. If you can't talk to your teacher, talk to your guidance counselor or someone else who will listen. It is critically important to approach learning tasks with a genuine anticipation of success.

9. It is sometimes helpful to turn subheadings into questions that you try to answer as you read. What this does is help to establish a purpose for reading. If you read not to serve any particular purpose or to learn anything in particular, that's probably what will happen—you won't.

10. If there are things about the topic of the selection that you are curious about, try to keep those curiosities in mind as you read. Comprehension has been defined as having *your*

questions answered. If you read with curiosity, your reading will have a better chance of answering your questions.

11. Think about the kinds of questions you usually see on tests in the class in which this reading assignment was made. If you can anticipate what might be required of you as a result of your reading, then your time can be spent more productively. It may help to make up a few questions that ask for the kinds of information you can anticipate being tested on. What kinds of things do you think *you* would ask of a person to find out if they understood the reading?

12. If your teacher provides study questions for you to use in reading an assignment, be sure you understand the questions before you begin reading. Ask for clarification if you think you need it. This will also help you to separate major points from explanatory detail and force a conscious effort into the act of reading.

Notetaking

Notetaking is a time-honored procedure for committing text to memory. When people take notes, they often attempt to outline what they are reading, and for good reason. An outline is a skeleton, a picture of the main parts, which can make the other parts easier to remember. An outline given to students before they read (which they can commit to memory before reading) or after they read (particularly for poorly written text) will help readers learn more from their reading (Guthrie, 1978). Outlining is, however, one of the most complex skills in learning because it requires analysis and synthesis of a very fine sort. Outlining requires that a student recognize the main ideas treated in a passage as well as the supporting details, examples, and reasons related to those main ideas.

Consider, however, that it is possible—even likely—that before a student can outline a text, he or she must understand the text. Recall in our discussion of readability in chapter 2 we suggested that textbooks do not always lend themselves to clear outlining. As one teacher expressed it to us recently, "I used to teach outlining, but not anymore; the texts I use just won't outline." If you're stuck with a book that won't outline easily, it is best to provide students the outline they need to understand what they're reading. Such modeling will help students begin to identify structural and semantic relationships themselves. If you happen to be working with a book that is reasonably well structured, here's a procedure for notetaking that most people find very effective. The procedure is sometimes called the Cornell method and its originator is Walter Pauk (1974).

This technique requires the student to draw a line lengthwise down the middle of a piece of notepaper. (Some looseleaf notebook paper comes already prepared in this format.) As the student reads or listens, major headings or concepts are recorded in the space to the left, supporting details in the space to the right. Only one side of the paper is used at a time. When it comes time to study, the paper is folded down the center line so that either the main ideas or the details are visible, but not both at once. In studying for an essay exam, the student tries to recall details when looking at the main ideas; in studying for a multiple choice test (to inefficient studiers, the multiple *guess* test), the student tries to recall main ideas when looking at the details. In this form, the student's notes are a mnemonic device for remembering, a tool for study that's much more efficient than reading or trying to recall strictly from memory.

Merely asking students to take notes in this fashion will be insufficient incentive, as you might guess. The most effective alternative is to model the procedure with your students. Assign a short selection to be read that has an organization that lends itself to easy notetaking (that is, has clearly stated main ideas and supporting details). Using an overhead projector transparency, construct your notes on the selection and share them with your students, discussing the decisions you each made. One variation of this procedure is to make notes on a selection in a group setting, again using a transparency and projector, allowing students a chance to see an outline take shape as they participate in its construction. Activities such as these can be repeated numerous times with the double benefit of teaching something about notetaking and providing a springboard for discussion of reading assignments.

■ Effective Use of Resource and Textbook Material

Few teachers at any level of school, including college, are aware of just how little their students know about how to use the resources available to them in their study. Yet one of the best uses of time in study is often the time spent tracking down additional information on a topic of special interest or difficulty. To give your students the edge in study skills, help them learn the resources that are available to them—atlases, almanacs, encyclopedias of various sorts, *Reader's Guide to Periodical Literature, Oxford Companions,* and even *Master-*

plots. Appropriate resources surely depend on the level of competence of students as well as their age and grade. You may want to meet with your school librarian and your public librarian to obtain a list of available resource books that are well suited for your students and your instructional purposes. In any case, one of the best favors you could do your students would be to keep them from thinking their textbook is the sole source of information available to them.

Students will also need help in effectively using their textbooks. Begin the year by showing students how to make the most of their textbook as a resource for learning. They particularly need to know how to use the table of contents, index, glossary, and any appendices to their book. This will help the industrious student find other references to concepts for which additional explanation would be of help.

■ Reviewing for and Taking Tests

Reviewing implies that some form of study has previously been conducted and that the purpose of review is to refresh one's memory. The best recommendations we can make for review follow our guidelines for contemplation. As we have said, learning will be difficult for students who insist on trying to memorize tidbits that teachers test. Rememberings are built on contemplations of understandings. If students learn and apply that principle, they will reduce the frustration potential found in efforts to remember without understanding. When students become impatient to remember and resort to memorization at the expense of understanding, they will ignore contemplations, and review will become relearning. Students must learn the advantages of contemplation. Think about how often adults, in nonacademic settings, naturally reinforce their understandings through contemplations; one of the first things you want to do when you have read something very good is to talk to someone about it, isn't it? You might suggest the following activities to your students as strategies for contemplation and review.

1. Immediately after reading, close your book and try to remember what you have read. Use your own shorthand to outline major points and important details.
2. Think back to any questions you might have asked before you began reading. Try to answer those questions without looking at the book.
3. If you discover you have trouble remembering something

you think you should remember, make a note of it so you can ask someone for more explanation or information that might help you.

4. Imagine yourself talking to the author or an expert in this field. What questions would you ask? What criticisms would you raise?

5. How might the information and ideas you just read have practical application for you?

6. Imagine you have been asked to present this information to a group of friends or associates; what would you choose to include in your presentation?

7. How does what you have learned from your reading fit your purposes and goals for reading it?

8. How much have you learned? How much do you have to learn to satisfy your objectives?

9. If there are things you have to remember but can't, try a mnemonic device. For example, if you need to remember the order of arithmetical operations (multiply, divide, add, subtract) you might memorize MiDAS. Try to associate familiar things with the things you are trying to remember. For example, if you were born in the year of a presidential election, you can remember that there will be such an election every year your age is divisible by four. Sometimes people remember things in rhymes—"Thirty days hath September, April, June . . ."

10. Try to imagine the circumstances in which you will have to recall what you have learned (for example, an oral report, a debate, a short quiz, or a final exam). Go over the material, trying to highlight in your memory what you can anticipate needing to know.

11. Reread! Anything worth reading once is worth reading twice. After all your other study and efforts at contemplations, a rereading will often be very easy and can serve to cement new understandings and information for future recall and use.

One big difference between successful and unsuccessful students is that successful students know how to show what they know when the time comes to do so. Bernice Bragstad and Sharon Stumpf (1982) suggest an activity they call "Becoming Test-Wise: Exam Error Checklist." By analyzing the errors they have made on tests, students can begin to see patterns in their preparation and test-taking behaviors that are costing them points on exams. As a series of questions, this is the checklist:

1. Did I incorrectly learn the material?
2. Did I neglect to study the material?
3. Did I take inadequate notes?
4. Did I misread the directions?
5. Did I misread the question itself?
6. Did I accidentally miss a question?
7. Did I consciously skip a question?
8. Did I run short of time?

In addition, for an essay exam:

9. Did I forget to write a thesis?
10. Did I inadequately develop the body of my essay?
11. Did I forget to write a conclusion?
12. Did I omit needed transitions? (p. 289)

Good test takers are test wise, and any words you can offer to the wise will allow them greater opportunity to show what they know on an exam. Many students have such deeply ingrained poor test-taking strategies that they actually think any alternative is tantamount to cheating! For example, some students protest in disbelief when we suggest to them that they might read through the alternative choices before reading the first part of a multiple choice item. Or, worse still, that they might first read the questions following a passage on a standardized test before they read the passage. When they do read the questions first, they find they can then read the passage with an important purpose in mind: to get the answer to the questions! If tests are to be more than tests of ability to take tests, then students will have to have instruction in the kind of behaviors that make good test scores possible. The checklist above will provide a starting point for that instruction.

FACTORS OF STUDY

By surveying the study habits of several hundred junior-high, senior-high, and college students, we have been able to identify three distinct factors that constitute the art of study. These three factors are (1) compulsiveness, (2) inquisitiveness, and (3) distractability (Estes & Richards, 1985).

■ Compulsivity: Hard Work Counts for Something

Good students are industrious, sometimes to the point of compulsivity. At the very least, they are very active in their pursuit of understanding. As they read, they *do* things to enhance their understanding and their remembering. An important conclusion we can draw from our research on study skills is that the doings we refer to are the difference between an "A" on tests and some lower grade. In other words, compulsivity in study habits may not distinguish "B" students from "C" students from "D" students, but it will distinguish the "A" student from the rest of the pack.

Successful students use a system to approach their study and direct their efforts with activities such as those we outlined for anticipation, realization, and contemplation. Successful students can be industrious, even compulsive, because they not only know what it means to study, they also know how to control their study. Successful students are aware of what to do when; they are also aware of options. A significant frustration for many learners, though, is their lack of awareness of how to approach their study. These students can't be compulsive because they are unfamiliar with any system or framework that could be used to study industriously. To help students become more industrious, even compulsive, we suggest you begin with those previewing, notetaking, and reviewing and test-taking activities we shared in this chapter.

■ Inquisitiveness: The Creative Process at Work

Inquisitiveness implies an extraordinarily high degree of curiosity, and it is a term that exactly represents the second factor of study we have identified. Much more clearly than either working hard (the compulsivity factor) or keeping one's mind on one's work (the distractability factor), inquisitiveness is the factor of study that best predicts how well a student is likely to score on a test. In general, the more inquisitive one is in completing homework assignments, the more likely one is to score well on tests. Instructionally, this means whatever a teacher can do to help students generate curiosity toward their homework assignments will stand those students in good stead when the time arises for a test on the material in the assignment. Many of the activities we have suggested under the headings anticipations, realizations, and contemplations are designed to make readers more active and inquisitive in their approach to study. Students who demonstrate inquisitiveness are those who stop from time to time in their study to capture the author's meaning by putting ideas in their own words, trying to relate the ideas they are learning to things they learned in other places. Inquisitive students are always trying to make sense of what they are learning. They test themselves as they are trying to learn. In short, they approach their study with an attitude of questioning, constantly thinking of ways to make what they are learning their own.

To help your students become inquisitive, explain and model for them at every possible opportunity activities that will engender for them the habit of inquisitiveness. You might recall in chapter 8 we noted that good questioning by students comes from stimulating questioning by teachers. In addition to serving as a role model for them, you might also have your students try paired questioning and ReQuest. You can do them and yourself no greater favor than to help them develop their inquisitive nature.

Distractability: Keeping One's Mind on the Work

Distractability is the clearest and strongest study characteristic we have been able to identify. Everyone suffers from some degree of distractability, the inability to stick to a task. However, because everyone suffers from it, distractability predicts nothing about how successful study will or won't be. Both good and bad studiers report that they are distractable. In many people, avoidance behaviors for study are quite refined. There's nothing like sitting down to study to remind one of all the things that need to be done first, or to arouse the pangs of hunger for a snack. Students for whom this is a real handicap often find they don't know what they've been reading when they come to the end of a page, they tend to daydream, they find it takes them rather long to get warmed up to the tasks of studying, and generally they find their periods of study are too short for them to accomplish much. But the difference between good and poor studiers is not in whether these things are true for them but in whether they are able, by some means, to control their distractability.

Unfortunately, many students have little or no concept of basic work-study habits that can help them be more efficient learners. They often study at haphazard times, whenever the mood strikes them, and in places that actually detract from rather than facilitate learning. Good work-study habits can foster students' awareness that dependable learning is based on the intent to remember by understanding. Simple exposure to information does not guarantee learning, nor does the passive repetition of an experience. When students learn to organize their study time and to establish a familiar place for study, they can become more proficient learners.

Efficient study can result from students' self-analysis of their use of time. A daily schedule, however, is a personal thing and should vary with each individual. Once established, it can indicate to a student how much studying is being done and give a better indication of how well the student is doing in a class. If a student is frustrated by his or her inability to learn, a motivating factor might be the realization of how much time and effort is being wasted. Few students are bored by learning; instead, they are frustrated and "turned off" by nonlearning. If a student can be encouraged to establish a reasonable daily routine where chunks of time for study can be set aside, it is likely that he or she will become more involved in study and perhaps more motivated to learn.

Finding the best place to study is another aspect of good study habits that can result in marked improvement in learning. Some students have no place where they feel comfortable studying. Usually, the best place is a special place, perhaps in a corner of a bedroom set aside for studying, or in a library carrel. *Where* may be as crucial as *how* one studies.

We think the important point to be made is the idea that distractability is controllable in a variety of ways. Perhaps most important among these is to establish an appropriate frame of mind for study. With tongue in cheek, Don Dansereau has suggested several ways to accomplish this in an unpublished paper entitled, "How to Create and Maintain a Crummy Mood." The following are some of his suggestions, with some elaboration from us:

Seven Ways to Create and Maintain a Crummy Mood for Study

1. The night before you know you'll have to do a lot of studying, be sure you don't get a good night's sleep. This is crucial. It is difficult to maintain a bad mood, to say, "I'm just not in the mood for study right now—maybe later," if you're rested and alert. If all else fails, force yourself to stay up two or three hours later than usual, and you'll probably be able to keep up the feeling of lethargy all day.

2. Don't plan ahead, and for goodness sake don't organize your study around a regular schedule. Be disorganized. Things like not being able to find what you need when you need it, forgetting when assignments are due, and postponing homework till the last minute are sure-fire ways to fight a proper mood for study and to insure that the study you do is practically useless.

3. Dwell on your failures and weaknesses; think about the things that you have the most trouble with in school. Blow these things out of proportion and you will begin to have a lousy self-image. People with poor self-image are the ones you see around you who have the best luck in maintaining a lousy mood. You'll want to be just like them.

4. While you're studying, watch the clock, count the pages you have left—anything to keep from becoming interested in the material. High interest in what you are studying will often put you in a mood to concentrate, which is just opposite the effect of the crummy mood you're trying to maintain.

5. Study in a place that is uncomfortable and not well lighted. If you strain your eyes, you'll naturally, often unconsciously, try to avoid the task of studying. You'll begin to feel tired even if you're not.

6. Before you sit down to study, tune the radio to something distracting. It is true that some people study well with background music, and for different people different kinds of music will suit. To avoid a good mood for study, pick something you dislike—maybe a news-only station or opera or a talk show on political issues.

7. Get together with friends to "study" when you know none of them have the least interest in studying. Chances are the group of you can find many ways to waste time together and forget all about studying. Misery loves company, you know.

Bernice Bragstad and Sharon Stumpf (1982) take a somewhat different approach to the problem of concentration. Students at the high school where they teach put together and published in the school newspaper a set of guidelines for creating and maintaining concentration. Bragstad and Stumpf suggest one way to devise such a set of guidelines is to survey staff and students with two questions: Based on your experience, (1) What interferes with concentration? and (2) What contributes to effective concentration?

This is the set of guidelines published in *The Lance,* LaFollette High School, Madison, Wisconsin:

CONCENTRATE? OF COURSE YOU CAN!

After being in high school for a few years, we juniors realize how many changes we experienced as freshmen. All of a sudden we were in classes with many students we didn't know. We had a different teacher for each class. We could participate in a great variety of activities. We had more free time about which we had to make decisions. We also had regular homework, which was required for credit in our classes. In addition, we had to become familiar with a new building and new expectations from those around us. Sometimes we felt muddled and confused, but we wanted to do well.

Effective concentration contributes to success, and lack of concentration contributes to failure. Concentration is important. Realizing that all the changes we were experiencing as freshmen did affect our concentration, we decided to give you some tips that we wish we had been given as freshmen.

What Interferes with Concentration?

1. Noise, people talking, music, TV. Having a quiet place to study is at the top of the list for upperclassmen. If your attention is divided or constantly interrupted, your mind will not be able to think effectively. Studying is thinking. Without these external interrupters, you can learn more and finish faster with improved concentration. Choose a quiet spot for study. If possible, choose the same place every day. Less distraction results in better concentration and improved learning.

2. Daydreaming. If your thoughts continually wander, stop and analyze yourself to determine the cause of the distraction. Whenever you find yourself daydreaming, make a mark on a piece of paper. Then work to reduce the marks per hour or per evening.

Another suggestion: give yourself a few minutes to daydream every hour so that you can concentrate the rest of the time. Don't let extensive daydreaming become a habit just to avoid the work of studying. Dig in and you'll soon involve those brain cells. Just quickly guide your attention back to studying when you begin to daydream.

3. Being Hungry and Tired. If you are hungry or tired, how about eating a little food or taking a short nap? Being alert when you study is important so that you become involved. Otherwise studying is just an obedience exercise. You can think and learn. Don't let hunger or fatigue be stumbling blocks for you.

4. Personal Problems. Not thinking about personal problems is difficult. All students have problems of one kind or another—so do adults. Even if there is no immediate solution, having the support of others feels good. Talking privately to your guidance counselor, who has had a lot of experience with problems, may help you in coping with or solving your problem. Even deciding that you will talk to someone may help you postpone thinking about a problem until you have finished studying. That "someone" may be a teacher, a friend, or your parents. We all need someone to listen. There are people who would like to help you.

What Develops Concentration?

1. Wanting to Learn! Every sophomore wants to learn what is in the Driver's Manual because getting a driver's license is important. The

desire to drive is so great that each sophomore is totally involved in learning. That is concentration.

Observe students in any class you take. You'll see some who are really paying attention and others whose attention is drifting from one thing to another.

Do you want to learn? This is a decision that you will have to make for yourself. No one can learn for you. Your mind is always active and ready to receive new ideas. Wanting to help your mind grow is a good stimulus for concentration.

2. Become Interested! The more you know about any subject, the more interested you become. You may not care about snakes, but if you really learned a lot about their habits and their problems, you might become fascinated. In high school try to find an interest in any course you take. Try to become an independent learner, instead of limping along with your teacher as your crutch. Don't expect your teacher to carry you. The teacher is there only as your assistant. You have the responsibility to learn. If you work, you'll very likely become interested. This helps concentration.

3. Being Organized. We have a few tips for this. First, make a weekly study schedule that you can usually follow. Be flexible if change is needed, but also be purposeful. Having a regular time for studying makes it easier to begin.

Second, know exactly what your assignments are and get the materials you need. Keep a detailed record of your assignments: the date, what the assignment is, the pages of relevant material in the text, and (after numbering the pages in your notebook for that course) the number of your notebook pages on the topic. One line in your notebook will look like this:

Date	Assignment	Pg-book	Pg-notebook
9/15	Factoring Prob. 1–15 Review.	35–40	15–16

Teachers and students claim that this continuing record is a reminder of make-up work after being absent. You'll also have a review record for a test.

Third, start studying the minute you sit down at your desk. If you always do this, you may find yourself concentrating with less effort.

Fourth, varying your activity by switching subjects gives you a change. Plan ahead for a break between subjects so you really work, or plan a little reward for yourself when you finish.

4. Competing with Yourself. Don't worry about all the work you have, just concentrate on what you are doing right now. Set a time when you think you should finish your science or English; then see if you can beat the clock. Timing yourself prevents you from daydreaming and poking along. You'll concentrate better when you're competing against the clock—even if you lose.

5. Being a Question Mark. Asking questions is a sign of intelligence. Listen carefully in class, but if you don't understand an assignment, be sure to ask the teacher for further explanation. You can't remember when you don't understand. In doing homework, if you know what to do and how to do it, you'll have less difficulty really "digging in."

6. Being Realistic. Expect to have some distractions. Unbroken concentration for long periods of time is not a common experience. When your thoughts wander, quickly refocus on your work. This single reaction saves time and emotional energy. In the face of distractions, your growing power of concentration will give you a sense of achievement. (Bragstad & Stumpf, pp. 197–199)

SUPPORT STRATEGIES FOR EFFECTIVE STUDY

■ ■ While the art of study requires industriousness, inquisitiveness, and an ability to cope with distractions, as well as a sophisticated repertoire of learning strategies and the knowledge of when to use them, another feature cannot be ignored. We refer to a dimension of learning that enables a student to use INSERT, SMART, and other strategies effectively; we're talking now about strategies that create a context for effective study. We want to highlight three of these so-called support strategies, drawing again on the work of our friend and colleague Dan Dansereau (1978):

1. Knowledge on the part of the reader as to exactly what will be expected as a result of reading and study.
2. Ability of the reader to focus on the task of reading, to concentrate, to cultivate a positive attitude toward the learning task.
3. Ability on the part of the reader to apply strategies efficiently and effectively, including ability to monitor the use of a strategy and to modify the strategy when necessary.

■ Knowledge of What's Expected

When students have a high degree of knowledge of what is likely to be tested from an assigned reading, they score higher on tests than if they have only the vague notion they will be tested on something from the reading. Good readers naturally focus on important information, and the fact that a specific bit of text is likely to be on a test tends to define that bit as important. One negative aspect of this phenomenon is that when students are repeatedly tested over minute detail, they will learn to read to remember minute details. (Much of what we teach students is more implicit than explicit.)

We hope we are not being unnecessarily repetitious here, but we cannot overemphasize the importance of the direct connection between how students approach learning and their perception of how they will be tested. Ideally, any test of comprehension would focus on the reasoning of the reader, not solely or even primarily on the product of the reasoning. If you agree, then you already know what students need to know about testing. They need to know the test will focus on the decisions they have made about the text and the reasons behind those decisions. They need to learn they will be asked to paraphrase what they have read. They need to know they will be asked to demonstrate an understanding of interrelationships and links among the ideas they have studied. When readers realize that certain strategies lead them to learn what they will be tested on, then learning strategies and tests of learning become compatible and complementary.

■ Ability to Focus and Concentrate

Recall the image of Rodin's "The Thinker." Were this sculpture alive, one has the feeling it would be difficult to distract the person. Likewise, professional athletes are known for their ablity to block out the distractions of crowd noises and extraneous events around them. It is, as we have already discussed, this power of concentration that we would hope to help all students develop. Not surprisingly, when students focus their attention and concentrate on learning, they learn the most. Dansereau (1978) offers several suggestions we have not mentioned that can help students learn to concentrate better.

First, help students determine when, how, and why they get distracted. They also need to assess the length of their distractions and their reaction to being distracted from a learning task. Students can also be encouraged to keep logs or diaries of their study sessions over a period of a week, after which they can analyze their study patterns.

Second, help students rectify bad habits, replacing them with effective study patterns. Awareness is the first step. Students need to be aware of the specifics of their own study habits. Often students have only a vague awareness that their study attempts will be frustrating. They do not approach study tasks with specific strategies in mind because they usually have no way to verbalize what it is they are doing when they study.

For our research on study skills, we have adapted a study skills inventory first published in 1934 by Gilbert Wren. Like other inventories of its kind (for example, Preston & Botel, 1967), the Wren inventory covers major areas of importance in study. Our adaptation of the scale is offered in reproducible form on p. 271, and we suggest you use it with your students and follow it up with a discussion of how and why various study habits might produce various results.

In responding to the inventory, students are asked to indicate "rarely or never," "sometimes," or "often or always" to a series of statements of study habits. Some items on the scale are worded positively, some are worded negatively. In scoring, we assign a value of 1 to "rarely or never" if the item is positive or assign a value of 3 to "rarely or never" if the item is negative. Likewise, we assign a value of 3 to "often or always" if the item is positive or assign a value of 1 to "often or always" if the item is negative.

Third, the most specific advice you can give students is that they approach the task of studying with determination to do specific things. If you provide them with specific directions for their reading and study, this will help them get on the right track. Also, suggest they "relax and clear their minds by counting breaths." Then, they should "imagine a period of successful study, then being distracted, followed by coping with the distraction." (Dansereau, 1978, p. 25) This will result in students beginning to gain control over the environment of their study as they find increasingly more success in applying learning strategies like those we have discussed.

■ Ability to Monitor Studying

It is important that students pay more attention to the monitoring aspect of their learning. With an increased awareness of effective learning strategies, students can benefit from an evaluation of their study. Notice that many of the learning strategies we have suggested include either a specific element that involves monitoring or the opportunity to include monitoring.

We suggest students use inspectional reading as a pre-reading strategy; they can then find places to use as monitoring checkpoints during study. This has the effect of breaking the text into manageable portions, and is particularly helpful when assignments are quite long. At each checkpoint, the reader can ask questions like, "How is it going?" "Are the decisions I'm making logical ones?" "What's going together with what?" "What do I seem to be missing?" "What can I

AN INVENTORY OF STUDY HABITS

Directions: This is a scale to measure your study habits. By understanding what you do when you study, your teacher will be better able to help you develop even better habits. As you read each of the statements below, think about how you usually study for this class. Then, indicate whether the statement is true for you "rarely or never," "sometimes," or "often or always."

	Rarely or Never	Sometimes	Often or Always
1. I try to judge how the writer's ideas make sense.			
2. I try to relate the writer's ideas to things I learned in other places.			
3. I try to memorize word for word most of the information.			
4. I try to understand the text well enough to put it in my own words without losing the author's meaning.			
5. I underline or set off in some way parts of what I'm reading.			
6. I take notes on what I'm reading.			
7. I test myself by answering end of chapter questions.			
8. I try to put the main points of the passage in my own words.			
9. I find it hard to keep my mind on what I'm studying; I don't know what I have been reading about when I get through.			
10. I go over the passage page by page and try to memorize the important points and details on each page.			
11. I have a tendency to daydream when trying to study.			
12. It takes me some time to get warmed up to the task; I am likely to waste time.			
13. I reread parts that I understand or have set off in some way.			
14. My periods of study are interrupted by outside interference such as telephone calls, visitors, and noises.			
15. I reread my notes on the passage.			
16. I find it hard to force myself to finish work by a certain time, under pressure.			
17. I have to wait for the mood to strike me or for an inspiration before starting a task; I am likely to waste time.			
18. I read the questions at the end of the chapter before I read the assignments.			

paraphrase?" "Can I image these ideas?" If problems start to arise, their causes can be more easily pinpointed. "Is the selection I am trying to study too long?" "Am I getting lost?" "Do I need additional background information?" These questions can help the reader control his or her own study behaviors by insuring that at any point in the study process, their effectiveness is being examined.

AN INQUIRY APPROACH TO READING AND REASONING

■ ■ Our object in this book is to share with teachers ways to help students become more accomplished as reader/learners. Among the most delightful discoveries enjoyed by an accomplished reader is the power and pleasure that comes from reasoning while reading. The reasoning reader controls the reading event, knows when he or she understands, knows when to alter strategies, and knows when any difficulty in comprehension is beyond his or her control. To help you help your students become accomplished as reader/learners, we have proposed ARC as a framework for learning and a guide for teaching. All of the ARC elements lead to a student's proficiency as a master of study. It takes time, patience, and courage for each of us and each of our students.

As a final thought, let us suggest that the ultimate gift any of us can offer to our students is the opportunity to claim mastery of the art of study. Toward that aim, we have found within the nature of inquiry itself a nine-step process that learners everywhere seem to activate. We have not discovered these steps, only been reminded that we have known them all along. The nine steps are:

1. Identify an area of inquiry.
2. Identify what is known about it.
3. Establish hypotheses.
4. Seek data.
5. Evaluate data.
6. Explain data.
7. Consider alternative explanations.
8. Establish additional questions.
9. Establish new hypotheses.

Students can learn to apply these formal steps of inquiry to any learning situation. As they become adept at making inquiry an integral part of their study, they will benefit from the following study plan:

An Inquiry Approach to Reading and Reasoning

1. Identify the topic of study.
2. Think long and hard about what you know about it. (If you could put everything that is known about that topic on one piece of paper, what would you write?)
3. What do you expect to learn about this topic? Why might you want to learn that?
4. Study the assignment.
5. Ask yourself: "What did I find out?"
6. Answer this for yourself: "What does it all mean?"
7. Ask this: "Is there any other way this might make sense?"
8. Identify what you did not learn that you thought you would have or should have learned. What questions do you still have?

If students learn to approach reading in the spirit of inquiry, they will learn to absorb new ideas into their personal frame of reference, and then those new ideas will serve to facilitate new learning. And so it goes, the cycle of reading. Anticipation leads to exploration and realization and subsequently to contemplation and further anticipation. And we have come full circle.

REFERENCES

Adams, A., Carnine, D., & Gersten, R. (1982). Instructional strategies for studying content area texts in the intermediate grades. *Reading Research Quarterly, 18,* 6–26.

Adams, J. L. (1980). *Conceptual blockbusting: A guide to better ideas.* New York: W. W. Norton.

Adler, M. J. & Van Doren, C. (1972). *How to read a book.* New York: Simon & Schuster.

Alvermann, D. E. & Boothby, P. R. (1983). A preliminary investigation of the differences in children's retention of "inconsiderate" text. *Reading Psychology, 4,* 237–246.

Anderson, J. R. (1980). *Cognitive psychology.* San Francisco: W. H. Freeman.

Anderson, R. C. & Freebody, P. (1981). Vocabulary knowledge. In J. T. Guthrie (Ed.), *Comprehension and teaching: Research reviews.* Newark, DE: International Reading Association.

Anderson, T. H., Armbruster, B. B., & Kantor, R. N. (1980). *How clearly written are children's textbooks? or Of bladderworts and alfa.* (Reading Education Report No. 16). Urbana, IL: University of Illinois Center for the Study of Reading.

Armbruster, B. B. & Anderson, T. H. (1982). *Problem/solution explanations in history textbooks, or So what if Governor Stanford missed the spike and hit the rail?* (Technical Report No. 252). Urbana, IL: University of Illinois Center for the Study of Reading.

Asher, S. R. (1978). *Influence of topic interest on Black children's and white children's reading comprehension.* (Technical Report No. 99). Urbana, IL: University of Illinois Center for the Study of Reading.

Ausubel, D. P. (1978). *Educational psychology: A cognitive view.* New York: Holt, Rinehart, and Winston.

Bach, R. (1977). *Illusions: The adventures of a reluctant messiah.* New York: Dell.

Baker, L. (1979). *Do I understand or do I not understand; That is the question.* (Reading Education Report No. 10). Urbana, IL: University of Illinois Center for the Study of Reading.

Banan, J. M. (1972) Negative human interaction. *Journal of Counseling Psychology, 19,* 81–82.

Baring-Gould, W. S. & Baring-Gould, C. (1967). *The annotated Mother Goose.* New York: Bramhall House.

Barnes, C. P. (1983). *Building better health, red level.* Evanston, IL: McDougal Littell.

Barron, R. F. (1969). The use of vocabulary as an advance organizer. In H. L. Herber & P. L. Sanders (Eds.), *Research in reading in the content areas: First year report.* Syracuse, NY: Syracuse University Reading and Language Arts Center.

Barron, R. F. (1979). Research for the classroom teacher: Recent developments on the structured overview as an advance organizer. In H. L. Herber

& J. D. Riley (Eds.), *Research in reading in the content areas: The fourth report.* Syracuse, NY: Syracuse University Reading and Language Arts Center, 171–177.

Bartlett, F. C. (1932). *Remembering: A study in experimental and social psychology.* London: Cambridge University.

Belloni, L. F. & Jongsma, E. A. (1978). The effects of interest on reading comprehension of low-achieving students. *Journal of Reading, 22,* 106–109.

Bernstein, M. R. (1955). Relationship between interest and reading comprehension. *Journal of Educational Research, 49,* 283–288.

Biology. (1979). New York: Worth.

Biology: Living systems. (1976). Columbus, OH: Charles E. Merrill.

Biological science: An ecological approach. (1973). Skokie, IL: Rand McNally.

Biological science: An inquiry into life. (1980). New York: Harcourt Brace Jovanovich.

Bloom, B. S. (1956). *Taxonomy of educational objectives, handbook I: Cognitive domain.* New York: McKay.

Bragstad, B. J. & Stumpf, S. M. (1982). *A guidebook for teaching study skills and motivation.* Boston: Allyn and Bacon.

Bransford, J. D. (1979). *Human cognition: Learning, understanding, and remembering.* Belmont, CA: Wadsworth.

Brooks, C. & Warren, R. P. (1979). *Modern rhetoric.* New York: Harcourt Brace Jovanovich.

Brown, A. L. (1980). Metacognitive development and reading. In R. J. Spiro, B. C. Bruce, & W. F. Brewer (Eds.), *Theoretical issues in reading comprehension.* Hillsdale, NJ: Erlbaum.

Brown, A. L. (1981). Metacognition: The development of selective attention strategies for learning from texts. In M. L. Kamil (Ed.), *Directions in Reading, Research, and Instruction, Thirtieth Yearbook of the National Reading Conference.* Washington, D.C.: The National Reading Conference, 21–43.

Brown, R. (1958). *Words and things.* New York: Free Press.

Buros, O. K. (1978). *Mental measurements yearbook.* Highland Park, NJ: Gryphon.

Business law. (1982). Boston: Houghton Mifflin.

Carlsen, G. R. (1980). *Books and the teenage reader: Second revised edition.* New York: Bantam.

Carver, R. P. (1974). *Improving reading comprehension: Measuring readability.* (Final report, Contract No. N00014-72-C-0240, Office of Naval Research). Silver Springs, MD: American Institute for Research. (ERIC Document Reproduction Service No. ED 092 920).

Christensen, F. & Christensen, B. (1976). *A new rhetoric.* New York: Harper & Row.

Concepts in science. (1980). New York: Harcourt Brace Jovanovich.

Cowan, E. & Cowan, G. (1980). *Writing.* New York: John Wiley & Sons.

Cramer, E. H. (1982). Reading comprehension and attitude of high and low imagers: A comparison. In J. A. Niles & L. A. Harris (Eds.), *New inquiries in reading research and instruction*. Rochester, NY: National Reading Conference.

Cunningham, P., Crawley, S. G., & Mountain, L. (1983). Vocabulary scavenger hunts: A scheme for schema development. *Reading Horizons, 24,* 45–50.

Dale, E. & Chall, J. S. (1948). *A formula for predicting readability*. Columbus, OH: Bureau of Educational Research, Ohio State University.

Dansereau, D. F. (1977). How to create and maintain a crummy mood. In Dansereau, D. F. (Ed.), *Instructional packet: Techniques of college learning*. Ft. Worth, TX: Texas Christian University.

Dansereau, D. F. (1978) The development of a learning strategies curriculum. In H. F. O'Neil (Ed.), *Learning strategies*. New York: Academic Press.

Davis, A. & Clark, E. (1981, October). High yield study skills instruction. Paper presented at annual meeting of Plains Regional Conference of the International Reading Conference, Des Moines, IA. (ERIC Document Reproduction Service No. ED 208 372).

Davis, H. B., Harris, G., Montoya, P., Schirrmacher, R., & Kahn, M. Kids have the answers, do you have the questions? *Instructor, XC, 4,* 63–68.

de Bono, E. (1983). The direct teaching of thinking as a skill. *Phi Delta Kappan, 64,* 703–708.

de Saint-Exupery, A. (1982), *The little prince*. New York: Harcourt Brace Jovanovich.

Dewey, J. (1897). My pedagogic creed. *The School Journal,* LIV, *3,* 77–80. Reprinted in M. S. Dworkin (Ed.) (1959), *Dewey on education*. New York: Teachers College Press.

Dewey, J. (1902). *The child and the curriculum*. Chicago: University of Chicago Press. Reprinted in M. S. Dworkin (Ed.) (1959), *Dewey on education*. New York: Teachers College Press.

Donaldson, M. (1978). *Children's minds*. New York: W. W. Norton.

Dooling, D. J. & Lachman, R. (1971). Effects of comprehension on retention of prose. *Journal of Experimental Psychology, 88,* 216–222.

Durkin, D. (1978–79). What classroom observations reveal about reading comprehension instruction. *Reading Research Quarterly, 14,* 481–533.

Eanet, M. G. & Manzo, A. V. (1976). REAP: A strategy for improving reading/writing/study skills, *Journal of Reading, 19,* 647–652.

Earle, R. A. (1976). *Teaching reading and mathematics,* Newark, DE: International Reading Association.

Earth Science. (1981). Englewood Cliffs, NJ: Prentice-Hall.

Edwards, A. L. (1957). *Techniques of attitude scale construction*. New York: Appleton-Century-Crofts.

Estes, T. H. & Vaughan, J. L. (1973). Reading interest and comprehension: Implications. *The Reading Teacher, 27,* 149–153.

Estes, T. H. (1979). The paradox of text: Will the real meaning please identify itself? *McGill Journal of Education, 16,* 81–92.

Estes, T. H., Estes, J. J., Richards, H. C., & Roettger, D. (1981). *Estes attitude scales: Measures of attitudes toward school subjects*. Austin, TX: Pro-Ed.

Estes, T. H. (1982). The nature and structure of text. In A. Berger & H. A. Robinson (Eds.), *Secondary school reading: What research reveals for classroom practice*. Urbana, IL: ERIC Clearinghouse on Reading and Communication Skills.

Estes, T. H. & Wetmore, M. E. (1983). Assessing the comprehensibility of text. *Reading Psychology, 4*, 37–51.

Estes, T. H. & Richards, H. C. (1985). Habits of study and test performance. *Journal of Reading Behavior. 17*, 1–13.

Fader, D. (1971). *The naked children*. New York: Macmillan.

Fader, D. (1976). *The new hooked on books*. New York: Berkley.

Ferguson, M. (1980). *The aquarian conspiracy*. Los Angeles: J. P. Tarcher.

Fry, E. (1977). Fry's readability graph: Clarifications, validity, and extension to level 17. *Journal of Reading, 21*, 242–252.

Gambrell, L. B. (1982). Induced mental imagery and the text prediction performance of first and third graders. In J. A. Niles & L. A. Harris (Eds.), *New inquiries in reading research and instruction*. Rochester, NY: National Reading Conference, 131–135.

Garner, R. (1982). Resolving comprehension failure through text lookbacks: Direct training and practice effects among good and poor comprehenders in grades 6 and 7. *Reading Psychology, 3*, 221–231.

Gillis, M. K. & Olson, M. W. (1982). Improving reading/study skills in a college content class. San Marcos, TX: Southwest Texas State University (ERIC Document Reproduction Service No. ED 225 103).

Goodlad, J. I. (1983). A study of schooling: Some findings and hypotheses. *Phi Delta Kappan, 64*, 465–470.

Goodman, K. S. (1965). A linguistic study of cues and miscues in reading. *Elementary English, 42*, 639–643.

Goodman, K. S. (1967). Reading: A psycholinguistic guessing game. *Journal of the Reading Specialist, 4*, 126–135.

Guthrie, J. (1978). Remembering content. *Journal of Reading, 22*, 64–66.

Guzak, F. J. (1967). Teacher questioning and reading. *Reading Teacher, 21*, 227–234.

Halliday, M. A. K., & Hasan, R. (1976). *Cohesion in English*. London: Longman.

Herber, H. L. (1970). *Teaching reading in content areas*. Englewood Cliffs, NJ: Prentice-Hall.

Herber, H. L. (1978). *Teaching reading in content areas*. (2nd ed.). Englewood Cliffs, NJ: Prentice-Hall.

Hirsh, E. D., Jr. (1977). *The philosophy of composition*. Chicago: University of Chicago.

Holley, C. D. & Dansereau, D. F. (1984). *Spatial learning strategies: Techniques, applications, and related issues*. Orlando, FL: Academic Press.

Impact of our past. (1972). New York: American Heritage.

Iser, W. (1974). The reading process: A phenomenological approach. In R. Cohen (Ed.), *New directions in literary history*. Baltimore: Johns Hopkins University.

It's our choice. (1972). New York: Globe Book.

Kintsch, W. (1979, April). *On comprehension*. Paper presented at the meeting of the American Educational Research Association, San Francisco.

Klare, G. R. (1982). Readability. In H. E. Mitzel (Ed.), *Encyclopedia of educational research* (5th ed.). New York: Free Press.

Kennedy, L. D. & Halinski, R. S. (1975). Measuring attitudes: An extra dimension. *Journal of Reading, 18,* 518–522.

Kronholz, J. (1980, September 18), Shed no more tears over the crocodile: It has snapped back. *The Wall Street Journal*, p. 1.

Langer, J. A. (1980). Relation between levels of prior knowledge and the organization of recall. In M. L. Kamil & A. J. Moe (Eds.), *Perspectives in reading research and instruction.* Washington, DC: National Reading Conference, 28–33.

Langer, J. A. (1981). From theory to practice: A prereading plan. *Journal of Reading, 25,* 152–156.

Langer, J. A. (1984). Examining background knowledge and text comprehension. *Reading Research Quarterly, 19,* 468–481.

Langer, J. A. & Nicholich, M. (1981). Prior knowledge and its relation to comprehension. *Journal of Reading Behavior, XIII*, 373–379.

Likert, R. S. (1932). A technique for the measurement of attitudes. *Archives of Psychology*, 140.

Mandler, J. M. & Johnson, N. S. (1977). Remembrance of things past: Story structure and recall. *Cognitive Psychology, 9,* 111–151.

Manzo, A. V. (1969). ReQuest procedure. *Journal of Reading, 13,* 123–126.

McLaughlin, G. H. (1969). SMOG grading—a new readability formula. *Journal of Reading, 12,* 639–646.

Meyer, B. J. F. (1975). *The organization of prose and its effect on memory.* Amsterdam: North Holland.

Meyer, B. J. F. (1977). What is remembered from prose: A function of passage structure. In R. O. Freedle (Ed.), *Discourse production and comprehension.* Norwood, NJ: Ablex.

Michener, J. (1974). *Centennial.* New York: Random House.

Minsky, M. (1975). Framework for representing knowledge. In P. H. Winston (Ed.), *The psychology of computer vision.* New York: McGraw-Hill.

Neisser, U. (1976). *Cognition and reality.* San Francisco: W. H. Freeman.

O'Conner, M. F. (1969). *Mystery and manners.* New York: Farrar, Straus, & Giroux.

Osborn, A. (1963). *Applied imagination.* New York: Scribner.

Our land and heritage. (1979). Lexington, MA: Ginn.

Pauk, W. (1973). The interest level: That's the thing. *Journal of Reading, 16,* 459–461.

Pauk, W. (1974). *How to study in college.* Boston: Houghton Mifflin.

Pearson, P. D. & Johnson, D. D. (1978). *Teaching reading comprehension.* New York: Holt, Rinehart, and Winston.

Petrosky, A. R. (1982). Reading achievement. In A. Berger & H. A. Robinson (Eds.), *Secondary school reading: What research reveals for classroom practice.* Urbana, IL: ERIC Clearinghouse on Reading and Communication Skills.

Petty, W. T., Herold, C. T., & Stoll, E. (1968). *The state of knowledge about the teaching of vocabulary*. Champaign, IL: National Council of Teachers of English.

Porter, D. & Popp, H. M. (1973). *An alternative to readability measures: Judging difficulty of children's trade books*. Paper presented at the annual meeting of the American Educational Research Association, February, 1973.

Preston, R. C. & Botel, M. (1967). *Study habits checklist*. Chicago: Science Research Associates.

Rankin, E. F. & Culhane, J. W. (1969). Comparable cloze and multiple-choice comprehension test scores. *Journal of Reading, 13*, 193–198.

Reading, thinking and writing: Results from the 1979–80 national assessment of reading and literature. (Report No. 11-L-01). Denver, CO: National Assessment of Educational Progress, 1981. (ERIC Document Reproduction Service No. ED 209 641).

Reading power and study skills for college work. (1978). New York: Harcourt Brace Jovanovich.

Rico, G. L. (1983). *Writing the natural way: Using right brain techniques to release your expressive power*. Los Angeles: J. P. Tarcher.

Robinson, R. D. (1971). *An introduction to the cloze procedure*. Newark, DE: International Reading Association.

Rogers, C. (1969). *Freedom to learn*. Columbus, OH: Charles E. Merrill.

Rogers, C. (1982). *Freedom to learn for the eighties*. Columbus, OH: Charles E. Merrill.

Rosenblatt, L. M. (1978). *The reader, the text, the poem*. Carbondale and Edwardsville, IL: Southern Illinois University.

Rothwell, C. L. (1983). Analysis of adolescents' ratings of text: Familiarity and importance. In P. L. Anders (Ed.), *Research on reading in secondary schools: Monograph Nos. 10–11*. Tucson, AZ: University of Arizona, 18–25.

Samson, R. W. (1975). *Thinking skills: A guide to logic and comprehension*. Stamford, CN: Innovative Sciences.

Sanders, N. M. (1969). *Classroom questions: What kinds?* New York: Harper & Row.

Schallert, D. L. & Kleiman, G. M. (1979). *Why the teacher is easier to understand than the textbook*. (Reading Education Report No. 9). Urbana, IL: University of Illinois Center for the Study of Reading.

Schrag, P. (1965). *Voices in the classroom: Public schools and public attitudes*. Boston: Beacon Press.

Science for a changing world. (1972). San Diego, CA: Benefic Press.

Shnayer, S. W. (1968). Some relationships between reading interest and reading comprehension. Paper presented at the annual convention of the International Reading Association, Boston, MA. (ERIC Document Reproduction Service No. ED 068 973).

Singer, H. (1975). The SEER technique: A noncomputational procedure for quickly estimating readability level. *Journal of Reading Behavior, 7*, 255–267.

Smith, S. L. (1979). Retellings as measures of comprehension: A perspective. In J. C. Harste & R. F. Carey (Eds.), *New perspectives on comprehension.* Bloomington, IN: School of Education, Indiana University.

Smith, W. H. (1980). What they didn't tell you about Jack and Jill: An aspect of reading comprehension. *Journal of Reading, 24,* 101–108.

Smith, F. (1978). *Understanding reading: A psycholinguistic analysis of reading and learning to read* (2nd ed.). New York: Holt, Rinehart, and Winston.

Smith, S. L., Carey, R. F., & Harste, J. C. (1982). The contexts of reading. In A. Berger & H. A. Robinson (Eds.), *Secondary school reading.* Urbana, IL: ERIC Clearinghouse on Reading and Communication Skills, and the National Conference on Research in English.

Spache, G. D. (1960). *Good reading for poor readers.* Champaign, IL: Garrard.

Spache, G. (1969). *Good reading for poor readers* (rev. ed.). Champaign, IL: Garrard.

Squire, J. (1964). *Responses of adolescents while reading four stories.* Research Report No. 2. Urbana, IL: National Council of Teachers of English.

Stauffer, R. G. (1969). *Teaching reading as a thinking process.* New York: Harper & Row.

Stauffer, R. G. (1975). *Directing the reading-thinking process.* New York: Harper & Row.

Steele, J. L. (1984). Recall and comprehension. Unpublished manuscript, University of Virginia, McGuffey Reading Center.

Stein, N. L. & Trabasso, T. (1982). What's in a story: An Approach to Comprehension and instruction. In R. Glasser (Ed.), *Advances in the psychology of instruction* (vol. 2). Hillsdale, NJ: Erlbaum.

Structure and function of the human body, Second edition. (1977). Philadelphia: J.B. Lippincott.

Tierney, R. J. & Mosenthal, J. (1980). *Discourse comprehension and production: Analyzing text structure and cohesion* (Tech. Rep. No. 152). Champaign, IL: University of Illinois Center for the Study of Reading (ERIC Document Reproduction Service No. ED 199 945).

Toffler, A. (1980). *The third wave.* New York: Bantam.

Upton, A. (1961). *Design for thinking.* Palo Alto, CA: Pacific Books.

Vaughan, J. L. (1976). Interpreting readability assessments. *Journal of Reading, 19,* 635–639.

Vaughan, J. L. (1982). Use the construct procedure to foster active reading and learning. *Journal of Reading, 25,* 412–422.

Vaughan, J. L., Castle, G., Gilbert, K., & Love, M. (1982). Varied approaches to preteaching vocabulary. In J. A. Niles & L. A. Harris, (Eds.), *New inquiries in reading research and instruction.* Rochester, NY: National Reading Conference, 94–97.

Vaughan, N. E. & Vaughan, J. L. (1983). On adolescents' comprehension: Perspectives from an earth science assignment. In P. L. Anders (Ed.), *Research on reading in secondary schools: Monograph Nos. 10–11.* Tucson, AZ: University of Arizona, 36–52.

Vaughan, J. L. (1984). Concept structuring: The technique and empirical evidence. In S. D. Holley and D. F. Dansereau (Eds.), *Spatial learning strategies.* New York: Academic Press.

Vaughan, N. E. (1984). *A comparative analysis of readers' comprehension as measured by free retellings, cued retellings, and hierarchically structured questions.* Unpublished doctoral dissertation. Commerce, TX: East Texas State University.

Vygotsky, L. S. (1962). *Thought and language.* Cambridge, MA: M.I.T.

We the people. (1977). Lexington, MA: D. C. Heath.

Wertsch, J. V. (1978). Adult-child interaction and the roots of metacognition. *The Quarterly Newsletter of the Institute of Comparative Human Development, 2,* 15–18.

Wetmore, M. E. (1984). Restructuring text to improve comprehensibility. Unpublished manuscript. Charlottesville, VA: University of Virginia School of Education.

Wigginton, E. (1972). *The foxfire book.* Garden City, NY.: Anchor.

Wigginton, E. (1973). *Foxfore 2.* Garden City, NY: Anchor.

Wigginton, E. (1975). *Moments: The foxfire experience.* Rabun Gap, GA: Foxfire Fund (Available from Ideas, Magnolia State Park, Nederland, CO, 80466.)

World history. (1974). Chicago: Follett.

Wrenn, G. C. (1941). *Study habits inventory.* Palo Alto, CA: Stanford University Press.

INDEX

Accomplished readers, 6, 7, 12, 141

Adams, A., 254

Adams, J. L., 196

Adler, Mortimer, 254

Alvermann, D. E., 55

Analogical thinking, *See* Thinking

Anderson, J. R., 151

Anderson, R. C., 197

Anderson, T. H., 9, 34, 141

Anticipation, 105–134
  in cycle of reading, 103, 104
  defined, 86, 105
  example of, 137
  purpose of, 112
  rationale for, 106–8
  of students' needs, 108–13
  the teacher's role in building, 113–34
  when students know a lot, 128–33
  when students know some, 122–27
  when students know little, 119–22

Appleby, A., 180

Application questions, 183
  example of, 185

ARC, 87–104
  and the cycle of reading, 102
  as framework for learning, 97
  guides, 95–100
  questions and activities summarized, 87–88
  and reading ability, 101
  and study skills, 253, 272

Armbruster, B. B., 9, 34, 35, 141

Asher, S. R., 231

Assessment
  of comprehension, 56–61ff
  instructional, 81–82
  of study skills, 270–71

Attitudes and interests, 231–51
  achievement, compared to, 238
  change in, 238–45
  and classroom climate, 239
  and classroom setting, 243–44
  comprehension, related to, 231–32

content reading lesson, related to, 234–35
  and curriculum factors, 241–43
  grade level in school, related to, 239
  and grades in school, 238–39
  related to learning, a demonstration, 232–34
  measurement of, 245–50
    Estes Attitude Scales, 246–47
    direct measures, 248–50
    guidelines for, 249–50
  and student characteristics, 244–45
  and teacher characteristics, 245
  and the teacher, 239–41

Ausubel, D., 105

Bach, Richard, 134

Background information, 13

Baker, L., 112

Banan, J. M., 240

Baring-Gould, W. S., 187

Baring-Gould, C., 187

Barron, R. F., 167, 168, 170

Bartlett, F. C., 231, 238

Beginnings and endings, 224–25

Belloni, L. F., 231

Bernstein, M. R., 231

Bloom, B. S., 182

Boothby, P. R., 55

Bragstad, B., 260, 265, 268

Brainstorming, 121–22
  as access to prior knowledge, 122
  as clustering, 131
  as step in categorical overview, 128

Bransford, J. D., 65, 107, 109

Brooks, C., 34

Brown, A. L., 151

Bruner, J., 180

Burke, C., 160

Buros, O. K., 250

Capote, Truman, 235

Carey, R. F., 12

Carlsen, R., 239

Carnine, D., 254

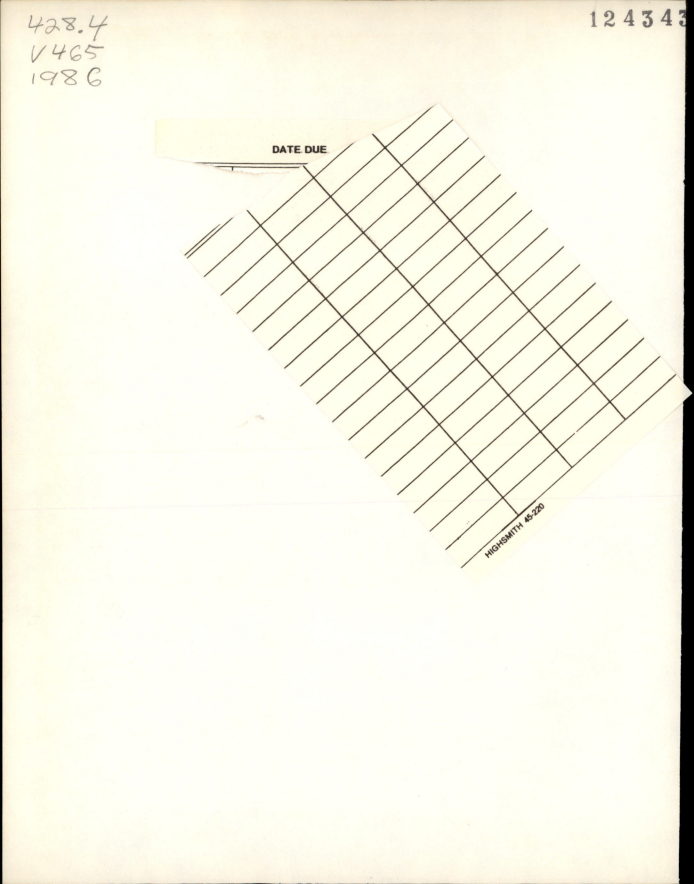

DATE DUE

HIGHSMITH 45-220